A Tale of Two Transformations

Bringing Lean and Agile Software Development to Life

Michael K. Levine

CRC Press
Taylor & Francis Group
Boca Raton   London   New York

CRC Press is an imprint of the
Taylor & Francis Group, an **informa** business

A PRODUCTIVITY PRESS BOOK

CRC Press
Taylor & Francis Group
6000 Broken Sound Parkway NW, Suite 300
Boca Raton, FL 33487-2742

© 2012 by Taylor & Francis Group, LLC
CRC Press is an imprint of Taylor & Francis Group, an Informa business

No claim to original U.S. Government works

Printed in the United States of America on acid-free paper
Version Date: 20110617

International Standard Book Number: 978-1-4398-7975-7 (Hardback)

Library of Congress Cataloging-in-Publication Data

Levine, Michael K.
    A tale of two transformations : bringing lean and agile software development to life / Michael K. Levine.
        p. cm.
    Includes bibliographical references and index.
    ISBN 978-1-4398-7975-7
    1. Information technology--Management. 2. Information technology projects--Management. 3. Agile software development. I. Title.

HD30.2.L475 2012
005.068'4--dc23   2011023936

Visit the Taylor & Francis Web site at
http://www.taylorandfrancis.com

and the CRC Press Web site at
http://www.crcpress.com

A Tale of Two Transformations

Bringing Lean and Agile Software Development to Life

Contents

List of Figures

Introduction

THE CHALLENGE: IMPROVE SOFTWARE DEVELOPMENT PERFORMANCE

Are you frustrated that your software development projects deliver less than promised, at more cost than you would expect? Have you heard the promise of Lean and Agile software development, but you don't know how to get your organization to adopt it effectively? Does your career success depend on improving your organization's ability to deliver software-based business or product improvements? If so, this book is for you.

Software development is often a frustrating and difficult endeavor for business leaders. They are typically neither trained nor experienced in technology, but their success may be dependent on technological success. Likewise, technology leaders may understand what an effective environment looks like, but they may not have the management skills or experience to move there. If a development organization needs improvement, what is the best way to make it?

That is the question faced by the two narrators of this book, who tell the tales of the transformations they wrought in their two very different companies. You will have a ring-side seat at their sides, so you can follow their thought processes and learn from their successes and failures. By reading these intertwined, entertaining stories about two companies—MCCA and FinServia—you can get some ideas on how you might go about making change in your own organization.

THE COMPANIES

MCCA was a promising mid-sized company, bought by a private equity firm, and set on a path of rapid growth. Both its operations and its product development (which was primarily software based) were chaotic, dependent entirely on the heroic efforts of a few dedicated and tireless individuals; its results were alternately spectacular and miserable. Its challenge was to standardize and improve its operations, and accelerate and make reliable its product development. Adding the right structure to the chaos was the goal.

FinServia, on the other hand, was a newly independent division of a much larger company. Its products and services had ossified, its customers hanging on out of habit and to avoid switching costs. Its operations and product development were highly regimented, slow to change, late to market, and behind the competition. FinServia's parent company had recently failed in a major effort to strategically integrate its operations with other divisions, and for lack of a better idea, had turned it loose to try to compete on its own. Its challenge was to loosen the death grip of bureaucracy and wasteful process, and accelerate and make reliable its product development. Reducing initiative-killing overhead and giving people the room and structure to learn was the goal.

THE NARRATORS

This book is the tale of the transformations of these two companies, toward a common operational and product development process goal: Lean operations and Lean/Agile software development. The tales will interlock through our two narrators, Jim "Wes" Wesleyan and Mary O'Connell. Wes and Mary are a new couple, just starting their life together, as they help lead the change at their respective companies. They have varied experience with Lean/Agile software development, but they are both committed to it as a next-stage vision for their organizations, even though the companies start from very different places.

To illustrate a broader set of transformational challenges and approaches, our two narrators have very different backgrounds and temperaments. Our lead narrator, Wes, is a polished ex-consultant, trained initially in law but never practicing, skilled at communication and learning but not expert in product or software development. In contrast, Mary is a highly expert software product development leader, strongly technical, with passionate and committed views of how things should be done, and little tolerance for the fools who would do it differently. We will have the good fortune to listen in on their conversations as they guide each other in their own transformation projects.

THE CHANGE MODEL

Wes and Mary struggle and eventually come to grips with one of the critical leadership choices we all face as we seek to make change: To what extent should leadership *direct* change, versus inviting it? If we know where we are going, why not just tell our teams, top-down, to go there? Is that even a possibility when we are seeking to create a Lean/Agile ecosystem, where respect for people, expertise, and problem solving are core principles? On the other hand, if we *invite* change and get broad participation, how can we be sure that the "right" change happens, at the "right" pace?

As Wes and Mary evolve their thinking on this critical issue, two models of Lean/Agile change emerge: one is to *drive people* (directive), and the other is *people driven* (participative). They explore the business conditions that point toward one or the other approach, and they adopt different approaches based on their different situations. We watch and listen as they execute their change models and see the implications of each. Their thinking and their (fictional) experiences can help you drive your own improvements.

THE GOAL: LEAN AND AGILE DEVELOPMENT

Lean product development and Agile software development techniques are the latest advances (skeptics will call them *fads*) in software development, much as Lean operations is the latest advance in operations. In operations, Lean is about standardizing whatever work can be standardized and empowering people to continuously improve the standardized process. Lean operations include the concepts of one-piece flow, cadence, visual management, and an emphasis on hands-on expertise and seeing for yourself.

The extension of these ideas to software development recognizes that, when doing new things with new teams and new technologies, the amount of work that can be standardized is limited. Instead, emphasis is placed on harnessing the thoughts and ideas of many people, distilling those ideas into code that runs, and continually evaluating and adjusting to provide incremental and steadily increasing value. Often, the more the value, the less certain and predictable the development process, because new things are being conceived and built in new ways, by groups of people working together in new ways. Lean product development and agile software development provide frameworks and techniques that facilitate this creative process, accelerating learning and reducing risks of failure, while sharing some of the Lean operating principles such as one-piece flow and visual management.

This is book is not a primer on Lean operations or Lean/Agile software development; if you're unfamiliar and interested in a primer, there are other books, including my first book, *A Tale of Two Systems*.[1] That is not to say that you shouldn't read this book if you aren't already well-versed in Lean and Agile; far from it: an in-depth understanding of Lean and Agile is not a prerequisite to read on. Our narrators will explain enough about their goals to keep newcomers from being lost.

THE BOOK

This book is about how to transform your organization to become Lean and Agile. The two fictional companies, MCCA and FinServia, represent two poles along the spectrum of companies requiring change. One is chaotic and lacks defined processes to a frightening extent, whereas the other is so tightly controlled and process driven that it is essentially frozen. Your organization is probably somewhere in the middle, or perhaps contains elements of both. By reading an engaging story, told through the eyes of two business leaders who are not specialists in change management (like most of us), you will gain an appreciation for what is required to bring Lean and Agile change to your organization.

The book is organized into five parts that take place over ten months. Along the way, signposts and guides are included (see the format in the chart), at the end of each chapter, to help you keep track of the two transformations, and to point out what you should be learning from the tales.

Signposts	Signposts will summarize the major events of the chapter with respect to each project.
Change Guides	Guides will point out lessons, as we see them now, at this stage of both transformations.
Coming Up Next	Coming Up Next will give you a preview of the next chapter, including who will be narrating and what the topic will be.

At the end of the book, in Chapter 14, I summarize the conclusions and principles based on my own twenty-five years of experience and studies in business. The principles will be illustrated with examples from the tales, giving you a final chance to consolidate your thinking and providing guidance on how to transform your organization.

In both these tales, the change leaders had positions of formal authority within a defined domain, and they had strong support from their senior leadership. This book is about how to *make* change, not about how to build the case for change among nonreceptive leadership. We will, of course, be concerned about building support within the organizations that need to change, but in the context of alignment of goals and general approach with the top management. This book offers little in the way of how to get senior leaders to align with goals and approaches that differ from their firmly held conceptions, in a way that would enable those who desire change in an inhospitable environment to succeed. (Perhaps that is a topic for a follow-on book.) If you're facing those circumstances, my only advice is for you to find a way to make the changes in the scope under your own control, or if you need to work in an organization better aligned with your beliefs, find a different organization in which to pursue your career goals.

THE DISCLAIMER

Before we get started, I have one disclaimer: the events and people in this book are all fictional. This is not a story of any single project, any specific person, or any real company; it's a universe I constructed for the sole purpose of instruction and entertainment. Neither is it about the specific technical debates, the nature of the systems being built, or the businesses in which the fictional companies compete; I created all of these merely as a foil to illustrate the principles. I caution readers against drawing conclusions from this fiction about people or events in real life.

Furthermore, all the opinions, perspectives, and conclusions are mine and mine alone. While I have learned much from my associates and experiences, all of the opinions expressed are personal and do not reflect any company's policies or perspectives in any way.

Finally, I am not an academic expert in change management, and this book is not firmly grounded in extensive research. I have not spent my career guiding change in dozens of organizations, and I have not formally studied a broad set of change initiatives. It is based on my own experience, studies, and conclusions alone. I make no claim that what I show and advocate in this book is "the best" or "the only" way to lead. I write this to entertain, to provoke thought, and to provide whatever guidance I can. My hope is that readers engage with the tales, reflect on the guides at the end of each chapter, and take whatever approaches, advice, and techniques make sense in their own situations.

ENDNOTE

[1] Michael Levine, *Tale of Two Systems: Lean and Agile Software Development for Business Leaders* (Boca Raton, FL: CRC Press, 2009). Toyota's chief engineer system is described in *Toyota Product Development System,* James M. Morgan and Jeffrey K. Liker (New York: Productivity Press, 2006).

Cast of Characters

MCCA (SEE FIGURE 0.1)

Connie Esposito, Vice President, Operations. Connie is an experienced Lean operations leader, grounded in her time at the Toyota–GM joint venture NUUMI plant in Northern California. She is now facing her first exposure to a non-Lean operation, and is determined to change it.

Cynthia Evans-Goldenbogen, Vice President, Human Resources and Communications.

Ernie Gatherington, founder and ex-owner of MCCA. Ernie is 64 years old and retired.

Franklin McDonald, Partner at Fletcher, Wilkens, and Johnson (FWJ), the private equity firm that owns MCCA. Frank, as his friends know him, is focused on making MCCA worth much more than FWJ paid for it, and then finding a lucrative "exit strategy."

Hannah Hoffman, Project Liaison, MCCA. Hannah evolves into MCCA's Program Manager.

Jack Langley, Vice President, Sales. A long-time sales leader, Jack prides himself on being able to sell anything, even if it doesn't exist yet!

Janet Livingston, User Experience Manager. Janet came to this position from the help desk.

Jasna Pikula, Junior Developer, and Rico DeSilva's protégé.

Jim "Wes" Wesleyan, Vice President, Product Development and Technology, and one of our narrators. Wes is engaged to be married to Mary O'Connell, our other narrator. He is just joining MCCA, reuniting with his old boss and mentor, Lynn Hollander.

Joan Dillingsworth, Financial Analyst. Joan becomes the Product Manager.

Lincoln Felsing, Test Manager. Lincoln is an external hire with a background in development; he has done Agile testing.

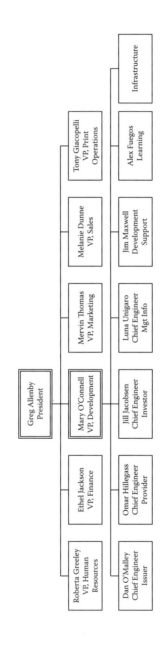

FIGURE 0.1
MCCA, partial organization chart (mid-year).

Lynn Hollander, President. Lynn came to MCCA as a financially savvy turnaround expert from the private equity firm (FWJ) that recently purchased it.

Melissa Groves, Saleswoman. Jack Langley's junior colleague on the San Diego National account.

Narish Marumen, Release Manager. Narish is the longtime leader in the MCCA datacenter/network group.

Phillip Glass, Development Manager.

Rico DeSilva, Lead Developer. Rico is a tightly wound, brilliant programmer.

Sasha Bilokov, Vice President, Finance, and Chief Financial Officer. Sasha is also accountable for administrative technology such as e-mail, networks, and data centers.

SAN DIEGO NATIONAL INSURANCE (MCCA CUSTOMER)

Daphne Zellern, Technology Support. Daphne supports Pervez Milligan and Emilio Fernandez, and is responsible for risk evaluation of the MCCA services and for integrating MCCA's technology to San Diego National's existing systems.

Emilio Fernandez, Records Manager. Emilio manages the MCCA relationship for San Diego National, and was the sponsor for the new, larger relationship with the claims management group.

Katie Flambeau, Claims Operations. Works in Pervez Milligan's department and is a hip young manager and a driving force for improving MCCA's products.

Pervez Milligan, Claims Management. Pervez has partnered with Emilio Fernandez to hire MCCA to add claims data, searching capabilities, and data extraction to the existing imaging system.

FINSERVIA (SEE FIGURE 0.2)

Alex Fuegos, Learning Leader. Alex joins from Cremins Corporation, Mary's ex-employer, where he served as Project Manager with Neville Roberts on several successful Lean and Agile software development projects.

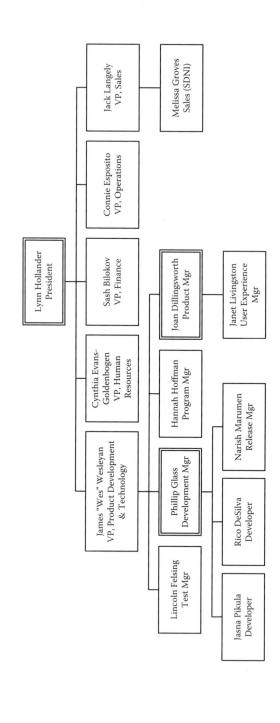

FIGURE 0.2
FinServia, partial organization chart (mid-year).

Dan O'Malley, Chief Engineer, Issuer. Dan is an old friend of Mervin Thomas and worked at Amalgamated with him. He is proficient in the needs of security issuers, but needs development in technology leadership. Joins FinServia at mid-year as part of Mary O'Connell's revamp.

Ethel Jackson, Vice President, Finance.

Greg Allenby, President. Greg has been Mary's boss before, and is a strong supporter of Lean and agile.

Jill Jacobsen, Chief Engineer, Investor. Jill was found by a recruiter and is an unknown quantity at FinServia. Jill was a development manager at Prosperity Investments. She joins FinServia at mid-year as part of Mary O'Connell's revamp.

Jim Maxwell (Max), lead developer for GRI, joins FinServia as lead of the Development Support Group.

Josh Lambert, Outside Counsel. Josh supports vendor contracts (especially GRI).

Luna Unigaro, Chief Engineer, Management Information. Luna was a contractor at Cremins, doing management reporting. She joins FinServia at mid-year as part of Mary O'Connell's revamp.

Mary O'Connell, Senior Vice President, Technology Development, and one of our narrators. Mary is engaged to be married to James "Wes" Wesleyan, our other narrator.

Melanie Dunne, Vice President, Sales.

Mervin Thomas, Vice President, Marketing. Mervin joined FinServia a month prior to Mary, coming from a company that had been one of FinServia's largest customers (Amalgamated Enterprises, or AE). Mervin had been AE's Stockholder Services manager. AE left FinServia in favor of one of its more technologically nimble competitors. Mervin was recruited to join FinServia to help guide its renaissance.

Omar Hillegass, Chief Engineer, Provider, and a recent transfer from FinServia's financial printing division.

Roberta Greeley, Vice President, Human Resources. Roberta is a longtime Cremins HR professional, who joined in the spinout. She had been the closest thing to an HR lead for the Cremins operations that were spun out to become FinServia.

Tanisha Clark, Manager of the GRI relationship.

Tony Giacopelli, VP Print Operations.

GLOBAL RESOURCES, INCORPORATED (GRI)

Manish Jhawar, Agile consultant.

Margaret Olson, Organizational Development consultant.

Masami Sato, Lean Product Development consultant.

Trevor McDonald, Trevor was the lead project liaison for Cremins Corporation and an author of "The Process."

Wayne Mellinger, Relationship Manager for Cremins Corp. and FinServia. Wayne is Mary's counterpart as she realigns the GRI link.

OTHER CHARACTERS

Neville Roberts, President, Cremins Real Estate Division. Neville is an accomplished software development leader, a Chief Engineer, and a good friend and colleague of Mary O'Connell. Neville serves as an informal sounding board and advisor for Mary and Wes.

Figure 0.3 provides a list of acronyms and their descriptions that are used in the book.

Acronym	Description
AE	Amalgamated Enterprises, the company from which Mervin Thomas, FinServia's VP of Marketing, emerged
BUM	Business Unit Manager, an acronym from the Microsoft Solutions Framework
CE	Chief Engineer, a Toyota-based, Lean Product Development concept. CEs are the senior driving force for each of Toyota's new-car developments. The CE at Toyota is a revered figure, combining top-notch engineering skills, customer focus, and leadership abilities.
CFS	Cremins Financial Services, the predecessor company of FinServia
DBA	Data Base Administrator
GRI	Global Resources, Inc., a technology outsourcing and consulting firm
LPD	Lean Product Development
MPS	MCCA Production System
MSF	Microsoft Solutions Framework, a codification of best practices from Microsoft
NUMMI	New United Motor Manufacturing Company, a joint venture between Toyota and GM
SDNI	San Diego National Insurance Company, MCCA's lead customer for its new products
TPS	Toyota Production System

FIGURE 0.3
Acronyms and abbreviations.

Section I

Setting the Stage for Change
February

1

Wes's Challenge at MCCA: February

Narrator: Wes

It felt good to be back at the Shelter Island Hotel, listening to the barking seals on the rocks outside my open window in the depths of winter. Quite a welcome change from last year at this time, when I was suffering through both the miserable Minnesota weather and the first failure of my career. I am here in San Diego to finalize my new position with MCCA. I am meeting with Lynn Hollander, the ex-partner at Griffin Consulting, for whom I had worked for nearly a decade, who is now MCCA's president. We had a basic agreement on title, compensation, and such, and now needed to finish the dialogue about my role and Lynn's expectations.

I write while I wait in my room for Mary and her kids to arrive. We've planned to walk over to Humphrey's and see an outdoor concert tonight. We announced our engagement a few months ago at the time I quit my job at Cremins Corporation. I need to finish landing a job and find a temporary place to live, while Mary and I plan the beginning of our life together and her kids gradually get used to the idea of me as surrogate dad. Mary is also taking on a new role, working for her favorite ex-boss in a brand new challenge. But I will leave that to her to describe for you.

The career failure I mentioned was Cremins United, a heroic attempt to transform a declining company through implementation of a broadly encompassing software system.[1] My role was chief of staff to the Project Control Authority (PCA), the committee that was responsible for the project. The failure was all the more painful in that it was my first career role within an operating company. My career up until the PCA was as a consultant at Griffin, advising clients in finance and marketing. I could now testify that being directly responsible for results was a lot more engaging and exciting than being the outside expert. I also knew that I wanted to try it again; this time, I swore to myself, I wasn't going to fail.

Lynn Hollander wanted to give me that chance at redemption. She had left Griffin several years ago to join Fletcher, Wilkens, and Johnson (FWJ), a private equity firm, as a sort of "fix-up" doctor, evaluating new investments and sometimes entering newly purchased companies as part of the team tasked with making rapid and dramatic improvements. She was gifted at quickly taking stock of a situation, understanding astutely, and making plans to improve strategy and efficiency. She could also turn those plans into action, a rare combination of talents. I had only talked with Lynn a couple times over the last several years; just enough to know that the constant stress and change associated with the stream of new companies and challenges was taking a toll on her. Too much travel, a bit too much drinking, too much pressure on her marriage.

Six months ago, she had taken a more stable role as president/CEO of MCCA, a struggling but promising company headquartered just north of here. She had a sizable equity stake as well, and she was offering me a somewhat smaller equity stake and a chance to help her turn the company around. A very fortuitous turn of events in all respects, since Mary lived not more than twenty miles away.

Lynn and I met both yesterday and today. I had learned more about MCCA and what Lynn was trying to do with it, and I got a sense of what my role would be, at least initially. I also had a chance to meet some of the MCCA leaders, most of whom seemed congenial enough, with the possible exception of Jack Langley, the Vice President (VP) of Sales. Jack appears to be one of those classic arrogant, money-driven, out-for-himself sales types that I had seen in too many companies during my consulting days. Lynn assured me that he wasn't as bad as he seemed, and that he was a key part of MCCA's future—I guess we'll see about that.

MCCA'S PAST (IN MICROFILM) VERSUS ITS FUTURE (IN INFORMATION MANAGEMENT)

I knew that Lynn was thinking through a rebranding effort, but for now MCCA remained the company's identity. It had begun life as Microfilm Creation Corporation of America. Founder Erwin Gatherington (whom everyone called Ernie) came out of one of the California banks, where he spotted an opportunity to get in on the ground floor of what became a substantial business for a decade or so. He bought some film machines and began offering a service to convert paper to microfilm. This grew rapidly, with branches opened across California and several other cities in the western United States, ultimately growing into a national leader in imaging and output services. The business changed continually as it grew, adding microfiche, then taking input directly from computer tapes, and adding imaging services and on-site operations for large companies and governmental units.

The microfilm/fiche business is now about dead, and imaging services has not proven to be as profitable as the niche it is replacing. Nevertheless, MCCA has the potential for a bright future. Lynn's partners at FWJ had seen MCCA's promise as a platform for a new, high-growth business—information management. With proper guidance and investment, FWJ's leaders believed, MCCA could become a very valuable company; accordingly, they bought the firm and appointed Lynn to run it.

Like most of the evolutions in MCCA's past, this one began with the sales team, which since Ernie's retirement, was led by Jack Langley. Jack was a master at staying in touch with MCCA's customer base and listening to what they wanted and needed, and finding a way to sell it to them. I understood from earlier talks with Lynn that Jack could, and did, sell products to customers that the technology and operations groups hadn't yet created! Sometimes this worked out well, sometimes not so well.

Two years ago, a longtime customer, San Diego National Insurance (SDNI), asked Jack if instead of storing images for them of the documents that supported claims, could MCCA store the text of documents and provide searchable access to the information. That would be a great benefit to SDNI, giving their adjusters, analysts, fraud group, and several other areas more direct access to this critical information than they had today. Jack said of course MCCA could provide this, explaining that it was just another module on top of MCCA's existing image storage system, and he proceeded to sell a system to do just that.

That MCCA didn't have such a module and had no plans to build one was not a material barrier to making the sale; those facts did, on the other hand, shape MCCA's future. Jack's counterparts at SDNI weren't the most sophisticated buyers, but they were canny enough to get a contract with stiff penalties for nondelivery. MCCA's internal sales controls were informal at best, so Jack was able to drive the deal through the flaccid approval process with high projected profit margins and a concomitantly large commission check.

This turn of events left the problem of delivery firmly in the lap of Phillip Glass, the manager of MCCA's technology department. When I met Phillip for a few minutes today (he doesn't like to be called Phil), I could easily fathom why Jack called him "Eeyore." Like Pooh's donkey friend, Phillip seemed perpetually depressed and beleaguered, as if the whole world was arrayed against him and he had no chance at all. I found it remarkable how much Phillip and his small team of developers had created over the last ten years, and how little credit he got or claimed for the success the company had achieved. Phillip and his team had created the software tools to capture, store, and view images, and even though they were struggling to support existing business, Phillip had gamely turned to his tormenter Jack's latest challenge. It was Phillip's new creation that drew FWJ's attention, and Jack's contractual mess that made Ernie amenable to it.

Ernie was now sixty-four, with a couple of beautiful grandchildren, a second home in the desert, and early-stage emphysema from his years of smoking. As the latest crisis/opportunity in his business became clear to him, he had decided he didn't have the energy or interest to keep at it. He had brought MCCA through several generations already, and he was ready to sit this one out.

Ernie was confident he could negotiate a reasonable settlement with SDNI if MCCA couldn't deliver, but he was also convinced that Jack and SDNI had stumbled on a goldmine. In the same way that technology advances had destroyed one incarnation of MCCA after another (microfilm to fiche, fiche to image, service bureau to custom in-house servicing, PC-based viewing to Internet browsing), each advance had given way to larger and more profitable incarnations, while the older businesses threw off cash in their declining years and enabled the next transition. This latest transition was especially promising because the imaging business continued to grow, and it showed some promises of becoming more profitable if MCCA could solve some operational problems. And now this new opportunity could grow right on top of the existing business, providing existing customers with new capabilities that many would eventually recognize that they needed.

Knowing Phillip as he did, Ernie had confidence that eventually a great product would evolve; the unanswerable questions were when and how?

An intriguing dimension to this new transformation was taking an operations company, with relatively well-known capabilities that it applied serially to new opportunities in a fairly reliable way, and evolving it to also become a software product development company. I had learned at

Cremins how different the two endeavors were: one was all about standardizing process, measuring variation, and doing continual improvement, whereas the other was all about accelerating learning to accomplish new things effectively. (In "Lean" terms, this was the difference between Lean operations and Lean product development.) I had also learned, with a lot of pain, the perils of mistaking new software development projects for repeatable operations and forcing preset notions of process onto them.

Most of this information about MCCA's opportunities I learned from the sale prospectus Ernie's accounting firm had provided to FWJ, which Lynn had shipped off to me a few weeks ago. I was expecting to learn more from Lynn yesterday, and I sure did! But before I got a chance to talk with Lynn directly, I had an opportunity to see firsthand some of the tensions into which I would be jumping in my new job. This particular squabble concerned a parallel transformation at MCCA, implementing Lean operations, and like many squabbles at MCCA, Jack Langley was squarely in the middle of it.

MCCA'S TRANSFORMATION GOAL: FIX OPERATIONS AND BUILD NEW TECHNOLOGY PRODUCTS

As I sat quietly in Lynn's outer office waiting for our meeting to begin, an agitated couple entered the waiting area and approached Janice, Lynn's assistant. The man appeared to be in his late forties, tall and large but trim; a striking-looking ex-athlete who had maintained his physical condition. He was dressed in a dark blue suit, black wingtips, and a power silk tie, and I caught a whiff of his cologne as he strolled past me. The woman was a striking contrast to him: she was rather short and plain-looking, in a frumpy dress, but with bright intelligent eyes.

As the man reached Janice's desk, he turned off his agitated demeanor as if turning a switch. He gave Janice a big smile, apologized for coming in without an appointment, and asked if it might be possible for Lynn to give Connie and him a fAew minutes. I made the connection: the woman must be Connie Esposito, Lynn's new head of Operations; a moment later, I realized that the large man must be Jack Langley, head of Sales.

"Sorry, Jack, Lynn is on a call now, and she's already late for her next appointment," Janice replied, nodding my way.

"We really need a few minutes with Lynn," Connie argued. "Jack is catching a plane at noon, and my reorganization is supposed to be announced this afternoon. Jack has problems with parts of it, and I don't want to wait to get going."

I saw the chance to meet two of my new peers and jumped at it. "Excuse me, but maybe I can help. I'm Jim Wesleyan, in to talk with Lynn about the product development position. I've got a couple hours with Lynn this morning, but I'm sure we could spare a few minutes for your consultation. How about you go next, and I'll just wait until you are done?"

Jack and Connie both turned toward me, extended their hands, and welcomed me. "Lynn told us you were coming in today," said Jack, "glad to meet you." His hand was big and beefy, his grip firm but not crushing. Connie added, "Thanks so much for volunteering some time, Jim. We'll try to be quick."

I was about to explain that I prefer to be called "Wes" when Lynn's office door opened and out she came. She saw me, her eyes brightened, and she hurried over and gave me a brief "business" hug. I was a little surprised by the hug; I don't think she'd hugged me in ten years at Griffin, although I knew she thought affectionately of me. Perhaps the new gig was agreeing with her!

"You've met Wes?" Lynn asked, smiling at me.

Connie and Jack assured Lynn that we'd been properly introduced. Janice then interrupted and asked Lynn to come over to her desk, where they quietly conferred for a few moments while Connie, Jack, and I waited awkwardly. A decision reached, Lynn walked back over to us and pronounced, "Let's all go into my office and we can talk over whatever it is that's bothering you two. Wes is going to be joining our team, so I'd like him to listen in if you don't mind." Jack and Connie looked at each other, then at me, and then nodded, shrugged, and into Lynn's office we marched.

Lynn was best described as elegant. She was now in her mid-fifties, I thought, and still looked as great as ever. She was thin, perhaps five and a half feet tall, with long jet-black hair surrounding her wire-framed glasses. She was wearing one of her usual tailored suits, although she'd left the jacket neatly on a hanger on the back of her door. People who didn't know her well would describe her as outgoing; those who did know her well saw her as reserved and difficult to get to close to. Lynn had a constantly probing, intense intelligence, of which I had initially, many years ago, been afraid until I had earned her trust. I remember when I finally felt the sunshine of being on the inside of Lynn's circle of trust—what a great feeling that had been.

After my time at Cremins Corporation, Lynn's office was a bit of a throw-back. Cremins had adopted the current trend of all modular furniture, not hard walls. No one had an office at Cremins, not even the most senior officers, unless they were lucky enough to be in temporary, rented space that didn't justify receiving the standard facilities treatment. MCCA had never adopted any particular policy on facilities, mostly just leaving properties as they found them, or doing whatever the local leadership chose. Lynn's office reflected the tastes of its previous occupant, Ernie Gatherington, which were, in a word, imperial.

Lynn's desk was enormous. It must have been ten feet wide, massive and wooden. A table jutted out from the end as if growing from the edge, allowing Lynn to hold court with her entire team while sitting at her desk. Wanting less formality at the moment, she gestured the three of us toward the couch and chairs arranged neatly at the far end of her lair. Once we were settled, Jack got right to it.

"Lynn, it's about Connie's plan for our operations. I know we've been over this, and I thought I could accept the changes, but as I talked over the plan with my team, I've come to realize I just can't go along with it. It undermines the basic way we've done business, and it puts my sales force into positions of glorified order transmitters. If we do that, I'll lose my best people: they'll go to other companies and take our business with them."

"Jack," said Connie, aggressively beginning to defend herself, "profits are low and customer loyalty is weak. Our operations are an embarrass-ment! I was hired to fix the operations, to build the customer base, and generate the cash we need to invest in the technology products Wes is being hired to drive for us. Unless Lynn has changed her mind about our strategy," she said, looking with a steady gaze at her boss, "we're going to do what we've already agreed to." I admired how Connie was standing her ground calmly, while looking to Lynn to confirm her position. I was start-ing to like her already.

Jack seemed to be bouncing back and forth within himself from angry and about to explode to patronizingly calm and reasonable. Not waiting for Lynn to give a nod one way or the other, he responded to Connie. "That's not the point, Connie. We all know we have a challenge to improve our profits, but putting a bureaucracy between our sales team and the operations teams that support our customers is not the way to do it."

Lynn looked over at me, gave me a knowing smile and nod as if to welcome me to the team, and entered the fray, trying to keep her sales prima donna and her operations workhorse from sundering her new company apart.

"Jack, Connie, let's take a step back and remind ourselves of what we are trying to do here," Lynn calmly framed the debate. "Jack, interrupt me if you disagree with any of this. We've got a nice base of document-oriented operations outsourcing, which doesn't make much money and has a lot of customers hovering between marginal satisfaction and complete disdain for us. We think there is still growth in that market, but our longer-term growth opportunity is to leverage that base into the broader organizational information/knowledge management market. To do that, we need to get our customers to respect us enough to give us the opportunity to do more for them; we need to improve our cash flow to finance our new investments; and we need to make adding customers a more reliable experience for both us and them. You still with me, Jack?"

"I am, Lynn." Jack looked over in my direction and said to me, "Wes, this is the discussion we've been having since Ernie began thinking about retirement, and we put together the prospectus to sell the company." Readdressing Lynn and Connie, he continued, "This is not about any disagreement with basic strategy. It's about how we engage our customers and ensure we meet their needs. We've always run our business as local operations—the sales district manager in charge, and the local operations managers responsible to the sales managers. That's where our flexibility and closeness to customers has come from. Once we break that model, we'll become a slow-moving, unresponsive bureaucracy like our competitors."

Connie was about to speak up, but Lynn, with a simple touch of her hand on Connie's forearm, quieted her. This was Lynn's battle, Connie was simply her lieutenant in it, and Lynn was going to fight it. "I am completely with you, Jack, about staying close to our customers and being flexible in meeting their needs, and I appreciate your passion in fighting to maintain that. However, we are going to change how we accomplish that. The value streams of our operations—the basic services we provide our customers—are very similar from location to location, but we do the work in dozens of different ways. The variety in how we do the work prevents us from optimizing it, making us slower to respond to customers than we could be, and driving up our costs and driving down our quality."

"And Jack," Lynn went on, "I've heard you yourself complain about the weak operations managers and the burden their failures put on your team. Connie and I agree completely with you that our managers are under-trained and led, and that they need dramatic improvements."

I studied Jack's reaction, while admiring how Lynn had retreated to the areas of common agreement and gotten Jack agreeing with her at the level of goals. Now we were back to tactics, and Lynn left little room for doubt on what she was demanding.

"Here's my bottom line, Jack. Our operations can be standardized, and we are going to standardize them. Our managers are not as skilled as they should be, and we are going to teach them. If we don't give our leaders the skills and responsibility to manage and continuously improve standardized operations to meet customer values, we would become the rigid, distant bureaucracy you fear. But with Connie's help, we will do both at once, and we will become the high-quality, low-cost, responsive operation we must to support our growth. Are you with me on the basics, Jack?"

Jack fidgeted. He had signed on to Lynn's fundamental strategies, and he wanted to see Operations improve so he had fewer problems getting in the way of sales. On the other hand, he could not stomach losing control, and he feared what Connie's new structure would mean for him. I could see him struggling with how to respond, and his response proved his interpersonal sophistication—backing off a little, but still trying to salvage as much as he could. "Of course, Lynn. But can we work on some mechanisms to ensure that Operations stays close to customers and the sales force? The organizational structure and Connie's announcement talk to efficiency and standardization but hardly mention responsiveness and sales support. I'm worried about the impact on our sales force."

Now Connie spoke up. "Jack, I'm happy to work with you to change the communication and to fine-tune the Operations–Sales relationships. In my mind, the changes are all about serving our customers better; perhaps that didn't come out as strongly as it should have in the announcement because I just took that for granted. My job—and the job of our entire operations team—is to provide value to customers, and we depend on you and your team to partner with us in doing that and in finding new customers."

Jack appeared to be satisfied with this statement, so Lynn summarized and closed out this very interesting interruption to our meeting. "Very well. How about you two connect with Cynthia in HR and see if you can modify the announcement, and let's see if we can get it out by the end of the week. A couple days to improve it won't hurt anything. And then I'd like to see something from you two by the end of the month on how sales and operations will work together more effectively in customer acquisition and customer support. Just outline the basic mechanisms, and if you have any more disagreements you can't resolve, get them on the table and bring them to the senior staff meeting. I'd rather have the disagreements out in the open for us to work on than festering between you two, so long as we're all in basic agreement on what we are working toward. Now, out of my office and let me get back to work on getting Wes on board!"

As Jack and Connie left the room, Lynn rolled her eyes and gave me a wry smile as she turned her attention to me. She asked about Mary and my move to San Diego. I explained I was staying at a hotel for the week while I found a place to live and finalized the new position. Mary and I didn't think it appropriate to live together with her kids until we were actually married, and we weren't quite ready for that. After all, I explained, we had never even lived in the same city together before, so we want to give ourselves a little time to be sure.

"Sounds like a good plan, Wes," Lynn said. "Too bad you won't have the same trial period with us, although you did just get a preview. What do you think of the two of them?"

"Well," I gave myself a moment to think. "Both Jack and Connie are certainly passionate about their work. I admire how they both stood up for what they wanted, although Jack seemed initially more interested in defending the status quo and control of the sales force than supporting the vision you've laid out. I'm betting there are more fireworks to come in that relationship. I'm also betting that Jack and I will have similar issues as I try to do what you want of me."

"Yes, I'm sure you'll have your own set of troubles with Jack. But he's an aggressive salesman, and his team really likes him. He knows our customers well, and he has some strong relationships with them, especially San Diego National Insurance, our lead customer for our information management suite. I'm hoping to get his commitment and energy around our plans."

After just that brief exposure to Jack, I had my doubts, but I thought it better to move on, so I didn't say anything. Lynn filled the silence by moving on to the substance of our meeting.

WES'S NEW ROLE: NEW PRODUCT DEVELOPMENT, INCLUDING TECHNOLOGY

"Wes," Lynn said, "how about I summarize the role I have in mind for you, and then we can go over how we work together?" I nodded; I had written out an agenda for us, and Lynn's suggestion was on the same path.

"As you've seen, our short-term challenge is to get our existing operations straightened out and profitable, to get our customers liking us so they'll eventually buy more and be good references, and to begin to build business again in our operations outsourcing business. You won't have much of a leadership role in that—that's primarily Connie's realm.

"On its own, improving our operations and restarting new business development can do good things for us. Right now, our operating cash flow is marginal, and we have a tough time getting new customers because our reputation among existing customers is so uneven. Once we fix operations, we should be solidly profitable, with about 10% net margins, and decent cash flow, although we'll need ongoing cash flow to support growth. Each new significant piece of operating business we pick up normally requires some investment, whether it's new hardware, facilities, or just start-up costs. New business usually entails some risks as well, because we often need to do fix-priced contracts or offer performance guarantees that, so far, we don't always meet."

I had seen this type of operations-outsourcing business a couple of times in my consulting career, and I had never been enamored of them. An awful lot of things need to go right in order to make steady profits and grow, and from what I had seen, MCCA wasn't in the strongest position to make this happen.

"Sounds like Connie's work is necessary for our success, but not sufficient," I responded.

"That's right, Wes," said Lynn. "Without her succeeding, we don't have a chance. It's her job to build out the base for you and your new team. FWJ didn't buy MCCA to get a slow-growing, capital-intensive, blocking-and-tackling operations-outsourcing company. Excelling at Operations that can limit our risks, but it's what we do with the new software and related services that will determine whether or not we succeed.

"Your mission is simple: build the information management business. We know there is a very large opportunity—most medium-to-large organizations do a poor job of managing their knowledge. Solutions are fragmented, expensive, and rudimentary. Most companies now have an intranet with documentation in many different formats, making it tough to search, with only accidental connections among the people who have and need knowledge and the electronic stores of the knowledge. In addition, most of these organizations have dozens or hundreds of partial solutions, ranging from document-imaging warehouses, team support tools, shared drives on local area networks, and the like. There are probably dozens of companies that are trying to provide new solutions, but none of them have meaningful traction yet."

I had read the material on the markets and competitors that FWJ had put together as it evaluated the MCCA opportunity and one thing had puzzled me. "Lynn, why is it that no one has been able to capitalize on this opportunity, which seems so large? And why do you and your partners think MCCA will be able to do so?"

"What do you think?" Lynn turned the question around on me, as she was wont to do.

I thought back on my recent experience at Cremins Corporation, a company that could certainly fit the profile of target customers. "I guess the problem space is so fragmented that it's difficult to configure a product that meets a broad set of needs. Each group within a large organization has its own needs, which overlap in confusing ways with other groups with different needs. Also, the solution would be expensive and demanding to buy, install, and manage, so potential buyers would be troubled to put together a business case, get priority set, and execute on the project to implement."

"Well done, Wes: that's very close to our analysis," affirmed Lynn, "and it speaks to why MCCA has a good shot at this. MCCA is already in many of our customers' shops, taking care of some parts of their knowledge management. Mostly it's just image management, but we have a core set of skills, admittedly uneven, that we can build on. We also have an outstanding piece of software that the experts we consulted believe could be extended to be an excellent solution in this space, which we can host for our customers and lower the barriers to adoption. We have a strong partnership with San Diego National Insurance, which can help us drive our product forward. And finally, we have FWJ's backing, providing us with some needed capital and guidance.

"Does that make sense, Wes? Are you excited by the opportunity?" Lynn checked me for agreement.

"Very much so, Lynn. Looks like a lot of the ingredients for success are here."

WES'S NEW ORGANIZATION AND PEOPLE

Lynn then moved on to my role. "We're expecting you to help us deliver it. Let's cover a couple of things for you. How about we start with your organization, then some short- and longer-term expectations around delivery, then I let you ask whatever questions you may still have?" I nodded, and Lynn continued.

"Your title is Vice President of Product Management. You'll have responsibility for marketing and product development, which includes all the product-related software development. We're going to keep the administrative technologies, like our internal financial system, e-mail system, networks, and datacenters, out of your hair, and have those report up through Sasha, our CFO. You'll find your organization has some great talent, especially in software development, but it's missing many of the roles and staff that you'll need to have."

"What will my accountabilities be? Will I have profit and loss responsibility for the products?" I asked. I had seen product management groups range from top dogs (as in the consumer products model, most notably, at Procter & Gamble) to a weak support function in sales-driven cultures.

"Our goal is to get to profit and loss (P&L) ownership," Lynn answered. "We can't start there, because your group just couldn't handle it. Today, profitability management is a hodgepodge of sales, operations, and finance, none of it done very well. We'll need to come up with some simple mechanisms to get to P&L by product, and you'll need to build the people and processes to manage. But more important, you'll need to build out the products and services we need.

"The basis for our new products is underway: our work with SDNI. You need to get to know your new organization and people and the San Diego work, and then come back to me and your teammates in a month or so and tell us what you think. Our goal is to capture a big slice of the information management market before major competitors get established. We'd like to have a solid product offering in the market in a year or so, and within two years, we'd like to be seeing some rapid revenue growth. We'll give you a milestone at one month for your preliminary thoughts; then at two months, we'd like to see some broad outlines of a plan. You okay with that?"

"Sure," I replied, "that sounds good. Can I test a few boundaries with you?"

"Of course. Where would you like to start?" Lynn asked.

"Money, of course. You say my group is understaffed and undertalented, so I will need to build it out. How much money are we thinking we have to invest? And for how long, before the new investment needs to start paying for itself? Is this a spend-a-lot-to-get-a-big-offering-to-market-quickly sort of approach? Or is it more a cautiously-invest-and-see-what-happens approach?" I had seen both strategies during the course of my consulting career. Companies funded and controlled by venture capital tended to go the first route, because the venture companies tended to seek very big wins and accept some losses. In contrast, privately funded companies (including private equity like MCCA's new owner) tended toward the more cautious approach.

"More the latter," Lynn explained. "We have put together a budget for you for the rest of this year and next, along with some revenue expectations. You can hire 20 to 30 new people over this year, depending on what other expenses you have. We did this budget when we put together our bid for the company and made our planned investment. After you've had a chance to get to know your team and the market better, we'd like to hear from you as to the reasonableness of the expectations, and if they are unreasonable, there may be a chance to adjust. Don't be afraid to ask for more resources if the opportunity to profitably accelerate growth is available."

"Let's talk about people. Do you have any insights on who are the key people, any promises made, or things I need to be aware of?" I asked.

"Good question," responded Lynn. "We have around 30 people in your group now, mostly developers, with a few project managers and analysts. Phillip Glass is the Development manager; right now, everyone in Development reports to him. I think you'll like him, but my guess is you'll have to quickly decide what to do with him. He's been with MCCA for many years, and he knows our technology and people well. His people trust him and will do anything for him—I think because they believe he protects them from Jack, which seems to be one of his primary roles. Jack calls him Eeyore, after the donkey in *Winnie the Pooh*. You remember Eeyore?" Lynn asked.

"Of course: '*Thanks for noticing me*,'" I drawled slowly, low in the register, with my eyes staring at my shoes, as I did my best Eeyore imitation. "So he's a pretty gloomy guy?"

"He is. Phillip is reserved, not very verbal, takes what Jack dishes out, and does his best to deliver on the promises Jack and his team make. He's a stickler for accuracy and detail, always correcting people for minor transgressions of understanding. He doesn't have much confidence in himself, despite delivering pretty well over the years. Seems very smart, logical, and he loves the systems he and his team have built, like they're his children. Sometimes, it seems he's more interested in the logical whole of the software than what we are trying to do with it."

I thought for a moment, then tested a conclusion: "Sounds like he's someone I need on my side, but maybe not in his current role? I think I'll wind up between Jack and the development team, along with some other new roles we'll establish, so if we remove that burden, perhaps he'd be more productive and happy."

"That's probably right. There is a group of developers who are close to Phillip; many of them are smokers who spend time outside in the parking lot a couple of times a day. If you can keep Phillip on point for that group, keeping them focused and productive, you may have a win there. But for goodness sake, Wes, don't take up smoking just to fit in!"

I did like to be liked, but that would be going too far even for me!

Lynn continued, "There is one member of that group who is in a class by himself, Rico DeSilva. Rico is, by all accounts, a technical wizard. He's the guy everyone goes to when they can't figure out a production problem, or to build a customer feature that needs to be done on an unreasonable time-frame or is impossibly complex. He knows he's good, and over the years, he has used the threat of leaving us to secure a very handsome salary. He can be charming, but occasionally he throws temper tantrums. Rico gets annoyed at stupidity more than anything, and he hates any structure other than just being told what customers want and being set free to build it. He's a prima donna, and you'll need to handle him with kid gloves."

"OK, Lynn, so besides these two challenges, do you have any winners for me?" I hoped.

"There is one other who you might find interesting. Her name is Hannah Hoffman, originally from Austria, quite brilliant actually. She began here four years ago as a contract programmer, loved that work, but she kept getting pushed into project management and requirements work because she is an excellent communicator. She seems to be the leader in providing what structure there is in Phillip's group. She may have potential to do more.

"Those are the only three people in development that stick out for me, Wes," Lynn summarized. "What else can I tell you?"

"Is there any product management material around? Someone who knows our customers, can think strategically, is financially savvy, has some people skills? Ideally, I'd like to find some people who can do product management, technology leadership, and project management all in one package, as a chief engineer,[2] but it sounds like we don't have that type of skill set." Lynn and I had talked about Chief Engineers earlier, when I explained my role at Cremins Corporation and I told her about Mary.

"You're right about that," Lynn agreed. "MCCA is an immature organization, even in our core competencies of sales, operations, and technology. The intermediate roles—like program management, product management, and so on—are basically voids. However, there is one bright young woman in finance whom I've had my eye on: Joan Dillingsworth. She's just a couple years out of school, has an MBA in finance, and she's been involved in new deal negotiation and contracts. You should probably check her out."

"I'll do that; she sounds promising," I said. "Looks like I have a lot of work to do on the people and organizational fronts. Mary has a saying, 'build people before you build software.' That will be one of my first orders of business."

Lynn nodded, but I could see she wasn't completely in agreement. "Of course, you need to build your team; unfortunately, you don't get the luxury of waiting for your team to coalesce before delivering. We have some critical deliveries committed to SDNI, and our coming-out party is in only five months, in July. That's when we plan to launch our new product and operational strategies. You don't get a 'time-out' to rebuild."

Lynn told me in an earlier conversation, when she laid out her strategy for the company, about the annual DocWorld conference scheduled for late July, which was fortuitously in San Diego this year. Many of our customers, prospects, industry analysts, and journalists would be there. We were aiming to do a relaunch of MCCA, with our new product strategy and positioning at that time.

"I understand, Lynn. The world doesn't stop for us improve. We need to do that while doing business, and get better all along," I reassured her. "I do have one final topic to cover before I get going. Can you give me some guidance on how much I should involve my peers, you, and FWJ in my plans? How open and collaborative do you want this to be?"

"Why don't you answer that one, Wes? What kind of team and culture do you want to help us create here?" Lynn again turned my question back to me.

I had given a lot of thought to this question when I left Cremins Corporation and began looking for my next job. I summarized for Lynn, "I'd prefer to be on a true management team, where we are open with each other, help ensuring that we make good decisions, and are all committed to joint plans. My last job was much more hierarchical and competitive, and I didn't enjoy that much."

"I'd prefer that as well, Wes," Lynn answered. "We have some way to go to build out that type of team. Many of us are new to each other, some are new to their roles, and we are just beginning to form. We also have a lot to do, with limited resources and leadership, so our leaders need to be free to make decisions when needed, without running everything past me or the management group. If you do your best to balance quick and decisive action with keeping the management group involved, and if you work hard to form good relationships with your peers, we should be all right. As for me, I would like you to keep me regularly informed of what you are finding and planning. Just send me informal e-mails or stop in and chat. Lay out your plans, talk them over with me, and then go execute them. Err on the side of overcommunicating with me to begin with, and we can relax that over time."

That all sounded good to me, and I told Lynn so. I was now good to go: I had my new boss's perspectives and boundaries, my mission, and some guidance on how to proceed. Now all I had to do was learn about my new company, our people, products and technologies, our customers, and our competitors; make and sell some plans to my boss and my peers and execute on them—all while not disrupting efforts already underway with our most important customer. I'd better get started!

Signposts	Transforming MCCA
	• MCCA was recently sold to a private equity firm. Lynn Hollander, the new CEO, needs to make it grow; to do so, she needs operational improvements to earn customers' trust in preparation for new products, and to improve cash flow to support the new product development Wes is being hired to lead.
	• Connie Esposito, the new VP of Operations, is facing change resistance from Jack Langley, the long-term VP of Sales. Lynn supports Connie while giving Jack a chance to save face.
	• Wes aligns with Lynn Hollander on marching orders. Priority: develop the new suite of information management products soon, while building longer-term capabilities.
	• Lynn gives Wes her perception of available talent (some) and gaps (many), and sets boundaries on the money available (some) and decision-making processes (be inclusive, but don't overdo it).
Making Change: Guides from Wes	• **Set a simple and compelling vision**, as Lynn has for MCCA. Continually retreat to this common position when conflict over tactics arises, as Lynn did in the Jack–Connie debate.

- **Combine existing leadership with new talent**; give current team members a chance to adopt and lead, with the help of new blood. Lynn is doing this with Jack, Connie, and Wes, and Wes is focused on this as well. *"Build People before Building Software."*
- **As a change leader, be sure you understand your superiors' objectives and your boundaries**—be they people, money, or management process.

Coming Up Next

Around the same time, Mary O'Connell explores her new challenge at FinServia. It's quite different from Wes's at MCCA, although as we'll see later, the same change principles apply.

ENDNOTES

1. Levine, *Tale of Two Systems.*
2. Toyota's Chief Engineer system is described in Morgan and Liker, *Toyota Product Development System.*

2

Mary's Challenge at FinServia: February

Narrator: Mary

In my career so far, I've had two kinds of jobs: some were consuming, frustrating, and challenging; others were productive, comfortable, and friendly. My last two were in that order: the earlier, a frustrating two-and-a-half year stint on the Cremins United project, the most recent a comfortable year leading the product development team in our Real Estate Services division. I wonder what's wrong with me that I can only shortly endure a comfortable job before I want to try something new. My mother says I always need to be testing myself, and I suppose that's true—at work, skiing, or even driving around San Diego.

In a lot of ways I love my current job. My boss, Neville, is a wise and gentle man, an engineer by training and nature. He and I see eye to eye on most things, and he trusts me to do my job and contribute to the management team. I'm good at my work, I know the systems and people well, and I can see the positive impacts of my leadership. I'm appreciated and fairly well rewarded. I even have a lot of friends here, and several of them work on my team. And most of the time I don't have to travel, which is important to me and my children. So what am I doing leaving this gig for the Financial Services Group?

Basically, my mom's right: it's a test for me, a challenge I can enter every day when I go to work. I know how to develop software; it's what I've done for my whole career, beginning as a junior programmer twenty years ago. I grew up with great leaders, one of whom, Greg Allenby, is again going to be my boss at FinServia. Together, over a decade or more, we explored different ways to develop software, settling on a people- and learning-centered approach, based on the belief that success comes from getting the right people in the right roles, learning quickly together to grow knowledge and turn that knowledge into code. In the last several years, this basic idea, plus many other valuable and related ideas, has been popularized as "Lean and Agile Software Development."

I've never been much for theory; I'm more about doing than reflecting and explaining. My husband-to-be, Wes, is more of the theorist and explainer, the level-headed, thoughtful observer and planner. However, the experience I had with the Cremins United project (which Wes and our friend Beth Dumas wrote about in *A Tale of Two Systems*) taught me some lessons about the harm that mistaken models of software development can inflict on people and a company. So when Greg asked me to join him again, to help him take the rigid and ineffective software regime in the Cremins Financial Services group and turn it into an industry-leading money-making machine, I just couldn't resist. I know how to do software development; now I get a chance to learn how to make a company do software development!

FINSERVIA'S TROUBLES: GLACIAL, UNRESPONSIVE PRODUCT DEVELOPMENT

Cremins Financial Services (CFS) is in a bit of a trouble, as Neville would understate it. It has had a long and profitable run printing annual and quarterly financial reports and the like for brokerages, banks, and insurance companies, work that is now slowing down, as the company's customers migrate to electronic communication instead of printed. Unfortunately, Cremins hasn't done very well in providing those new electronic tools. One critical element of the struggle had its roots fifteen years ago, when Cremins Corporation participated in a management fad of the moment and concluded that computer technology was not a "critical competency" for it—and then outsourced almost all of its computer support to Global Resources, Inc. (GRI).

Initially, the GRI arrangement worked fairly well. GRI took on most of Cremins' staff; moved its datacenters into shared, lower-cost megacenters; and drove down Cremins' costs. Cremins kept a small cadre of vendor management staff, who were responsible for service-level management, financial and contract management, and requirements and acceptance testing for new functionality. At the time, Cremins' culture around manufacturing (i.e., printing) was adopting Six Sigma concepts: driving out the variation in process through relentless standardization to ensure conformance to specification. It mistakenly applied the same ideas to its software development process, a decision that was embraced and abetted by GRI.

At the same time, GRI was putting into place a highly disciplined software development methodology designed for the primary purpose of ensuring reliable profitability of its outsourcing contracts and avoidance of legal liability claims. Cremins' vendor managers and the methods group at GRI formed an unholy alliance and created a monster they called the Cremins Development and Risk Control Process, which just about everyone called The Process (as though they were talking about *The Creature from the Black Lagoon*, and usually accompanied by air quotes!). This combination of events ensured that Cremins' Financial Service business would be unable to adjust to the coming electronic migration spurred by the invention and growth of the Internet. In combination, the misapplication of Six Sigma ideas and the divergence of GRI's financial self-interest from Cremins' need for market-driven speed destroyed the future of Cremins' financial services business.

Let me take a brief aside here. I mentioned above that my temperament is more direct and judgmental than Wes's. Most of the time, I don't naturally see both sides of an argument, and I'm impatient with incompetence and closed-mindedness. I need to work very hard to restrain myself when working with people whom, in my younger days, I might have called "morons." When Wes and I agreed to work together to write this book, I told him I was going to write in my own voice, with my own opinions, and he was fine with that. He even encouraged me to be direct, so readers can get my unvarnished views. Expect no "fair and balanced" reporting from me!

The first realization that CFS might be in trouble came about five years ago. One of its customers, which was generally satisfied with its service, had been solicited by an upstart competitor. The competitor was offering to put its financial reports online and to solicit its shareholders for e-mail addresses and permission to stop physical mail in favor of online access. The competitor had its technical solution up and running, and it promised to implement the technology in just several months, in time for the customer's next major mailing. The CFS sales executive was given an opportunity to respond, and he found to his dismay that CFS would not be able to provide a competitive response in that time frame. One customer opportunity lost, with the prospect of many more to follow. The sales executive brought the problem to his management, and over the next several years, CFS began building its response to the Internet threat.

At the time, CFS had few technology capabilities in-house. A couple informal programmers in the plants, taking in data files from customers, doing some mail merges and the like; the rest had been ceded to GRI. The relationship was in the early stages, so naturally, CFS turned to GRI for help, through its vendor management group. Thus began CFS's attempt to compete more effectively, trendily called "eCFS."

The first step of The Process was to do a *scope and vision* document, as prelude to a contract. The Process prescribed a specific format and approach to this document, which posed a problem for CFS: it didn't have anyone with the experience or skills to do this type of documentation. CFS had been a fairly simple organization: it consisted of sales people who were out rounding up printing and mailing business from financial services companies; several printing plants; some operations teams in the plants who took files and data from customers and prepared the print jobs; and some finance/accounting staffers who managed pricing and costs. Of course, GRI was happy to assist. It provided project managers, business consultants, and systems analysts to work with the CFS sales executives to set a vision.

The executives didn't have a problem setting a vision. It was very simple—they knew where they were losing business at the time, so they asked for the same capabilities that were causing them trouble. The GRI consultants were much more sophisticated than this, however, and they convinced CFS to do a deeper, longer-term vision. Thus, the first work assignment under the eCFS contract: interview customers, research competitors, hold focus groups of sales executives, and specify in more detail the capabilities and products that CFS needed to continue to dominate its markets.

Six months and substantial dollars later, GRI produced a very impressive series of PowerPoint slides, laying out the challenge and the response. CFS management bought the pitch—why wouldn't it, since GRI basically spit back the same information CFS had fed in? CFS agreed to go to the next step: detailed requirements for what had now been transformed from a strategy (eCFS), to a technology product/project, also called eCFS. There was only muted disagreement on the CFS side, mostly from some of the programming staff in the plants and a few of the younger, more aggressive salesmen, who wanted to just start building the tools their customers were asking for. In retrospect, it is puzzling why CFS was so patient and compliant with GRI's approach, but it's fairly easily explained by CFS's near-total lack of technology expertise in the leadership team, and what seemed like plenty of time to address the threat.

Fortunately—or perhaps, with the benefit of hindsight, *unfortunately*—when the electronic onslaught began, CFS generally kept the printing work that remained, which tended at the beginning to be the vast majority.

Stockholders needed some time and incentives to stop receiving paper; only about 10% were ready to accept the offers to go paperless and all electronic. This kept CFS solvent, suffering slowly declining revenue instead of a more serious collapse, and it gave CFS the illusion of time to deal with eCFS as the "best practice" Process specified.

Another Work Assignment, another year, and another substantial chunk of cash, and the requirements were complete. Two full notebooks of documents were produced, beginning with bulleted lists of needs and features, drilling down into sketches of screens, screen flows, data flows, and data element lists and definitions. Half of one of the notebooks was full of something called *nonfunctional requirements* that laid out in quantitative detail that the system was to be reliable, fast, and secure. The documents were reviewed with the CFS vendor management team, which by now had added "certified requirements analysts" to "facilitate the gathering of requirements," and ultimately signed off on by designated sales team members, who solemnly swore that if GRI could provide technology to do what the notebooks asked for, eCFS would be a great success.

By then, the pattern was becoming clear. Another work assignment, another six months, another substantial chunk of cash, and GRI produced the functional and technical design documents. By this time, CFS's leaders, who were far from stupid, had realized that they really didn't want design documents; what they wanted was a working system. Appetites had been whetted, and customers were being lost: a system was needed! *How much would the system cost?* they asked, *and when can we have it?*

GRI quite reasonably gave CFS a choice. It could start doing the design and build at the same time, but it couldn't give any assurance on how much it would cost or when it would be done. In this case, CFS would simply pay for the assigned "resources" on a time-and-materials basis. Alternatively, if CFS would follow The Process, GRI would complete the design, and at that point, it would be willing to give CFS a fixed-price, fixed-time bid, subject (of course) only to change control. GRI explained to CFS's senior leaders, who had all come out of the sales force, that building before the design was complete was highly risky: imagine, they said, beginning to set the type on a job before you had agreed on typeface, color, quality of paper, number of copies printed, and so on? Of course, put that way, starting to build before completing design made no sense to CFS.

Per The Process, the design was completed, and a fixed-price bid was agreed on. To be sure the bid was fair, the CFS Vendor Management group solicited two competitive bids, both of which were at least double GRI's, much to CFS's surprise. No surprise to me or I'd guess anyone experienced with development—to jump in at that stage, even with all the documentation, would require either great stupidity or leaving a very large margin of costs to absorb the great uncertainties. By the time GRI had done the requirements and design, it had accumulated vastly more of the knowledge to build the solution than anyone else, so the competitive bidding was more form than substance.

The fixed bid was very comforting to CFS's senior managers. They didn't understand the technical design, but that didn't really matter, did it? GRI was a reputable company, with deep pockets, and was expert at this sort of thing. CFS had the functional specification that laid out the system in great detail and the service-level agreements that required the system to run well. CFS could simply hold GRI accountable; good contract administration was needed, not software development skills. The fixed bid, plus the internal expenses of the Vendor Management Group (which, by now, was growing to include Product Managers, who were kind of souped-up requirements analysts), were compared to the expected benefits, and a culminating Work Assignment was agreed on. The bid to do the entire system was prohibitively expensive, so the Assignment was for Phase I of an anticipated three phases.

And so began the development process. GRI brought in dozens of additional staff members—datacenter liaisons, security managers, java developers, database administrators, test managers, testers, documentation specialists, and process engineers—and work was undertaken at a furious pace. It seemed that the GRI staff worked all the time—late into the night, on weekends, on long phone calls with overseas development teams—and the system began to take shape. eCFS grew, adding staff to set pricing, build operational procedures, plan marketing and advertising, and plan User Acceptance Testing. But as the software moved forward toward completion, over another nine months, and as CFS grew more and more familiar with what they (and their predecessors on the team) had specified, some dissonance began to creep into the project.

The dissonance grew in two ways. First, the GRI team seemed to be continually asking for clarification and elaboration of the requirements and design, and each question seemed to result in a Change Order that added (unbudgeted) cost and time. Second, the CFS staff repeatedly found issues that needed to be addressed, whether caused by misunderstandings of the business needs going all the way back to initial requirements (which GRI rightly noted were signed off on quite some time ago), or by poor requirements (often found when putting together test cases or even while testing), or by the transformation of requirements to design, or by new business needs driven by competitors or customers/prospects, or by new market conditions. These new issues also usually resulted in a Change Order and added costs and time.

As Change Order costs and delays mounted, CFS management, led by the Vendor Management group, responded by working to perfect the serial requirements through coding flow. Checkpoints, walkthroughs, reviews, and audits were added, and a process to charge Change Orders back to the department that "caused" them was imposed.

Eventually, the end result was a new system, eCFS. It did put CFS back into the competitive game, with some functionality that leading competitors had much earlier. The infrastructure—servers, databases, network, monitoring—was good: those areas played to a real strength of GRI. System enhancements were rigorously prioritized and squeezed through The Process, resulting in a slow trickle of carefully managed improvements that met some customer needs, but that on the whole kept eCFS falling steadily behind its competitors. The Process had become institutionalized, with an assembly-line flow of requirements into designs into quarterly releases, with strict stage gates (requirements had to be done 9 months prior to release, design had to be done 6 months prior, etc.), and lots of people at CFS and GRI whose jobs were based on their fulfilling the roles specified.

And then Cremins Corporation made a change in strategy: it created Cremins United. This new strategy emphasized cross-divisional synergies and shifted focus and some resources away from the eCFS work. For two years, eCFS staggered slowly along, putting CFS increasingly far behind its competitors, until Cremins United failed, the strategy was abandoned, and CFS was spun out of Cremins Corporation as a separate unit known as FinServia, to sink or swim on its own. My old boss, Greg Allenby, who had been successfully running the software-intensive Real Estate Division, was named president of the new company, and he recruited me to join him. Revitalizing eCFS was now on the table, and I was to be the head chef.

Unfortunately, the time that CFS had frittered away now hurt. In the last few years, as "green" has become more fashionable and more and more people have become comfortable with the reliability of the Internet, the percentage of people choosing to work over the Internet instead of relying on print distribution had been creeping up. Competitors had continually improved functionality, such as offering the option of requesting a paper copy mailed whenever desired, managing proxy votes, and distributing coupons for products of the company in which stock was being held. The 10% take-up of initial offers to end mailing in favor of online access crept upward to 25% or more for initial solicitations, and over time, it has even reached 50% and higher, among more mature target populations. There is no sign of this slowing down yet, either. FinServia started with still significant but falling revenue and marginal and declining profitability. Greg and I, and the rest of our team, had a challenge on our hands!

FINSERVIA'S TRANSFORMATION GOAL: FASTER AND CHEAPER

It was a sunny but cool San Diego Friday afternoon. I had spent most of the day cleaning and packing my office as I wrapped up my job at Cremins' Real Estate Division and got ready to join FinServia on Monday. I met Greg Allenby, my new boss, at Lindy's in the foothills northeast of La Jolla. As I walked through the foliage-enshrouded pathway to the outdoor patio, I saw Greg sitting underneath a gas heater, watching the slowly moving koi in the small pond. Greg is a few years older than me, still with a full head of short curly hair and rimless glasses. Today, he was wearing his usual golf shirt and khakis, sipping a lemonade while he waited for me to arrive.

Greg and I had worked together off and on for more than a decade. He is a terrific leader—smart, visionary, expert, thoughtful, and caring, at least up to a point. I've rarely met anyone more focused on accomplishing whatever objectives are sought, and so long as a person is important to that objective, Greg cares. Otherwise, Greg has just a small circle of true friends. I believe I am somewhere in the middle. Over the years, I had always been important to Greg's objectives, and I hoped that I had sneaked over at least a bit into the friends circle. Even if that was true, Greg didn't show it today; he was all business.

"All ready to go, Mary?" he began.

"I am," I said. "Wes and I are going to relax around the house this weekend, and then bright and early Monday morning, I'll be in the office, and it's off to the races." I also mentioned that Neville and his wife were going to stop over Saturday afternoon, and that Wes and I were planning on picking his brain on our new work challenges.

"Give Neville my regards," said Greg. "Good idea to get some free consulting from him. We left the Real Estate Division in such good shape, he probably needs something to puzzle over again." Neville Roberts had worked with Greg and me for the past several years, and Neville now had Greg's old job.

"Well, Mary, what's your take on FinServia so far?" Greg asked.

I had spent a fair amount of time over the past month getting the lay of the land at FinServia, and I had developed a pretty good idea of what needed to be done. Now was the time to test my thoughts.

"We are in deep trouble," I started. "We're getting killed in the marketplace, and we don't have money or time to waste. We have to do, again, what we did in the real estate world fifteen years ago, when we transformed ourselves from a printer to a software and services provider. But this time, we don't have years; I just wish I knew how much time we *do* have."

Shaking his head, Greg agreed. "I'm not sure, either, Mary, but I know it isn't much. We have to cut costs quickly to stay ahead of the falling revenue, while speeding up our product development. Let's start on the product side. What do you think of Mervin? You feeling OK with your partnership with him?"

Mervin Thomas was the new VP of Marketing. He had joined FinServia just a month ago, recruited by Greg to provide the product vision and marketing approach. Prior to joining us, Mervin had been with Amalgamated Enterprises (AE) as manager of Stockholder Services, a hot-shot, ambitious young MBA climbing his way up. AE had taken its financial printing business from FinServia in favor of one of its more technologically nimble competitors three years ago, at Mervin's direction. Mervin had been recruited to join FinServia to help guide its renaissance.

"I am, Greg," I replied. "Normally, I would prefer that product management and engineering be under one Chief Engineer, as we did in Real Estate, but I have to admit that I know little about this business, and it's going to take me some time to get to know it. In the meantime, I have an awful lot to do in getting our software development to perform. I'm going to have to trust him, and your management of him, and focus my attention on the software development people and process."

"Excellent," said Greg. "We'll need to adapt our organization to the situation and people, and I think this should work well. Mervin has some great ideas about what we need to do, and I think he has the skills to help guide us. You'll need to help him a lot, and help me by providing 'adult supervision' if he needs it. Mervin is calling the new direction the Stockholder

Portal, a concept well beyond simply replacing print with online. It's about meeting the full set of needs of public companies worldwide to connect with their owners. There are some great revenue opportunities, and lots of competitive gaps."

I had reviewed Mervin's early stabs at a business plan, and it did indeed look promising. On the other hand, I thought his projected time frames to develop the technology functions required were unrealistic, and the development costs to do as much as he was proposing seriously underestimated. I was also worried about the length of the sales cycle. How long would it take from product completion to revenue realization? And how could we get our sales force to find opportunities, get them into the development pipeline when needed, and get them delivered? I voiced these concerns to Greg.

"I'm worried about all of that as well," Greg said. "I'm going to be spending a lot of time with our sales force, our customers, and our prospects, and working with you and Mervin from that direction. You need to get our development costs down, our development velocity way up, and improve our ability to change priorities quickly when we have a good revenue opportunity. Mary, I trust you to do this; you'll know what to do. Keep me generally informed, run the big decisions past me, but err on the side of asking for forgiveness instead of permission."

I knew that Greg trusted me, but this was more responsibility than he had ever given me before. Coming after the tightly controlled Cremins United project, it was both a breath of freedom and a bit scary. I wanted to check out one more important item: the GRI relationship.

"Greg, can you fill me in on the GRI contract, and your expectations around that? My sense is we should terminate the application development and support part of it as quickly as we can and maybe the computer operations as well. I want to start working on that right away," I said.

"GRI is going to be tricky, Mary," Greg explained. "We haven't redone our contract since the spinout of FinServia from Cremins; technically, the lawyers tell us that we are in default due to the change in control clause. GRI isn't pressing any advantage, thank goodness, probably because the commitment term in the contract has also expired. We are both going month to month, still paying the same rates as before, pending a determination of what path we want to take. You will need to determine what to do with GRI. Just be sensitive to how dependent we are on them now."

"Thanks, Greg. You know you can count on me. How about I take a bead on the situation next week, and update you next Friday?"

"Great. Welcome to FinServia, Mary. It's wonderful to have you here!"

As the California sun began to set to the west and the temperature began to dip, I could sense this latest career challenge beginning to heat up.

Signposts	Transforming FinServia
	• FinServia is in trouble. It has fallen far behind its competitors, and it needs rapid change if it is to survive.
	• Its product/software development processes have fossilized into a glacial, sterile series of rigid handoffs.
	• Mary is asked to focus on the product development: to drive down costs and increase velocity and flexibility. To do this, she needs to trust her team members in Marketing/Product Management and Sales.
Change Guides from Mary	• **Remember that "canned" methodologies like Lean and Agile often specify roles supposedly critical to success.** For Lean Product Development, as practiced by Toyota, it's the Chief Engineer; for Agile, the Product Owner and the self-managing team. In practice, each situation, each culture, each group of people has unique characteristics, perhaps demanding unique implementations. You must fit your role definitions to the situation at hand; many configurations can work, so long as you ensure all the key perspectives are represented.
	• **Identify the big risk areas and attack them first.** Don't do the "easy" stuff first; success there is meaningless. Get the business benefits! In FinServia's case, the big kahuna is the GRI relationship and all the baggage involved with it, so that's where initial focus must be.
Coming Up Next	The following day, Mary's wise friend and mentor Neville and his wife Cornelia join Mary and Wes for a backyard barbeque and a chat on their new work challenges. How will Neville counsel them on approaching their unique situations?

3

Setting Initial Approaches for Both Companies: February

Narrator: Wes

I was only slightly acquainted with Neville Roberts, despite his role as one of Mary's closest and most valued work colleagues. Neville had been Cremins' Real Estate Division's lead Chief Engineer (CE), the only CE senior to Mary, in many ways a mentor to and model for her. Today was an opportunity to get to know Neville a little better and a chance to talk through some early thoughts on how to approach my challenge at MCCA. Mary also wanted to run some ideas past Neville on what she was facing at FinServia.

Neville and his wife Cornelia had arrived at Mary's home an hour before, in the fading weak sunlight of a Southern California winter day. The four of us (Mary's children were with their father this weekend) sat on the deck in the backyard polishing off a bottle of Sonoma Pinot Noir that Cornelia brought, and we had gotten to know each other a little better. I had grilled up some steaks and Mary had put together the rest of dinner, which we moved into the house to consume as it began to cool off outside. During dinner, Mary and I each related our situations at work to Neville, preparing him for the after-dinner conversation we were about to begin. We had opened up another bottle and were relaxing in Mary's living room.

Neville and Cornelia made a striking couple. They were both in their mid-forties, both tall and healthy looking, in a California sort of way. Neville was lanky and big boned, with big hands and feet, a deep voice, and a prominent nose under his too-long bangs. Cornelia was just as tall, but small boned, with hands and feet that seemed almost too small for her length.

Neville was an unusual combination of engineer, marketing manager, and leader. He'd come to the United States twenty years ago from England to get his engineering degree at Cal Tech up in Pasadena, where he had married Cornelia, one of the few women attending the school at that time. He drifted from electrical engineering at Lockheed into the booming software field, and then into customer-facing and product development roles. Greg Allenby had found him four years ago for the Real Estate Division when Greg was building his initial management team, and Neville became a key member of the leadership group and the point person for the most important development projects. Cornelia was also an electrical engineer, one of the leading cell phone chip designers in the world. Luckily for us, she was interested in our kind of work and enjoyed listening to our conversation.

BUILDING A LEAN AND AGILE CHANGE MODEL

"Fascinating," Neville began. "It sounds like you both have a common destination: an organization that can develop customer-satisfying software quickly, without waste. You also have a common belief on the basic shape of that organization, which for the sake of simplicity we'll call Lean and Agile. You know generally what that organization needs to look like, in our three dimensions of *people, process, and tools*. Mary, do you still have our cheat sheet?"

I responded instead of Mary. "I have it in my briefcase, Neville. Let me grab it." I got up, found my briefcase, and took out my laminated copy of the Lean/Agile cheat sheet that Neville, Mary, and the Real Estate Division team had created a couple of years ago (Figure 3.1).[1]

As I handed it to Neville, I said, "I think I understand generally where we need to go, Neville, but I'm struggling with two things right now: some of the specifics on what to implement in my particular situation, and how to get there from here. There are so many changes to make, where do I begin?"

Mary chimed in as well. "I have the same questions, Neville. I've never had to lead an organization to change in this way. We built the Real Estate Division's Lean and Agile culture over almost ten years. When we started, we didn't have much of a guide other than our guts, and knowing that the conventional wisdom at that time didn't seem to work. As Lean came out of Toyota and Agile was developed, we learned, adapted, and implemented elements that made sense for what we needed at the time. It was the same way at Toyota: its Lean culture wasn't adopted all at once; it took decades for it to develop and mature.[2] Neither of us has decades!"

"Let's see if we can think this through a bit," Neville proposed. "We know that to build a top-performing software development organization we need to deal with *people, process,* and *tools*. It takes all three dimensions to succeed, with each reinforcing and supporting the other. You

Lean & Agile Development

- Towering technical competence
- Chief engineers
- Managers as teachers
- "Module development teams"
- Culture: value, eliminate waste, continuous improvement, reflection, problem solving

People

Purpose:
Lean operational value streams

Process

Tools

- Light project mgt: Milestones/ responsibilities/ "Go See"
- "Study" phase
- Integrating events
- Concurrent engineering
- Continuous Integration
- Agile development (sprints, scrum, agile planning, user stories)
  - One-piece flow/small batches
  - Test-driven development
  - Cadence & pull
  - Backlogs
  - Product owners
  - Enables "go see"
  - Eliminate handoffs

- Communication: One-page "A3's"
- Strategic alignment via "Policy Deployment"
- "Go See"
- Value stream mapping => Appropriate Process standardization
- Supplier partnerships
- Error proofing
- Team rooms

FIGURE 3.1
Lean and Agile software development. Adapted from J.M. Morgan and J.K. Liker. *The Toyota Product Development System* (New York: Productivity Press, 2006), 18.

need expert *people,* organized into appropriately focused teams, working in a culture dedicated to problem solving and elimination of waste. The people need to follow lightweight project *processes* that reinforce continual rapid cycles of learning, and have *tools* that make communication, learning, and partnering efficient. So there's no mystery about our destination; instead, what differs would be our starting point, eh? And perhaps the business conditions that could affect the path to our goals.

"So how about we start by talking about the various levers we could pull to make improvements, and then maybe we look at your two situations, how they are similar and how they vary? Do those variances point one way or another to which levers to pull, in which order, with which emphasis?"

Mary wasn't much of a theorist, and I could tell by the look on her face that she wasn't following Neville. She said so: "Neville, what the heck are you talking about? I don't need a general theory of change; I just want to pick your brain on what I need to do next!"

I had been a strategy consultant for years, and I thought I saw where Neville was going and its promise. "Mary, how about we try what Neville is proposing for a few minutes, and see if it's useful? After all, I need the same guidance you do, and perhaps we can both learn by comparing our two situations."

"Well, OK," Mary acceded. "Where do we start, Neville? You said something about change levers?"

"Perhaps I'm overcomplicating this," Neville said. "Think of it this way: What are the different approaches you can take to driving the transformations of your companies? I'll go first, starting with Wes's diagram. On which dimension of the triangle should you start to focus? Should you pick one, say, *people* or *process*, and put emphasis there? Or should you simultaneously try to change all three?"

"Ah, I see," said Mary. "That's a good question. Normally, I would say you have to start with people—that's what matters. In other words, if I could have a few great CEs, some awesome developers and product owners, and a culture focused on customer value and elimination of waste, I'd be there. But that would take so much time! I can't just order up a CE or two and a new culture."

"Perhaps you have to get to *people* through the other dimensions of the triangle," I conjectured. "If you change *process* and *tools*, will people grow?"

"We definitely saw that happen at Cremins," said Mary. "But it takes time. Maybe you can do both, work on *people* directly and indirectly."

"How about we postulate two ways of what I'll call *triangular change*, at least to get going here," Neville asked. He fished in his pocket for a pen, reached for my laminated Lean/Agile cheat sheet and some paper, and sketched out a picture to illustrate his point (Figure 3.2). "At each point in time, any particular organization has its own set of *people, process,* and *tools*, and a set of overarching business conditions, which together comprise its current reality. Our challenge is to figure out the best approach to move your organizations from where they are today, to where we would like them to be, in Lean/Agile Nirvana, as illustrated in Wes's picture (Figure 3.1).

"You can start with *people*, which you'd want to do for optimal alignment, and you'd need to do if you couldn't get enough traction going on *process* and *tools*. Or you can start with *process* and *tools*, if you know what you are doing and rapid action is more important than having the whole team's fingerprints on the change plan. Of course, in practice, you'll be pulling every lever you can, but as leaders, we need to have focus."

"I like it, Neville. How about I try to draw this up as we go?" I grabbed a notebook from my briefcase, and took a stab at a diagram. "How's this?" (Figure 3.3).

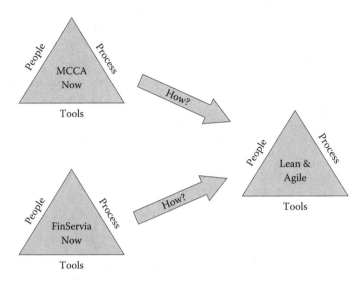

FIGURE 3.2
Three-dimensional Lean/Agile change.

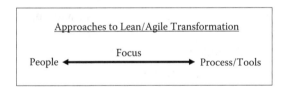

FIGURE 3.3
Dimensions of approach to Lean/Agile change.

Neville approved: "That looks good. Now, what's the next dimension?" he asked.

The concrete example we had just considered enabled Mary to see the value of Neville's explorations, and she was now enthusiastic about it. "I'm not sure if this is a new dimension or just an implication of the focus thought we already had, but how about a *leadership* approach? When we built the Real Estate Division, we were very participative—no one told us what we had to do, and we had no single leader driving us forward. Greg was in charge, no doubt, and he set the general tone and vision, but many of us explored ideas, experimented, and built the company together."

Cornelia, who had been quietly listening, now interjected. "At my company, we did just the opposite when we implemented Six Sigma years ago. We hired a new manufacturing director from a company deep into the methodology, and he required us to adopt it hook, line, and sinker. He brought in consultants, required every manager to get trained and become a black belt, allocated project money only to Six Sigma projects, inspected for control charts, you name it. It wasn't much fun, and we lost great people and became overly compliant and tentative, but our manufacturing quality improved pretty quickly."

Neville smiled at his wife, and he agreed with Mary, so I added a *leadership* dimension, from *participative* to *directive*. It seemed to me that *participative leadership* lined up with *focus* on *people*, so I put them together on the diagram, and showed it to our group (Figure 3.4). So far, so good.

"This is getting fun," said Mary. "I wonder how many of these dimensions we need."

Ever the consultant, I answered, "The magic number for consulting is usually three or four. People can't absorb and remember more than that very easily. Why don't we keep trying and see how many we come up with, and then we can whittle it down if we need to. I'm also wondering if the dimensional poles continue to line up, so we wind up having essentially two primary approaches, with variation, or if we wind up with something much more complex.

"In the meantime," I added, "I have another candidate. How about *pace*? At MCCA, I'm looking at a horizon of several years. True, we need to get some key things done quickly, but my boss is expecting that I'll have to add new talent and create a new culture that is simply absent right now. Lynn understands we have to build a software product development group, and she knows it will take time. My problem is to not screw up what's on track, while building out for the future. I think Mary has a completely different problem, which could call for a different approach."

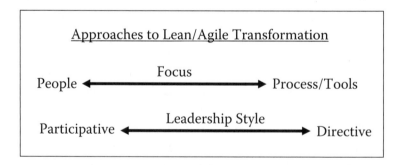

FIGURE 3.4
Approaches to Lean/Agile transformation.

"You're right about that, Wes," Mary nodded. "I don't have any time to spare. We are failing right now, and wasting a lot of money doing it. I have to drive radical change, and fast! There isn't all that much working now, so the risk of disruption is low."

"Perhaps we have two more dimensions here, eh, Wes?" queried Neville. "*Pace* and *disruption*? They are definitely related, but as we found with our *leadership* dimension, that seemed related to the *focus* issue as well. I think *disruption* does speak to a separate dimension as well, though for example, if you are putting together a whole new project, or a new partnership, or a new business, you don't have much to disrupt, and your approach could be very different than trying to modify an existing endeavor. Wes, can you draw up what we have so far?"

I took a moment and updated my picture (Figure 3.5). I struggled a bit to find generic names for the two sides of the chart, and it finally struck me: *People Driven* versus *Driving People*. I passed it around to Mary, Neville, and Cornelia, and Mary's living room was silent for a few moments as we all thought about it.

Neville gave his evaluation first. "I'm not sure if it's complete, or if it's exactly the right four dimensions," he said. "But it's certainly interesting, and it differentiates alternative approaches well. I like how it gives two basic approaches and some dimensions within each of them. Also your names for the two basic approaches are very clever, Wes."

"*Driving people* sounds a bit harsh to me, dear," said Mary. "Especially because *you* get the 'nice' side, being *people driven* and all, whereas *I* sound like a slave driver."

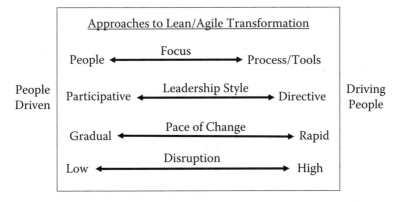

FIGURE 3.5
Approaches to Lean/Agile transformation (final).

"I'm open to better ideas," I shrugged, but I was pretty sure no one would have any.

Neville continued his evaluation. "Both of you were able to use characteristics of your own situations and connect them to the choices shown in the *people driven* and *driving people* dimensions. Unless one of you has a material improvement, I suggest we leave this alone for now, and move on to considering more about each of your situations. Once we have that better understood, we'll come back to this approach model, and see how well it stands up. Make sense?"

We all thought it did, so we let Neville take us back to considering our two situations.

COMPARING THE TWO OPPORTUNITIES, AND SELECTING AN APPROACH

Neville asked, "Wes, can you draw us one more of your consultant charts? I'd like us to identify some of the key characteristics describing how the situations you and Mary face differ. Then we can see how those variances could lead to the selection of one or the other poles of the change dimensions we just completed. For example, you said that although you had lots of opportunities to get better, you could also get much worse if you screwed up a change initiative, whereas Mary doesn't seem too worried that she could make it much worse."

"I think I see what you mean, Neville. Sure, I can do that. I think I'll call that characteristic *current performance*. Mary, can you list a few of the characteristics of FinServia that would drive your change approach in one direction or another?"

"Sure, I can think of several," Mary said, and proceeded to list several, which I wrote down while she talked:

- "Wes has a chance of getting by even if he does nothing, whereas if I do nothing, I surely fail.
- "I know just what I want my group to do, and I can tell them, whereas Wes has only a vague understanding of software development." [That hurt a little, but it was true; nevertheless, I called it *technical expertise of leader.*]

- "I like to tell people what to do, and I'm pretty good at it, whereas Wes is more of a team-building, listening type of guy." [True again and something I'm proud of, even though it sounded like a criticism coming from Mary.]
- "I have to cut costs and staff by a lot, and soon, whereas Wes has the luxury of adding people.
- "Wes is in big trouble if he loses a couple of the wrong people, who are holding the place together and without whom Wes can't possibly deliver on the big promises that Jackass Langley has made. I don't think I care too much if any particular people walk out." [Mary had started calling Jack Langley, MCCA's VP of Sales, Jackass soon after I described him to her. It made me a little wary of introducing them to each other.]
- "I'm sure my people have no chance of reforming themselves, no matter how much training or cajoling I give them. They are too entrenched in a system that gives them power and status and protects them from having to perform and think. In contrast, Wes's people seem to have promise because they are more chaotic than certainly wrong."

I grimaced a little at Mary, but I admired her list. I added one more point, about our managers:

- "Lynn, my boss, is not an expert in my area, and she knows I am not either, so she is likely to be hesitant about rapid change dictated by me. Lynn needs to be informed and convinced, and she needs to gauge the reaction of others on her team. Greg, on the other hand, knows as much as Mary does about software product development, and he is confident that Mary's expertise and perspective is similar to his. Mary has little convincing to do in order to move fast."

I finished my writing and handed it to Neville to review (Figure 3.6).

"I like it, Wes. It looks general enough to apply to a lot of situations, and it seems to fit these two very well," said Neville, "without being too formulaic." By the time Neville said this, Mary and Cornelia were looking over his shoulder at the chart, so Neville handed the document to Mary. Mary and Cornelia studied it; Cornelia was the first to speak.

Characteristic	MCCA	FinServia
Current Performance	Uneven; alternately great and terrible	Uniformly poor
Urgency of Change	Moderate; possible to stumble along	High; failure assured if not successful
Technical Expertise of Leader	Low; Wes is a facilitative with broad business skills, not expert in this business or software product development.	High; Mary is extraordinarily knowledgeable about software product development and can specify in detail how things should be done.
Style of Leader	Participative	Directive. Mary likes things to be done her way and isn't shy about telling people so.
Staff Trajectory	Growing	Shrinking
Individuals Critical to Mission	Some of the technical leaders	Probably none
Ability of Organization to Reform Itself, Given Support and Chance	Possible; not set in any particular way, see need to change (poor relationship with Sales)	Unlikely. Each person/group in the existing process is validated by their role in the process and likely not able to think outside their comfortable box.
Support from Senior Executives	Supportive, but wary	Very supportive and trusting

FIGURE 3.6
Comparing change characteristics: MCCA and FinServia.

"Looks clear enough to me, Mary," Cornelia said. "No doubt in my mind that your situation calls for the *driving people* approach. You start by directing *people* to use the *processes* and *tools* you know are right, and you intentionally disrupt the existing structures and methods to make rapid change. If you lose some people on the way, so what? There are too many of them anyhow; they aren't performing well now, and most likely, the least useful ones would bail on you. Get them going in a better direction, and see who falls in line with you. Build your participative, high-performing team later. Make bold moves, keep your peers and boss informed but not involved in your decisions, and move fast."

Cornelia continued, "As for you, Wes, you need to start with the *people* you have. They are critical to what's going on now; they have some excellent skills and abilities and they don't seem to be stuck in their current ways. In fact, it sounds like no one is really happy with how things work today. You'll probably have to add some new blood as well. But you can't start with *process* or *tools*, because even if you were willing and tried to specify exactly what should be done, you'd probably get it wrong. No offense."

"No offense taken, Cornelia," I agreed. "I know the direction we need to go, but not how to get there. I need my team's help. I'm hoping I can get the team to buy into a Lean and Agile direction, and then they can choose which *processes* and *tools* make the most sense for where we are and where we need to be."

Cornelia continued, wrapping up her assessment. "You will need to be cautious with your peers and boss: make sure they're buying into your program, because they won't automatically assume you are doing the right things. If all goes well, you avoid disruption, get fingerprints of everyone on the change needed, get widespread adoption in ways that best fit your group, and gradually transform the group into a high-performing Agile team."

"That would certainly be a great outcome," I agreed. "Hey," I exclaimed, turning to Mary. "I thought you said that Neville was the wise old man who would help us think through what to do. Looks to me like Cornelia is tonight's counselor."

Cornelia and Neville both laughed, and Cornelia was quick to protest. "That's all I've got, Wes. Anything more detailed and you'll have to look to Neville, unless you need some guidance on how to design a communications chip!"

WES AND MARY MAKE THEIR INITIAL PLANS

Mary had hoped to play some bridge tonight, so she started to move us towards a conclusion of our business discussions. "How about we spend just a few more minutes on this, and then we play a rubber or two of bridge?" she asked.

"Bridge would certainly be a good compatibility test for the two of you," joked Neville. "What else do you want to do, in just a few minutes?"

"How about Wes and I take turns going over our top five priorities, and see what you think, Neville? Would that be OK?" Mary asked. Now that we were beyond what Mary saw as "theorizing" and into specific action planning, Mary was back in her element.

"Sounds like fun," Neville said. "Let's hear your top five, and also give your next two events." I knew from seeing Neville work at Cremins that he was partial to what he called *integrating events*, a concept from Lean product development. Setting up a series of these events, which become targets for multiple groups and opportunities for all involved to see progress visually, was a foundation of Neville's approach.

"I go first," said Mary. "Here's what I think my top five priorities are:

1. **"Deal with the GRI contract.** I've got to take application development back from them if I have a chance of speeding it up and cutting costs.
2. **"Figure out my leadership team.** I know I'll be driving people, but I do need the right people to drive! I'm afraid my current group is woefully inadequate to the task ahead of us.
3. **"Change the development process to be more Agile.** Right now, we seem to be operating in contradiction to all of the Agile values:[3] we value *processes* and *tools* over *people* and *interactions*; we value documentation over working code; we value contract negotiation over collaboration; and we value following plans over responding to change. I'm thinking we push as quickly as we can into more a more Agile process, scrum, and hope the values start to seep in.
4. **"Get alignment with Mervin, my Product Owner.** I don't have control of the product concept and priorities, as I would ideally like, so we need to form the right partnership."

Then Mary paused. "I'm stuck. I can't think of a number five, so I'll stop there; that's enough. As for my integrating events, I'm choosing two:

- **"The first event is sharing my plan with Greg and my peers.** I'd like to do that in two weeks, and include the GRI resolution, a budget, an initial people action priority list, and an explanation of how we'll be going forward with release management and scrum.
- **"The second event will be our initial release planning session,** which I hope to do in 4 to 6 weeks.[4] We'll set aside three or four days, gather whatever leadership I've got by then, share some vision and plans, do

some training in the Lean and Agile techniques I'll be forcing on the group to start, and then build a rough backlog and release plan."

Having ticked off these 4 top priorities and 2 target events, Mary asked us if we had any comments.

"I might have your number 5, Mary," Neville commented. "Remember your focus on *process* and *tools* over *people*? You seem to have totally ignored the transformative power of *tools,* so how about this:

5. **"Select and implement an Agile management tool, to track the backlog, set up sprints, do reporting,** and so on. After all, if you're going to force people into a box, you might as well give them a good box right up front. I'd suggest you go with AgileFocus, since you already know it well."

"I like that idea," Mary beamed. "They offer hosting, so we don't have to worry about technology, and we can get started without too big an investment. Thanks, Neville!"

"Wes," Neville guided me, "your turn. List your top 5 priorities, plus 2 integrating events."

I had the advantage of thinking about my 5 while Mary elaborated on hers, and unlike her, I had come up with the full complement. I listed my top 5 priorities one by one, and we talked them through:

1. **Establish a better mechanism to link sales efforts and expressed customer interest with our ability and interest to deliver.** We don't want to discourage aggressive sales or uncovering new opportunities, but we also don't want Sales to be committing us to things we can't deliver. This was going to be a tough one, because it involved dealing with Jackass Langley, but I hoped that I could partner up with Connie on it and at least get some improvements underway.

2. **Figure out the Chief Engineer (CE) issue.** I conceptualized this as filling the gap between sales and development. Lean product development (as practiced at Toyota) combined the development leader with product management and program/project management into this revered figure, the CE.[5] In contrast, Agile had this dreamy conception of a *product owner* who could magically tell the developers just what the software should do, and didn't seem to have any project management at all from what I could tell, just a

self-organizing team and a scrum master.[6] I doubted either would work for me, but I didn't know what would.

3. **Be sure we could deliver what we'd already sold** to our customer, San Diego National Insurance.

4. **Implement release management.** We needed to establish a vision of where our new product was going to guide our sales force, or else they'd make something up and sell it!

5. **Gain broad alignment among Development, Sales, my peers, and my boss about what problems we now faced, and what we jointly needed to do to solve them.** I believed that moving in the Lean/Agile direction was the solution, but I needed them to believe it also, and to help take initiative in getting us there. This would take some combination of communication, training, coaching, directing, and leading—a combination I'd need to figure out.

Neville compared our two lists and said, "It's interesting how different your lists are. You both have some tasks in the area of release management, backlog management, and perhaps scrum, although the emphasis is different: Mary wants to get immediate cost reduction and faster results, whereas Wes wants to lay the basis for longer-term success and to control expectations. You also both have something in the CE space: Mary getting aligned with Mervin and getting some leadership in place, Wes more broadly figuring out how to do project and product management. You also have some critical differences, with Wes more focused on getting buy-in and building self-sustaining change, whereas Mary just wants to get it done, at least to begin with," he summarized. "Is that enough for tonight? We can explore some more over bridge, if you like."

"Wait a minute," I protested. "I need to tell you about my integrating events." My dinner companions briefly slowed their movement to the bridge table and listened to me for another moment. "The big one is our DocWorld conference in July, where we need to reveal our product strategy and set expectations in our market. I also need to stage something with my management team to set direction and gain agreement—not sure when to do that, but I'll set it soon. Is that specific enough?"

I could tell Neville was thinking over my events; he had one more thought for me. "Wes," he said, "I like the conference idea, but that's more about communication than integration. But OK, it's a target, and it'll focus energy and attention. As for aligning the management team, how about using an Agile idea to make your change? Could you get your team together and lay out a release plan for your transformation? And then manage it in sprints and scrums, and adjust at the end of each sprint, just as we do in developing software? [7] Might be a great way to ensure that it is truly *people driven* and adaptive. Then you can have the same type of cadence of integrating events for your change process as you do with your software process."

I had to think Neville's idea through for a moment; it seemed to make sense.

"Sounds right," I said after cogitating. "I'll need to think through exactly how to do that, but why not? Eat our own dog food, so to speak."[8]

"Speaking of dog food, Wes," Mary poked at me, "how would you like to try being my bridge partner?" Dissed, but I was game. I knew I was in trouble when Mary asked me if I played the Jacoby transfer. But I was intrigued by Neville's last idea, and ultimately would give it a try.

Signposts	• Wes and Mary consult with Neville, a Lean/Agile expert, on how they should approach the transformation efforts in front of them.
	• They postulate two basic kinds of change, *people driven* and *driving people*. The two approaches vary in emphasis on *people vs. tools* and *process*, participative vs. directive leadership, gradual vs. rapid change, and low vs. high disruption.
	• Mary and Wes compare the current states of their two organizations and their own leadership styles, and conclude that Wes will take the *people-driven* approach, whereas Mary will take the *drive people* approach, even though it sounds slightly evil.
	• Mary and Wes lay out their top 5 priorities and first 2 integrating events.
Change Guides from Wes	• **Make a plan, specific to your reality.** Although there are commonalities among situations (this book's thesis depends on it, posing "too much" and "not enough" structure cases), the *differences* are what matter. Draw out your own Lean/Agile triangle, and figure out what path might work best for you.
	• **Use integrating events.** Integrating events are as powerful an idea in making transformations as in making software or new products. They focus the mind and the organization and provide powerful feedback.
	• **Accelerate delivery.** As Wes's boss said, you get no timeout or forgiveness while making transformations. Even Mary, who is contemplating a consciously disruptive change, expects to accelerate delivery from Day 1.

- **Find outside wisdom.** One of the most powerful Lean product development tenets is *towering technical expertise*, and that applies both to the development and change processes. Even the most expert of us can use a mature viewpoint and honest sounding board.

Coming Up Next

Wes gets to know MCCA in more depth. He meets his development team, talks with Connie Esposito (MCCA Operations VP) to learn about her struggles with Sales, and visits with a key customer.

ENDNOTES

1. This diagram summarizes the Lean and Agile software development system as Michael Levine presented in *Tale of Two Systems*, 36-45. Readers unfamiliar with Lean and Agile software are safe to read ahead in this book, as the elements will be discussed in due course.
2. See, for example, Jeffrey K. Liker, *Toyota Way: 14 Management Principles from the World's Greatest Manufacturer* (New York: McGraw Hill, 2004).
3. For explanation of Agile values, see Agilemanifesto.org.
4. Release planning is described in Mike Cohen, User Stories Applied (Boston: Addison-Wesley, 2004), 9ff.
5. *Toyota Product Development System*, see note 3.
6. The role of the Agile product owner is described in Cohen, *User Stories Applied*.
7. The idea of using scrum to roll out Agile was presented in Ken Schwaber, *The Enterprise and Scrum* (Richmond, WA: Microsoft Press, 2007).
8. "Eating our own dog food" is slang for a company using products that it makes.

Section II

Understanding the Landscape
March

4

Getting to Know the MCCA
Team and Culture: March

Narrator: Wes

I am now several weeks into my new job at MCCA, gradually getting to know the place. I found an apartment, but it won't be ready until the first week in April, so I'm still at the Shelter Island Hotel. Not having a real place of my own has led me to work a lot—it's either work, spend time at Mary's, or hang out in a hotel room. Mary and I have chosen to limit our time together with her children, so they can get used to me gradually. As a result, even though we are now living just a few miles apart, I see her only two or three times a week. The good point about that is we would both like it to be more often, and we've started to talk about setting a date to tie the knot. The downside is I'm working almost all the time.

Being VP of Development is a very different feeling from either consulting or doing support work at Cremins. Here, I feel I'm doing the leadership myself, instead of helping others to lead. Fun—and scary. It would have been nice to start off in a better position than we are, but these are the cards I was dealt. I've been meeting people and working on the priorities I set at Mary's with Neville and Cornelia a few weeks ago.

In my first week, I planned to explore Development, Sales, and the links between them. It was mostly about discovery, getting to know my development team, and listening in more detail to Connie, our VP of Operations, whose struggles with Sales I had overheard on my first visit. I followed up these internal experiences with an enlightening visit to a key customer, San Diego National Insurance Company. I now believe I have a good bead on MCCA's situation and a much better sense for what needs to be done.

MEETING MY DEVELOPMENT TEAM

I started with Phillip Glass, the rather morose development manager. I had briefly met Phillip a few weeks earlier when I came to visit before I formally joined the company. Last week, I set up an hour for us to talk, and I set it for his office so he would be comfortable.

When I got to Phillip's office, though, he was nowhere to be seen. The office was a small square room, with no window, with just a small metal desk overflowing with computers, a desk chair, two guest chairs in front of the desk, and a file cabinet. I smiled at the small stuffed Eeyore on top of the file cabinet. It was good to see that Phillip had a sense of humor about himself. I waited for about ten minutes and then wandered out onto the floor to see if he was around. Perhaps he'd forgotten our appointment or had been diverted.

The development area was strikingly different from the executive area just a floor above. Instead of spacious offices lining the outside windowed walls, a narrow walkway separated the windows from a hodgepodge of cubes and desks. This walkway was, I later learned, a small triumph of the developers, who had requested the space to allow the light to be shared by everyone. Managers like Phillip were consigned to inside-wall offices only, to which they had readily agreed. And instead of company-provided coffee and tea areas, a few Mr. Coffees were set up around the floor on makeshift tables, with coffee cans adjacent for per-cup contributions. The next day, I asked my assistant to work with the executive floor's coffee provider to supply the developers as well—and this single act probably did more to earn me loyalty than anything else I did!

As I wandered the floor asking for Phillip, I eventually found him huddled with three young developers, all looking intensely at a screen. The developers looked much the worse for wear. Phillip saw me approach and reluctantly tore himself away from the huddle.

Phillip was as I remembered him—hair shaggy in an unfashionable way, an inch-long full beard, and large plastic-rimmed glasses straight from the 1970s, radiating an air of intensity and earnestness. He wore jeans, a t-shirt, and boots, looking more like an auto mechanic than one of the business executives just upstairs.

"Sorry, Mr. Wesleyan," he said, "I didn't notice the time." He turned to the bedraggled developers, excused himself, and led me back to his office.

"Please call me Wes. Is it OK to call you Phillip?" I asked. He nodded, and I continued, "Crisis of some sort, Phillip?"

"Just the usual. A salesman brought in a new deal a few weeks ago. It would have required that we drop what we were doing and take on a tough system conversion, from the failing system to ours. The deal went up to Finance, as usual, and the finance analyst asked me if we could get it done. My team was already working overtime and falling behind, so I finally got up the nerve to say no. I thought that was the end of it, until I got into the office yesterday morning. The salesman offered my developers a bonus if they would come in this weekend and do the work. I might never have known they'd done this if they hadn't gotten stuck on a format that hasn't been used since before they were born."

I was stunned. I was learning that this company was sales driven, but this was truly remarkable! Phillip's reaction was just as telling—he wasn't angry, he was taking it in stride.

"Is it okay if we talk for a bit now?" I asked.

Phillip looked at his watch and said, "Yes, of course. We had this time scheduled, and I think I've got the conversion past the hiccup. Here are the org charts, the people list, and the list of projects underway as you asked. Shall we start there?"

"Why don't we start by talking about ourselves. I'd like to learn more about you, your background, how you are enjoying your job, and where you want to go with your career. I can share the same about myself, and then we can dive into your organizational and project review."

Phillip hesitated. From what I had seen of this place so far, there didn't seem to be a lot of caring about him as a person, and I didn't peg Phillip as the type of person who thought about his own needs very often. But I had asked, and I was his new boss.

"Would you mind going first?" he asked. It was a reasonable request, which also would allow him to gauge how much he would share. The tone in his voice was somewhere between wary and curious, with a little resignation thrown in. To Phillip, so far, I was just one more change thrown at him, to which he'd have to adapt.

I gave Phillip a brief summary of my career—law school, consulting, Cremins Corporation, working with Lynn, and joining MCCA. I told him how excited I was to have this opportunity and how I wanted to partner with the existing people at MCCA to help the company grow. I relayed the essence of Lynn's strategy, to improve operations, keep growing the existing business, and build out our information management software and accelerate our growth. And I shared the five priorities I had set with Neville's help:

1. Establish a better relationship with Sales.
2. Determine project management and product management regimes (the Chief Engineer issue).
3. Deliver what we've promised to our customer, SDNI.
4. Implement release management.
5. Gain broad alignment and commitment to our plans.

Finally, I explained that I was attracted to the ideas of Lean and Agile software development, and I hoped to recruit a core team in product development to guide and drive our growth, perhaps using the Agile process of scrum.

Through all of this, Phillip paid rapt attention but didn't say much. When I stopped to probe for understanding, I got nods or OKs, but not much more. After I mentioned the scrum idea and stopped talking, Phillip gathered his thoughts and began to respond.

"That's quite an agenda. It's a good one, and I think you've hit on most of the key high-level needs. I don't know much about Lean and Agile, other than I've heard about them, and a few of our new developers are trying some of the techniques. We're going to need to talk about the San Diego National Insurance project: it's in trouble and needs some help. Your other items, if we could deal with them, would go a long way toward making projects like SNDI work better.

"We're going to have to spend time on many of these issues, Phillip," I said, "and I want to see what I can do to help. How about we focus today on getting to know each other, the sales interface, and next steps on the priorities I laid out, and we'll talk about SDNI in the next few days?"

"Sounds good," Phillip said. "I can start with me, I suppose. I've been with MCCA for 22 years: I joined as a programmer soon after Ernie started up. He began by getting printed reports on paper and microfilming them, but then he needed to start taking in electronic files and going direct to film and fiche. That's when he hired me. I spent my first year here setting up incoming file transmissions and formatting for output. Been here ever since."

"Have you always been the technology manager?" I asked.

"Since the day I got here," Phillip confirmed. "Ernie didn't know much about technology—he spent most of his time in Sales. A couple of times, I talked to him about getting someone else to be the manager, but he wouldn't hear of it. He trusted me, and he wasn't sure how else he could be confident in our technology."

"You say you considered moving out of the management role?" I asked. "Would you mind telling me about that? We're going to have opportunities to change our organization as we grow, and I'd like to be sure we provide you the best possible fit."

"I'm really not much of a manager, Wes, as I'm sure the salespeople have told you by now. I'm a programmer, a darn good one, and also a designer and troubleshooter. I wind up spending all my time fighting fires, in our systems, with customers, and with Sales, instead of doing what I love to do. Over the years, I've tried to hire project managers and analysts to relieve me of the work I don't like as well. But Ernie and the salespeople in his mold liked coming directly to the people who could do what needed to be done, and they never supported putting structure and process in the middle.

"I remember one time," Phillip explained, "just a few years ago. Ernie was out at one of our utility customers, and he heard about their need to put customer statements online. He calls me up, all excited, and asks if we can do it, and how much it would cost us. He wanted to make a proposal and a commitment right then and there. I asked him for some time to figure it out, and he said OK and gave me a couple of hours, said it could wait until after that afternoon's round of customer golf. I pulled Rico and a few others together, we gave him what he needed, and we had the business before the drinks were gone at the 19th hole.

"The problem," Phillip said, "is that we're doing bigger things now, with a lot more people involved, and I'm just not able to do what we used to do. Things are more complicated, the problems more diverse. We—"

At that moment, we were interrupted by a young woman, hurrying into Phillip's office, breathless. "Phillip, can you come now? Rico just went off the deep end."

Phillip swore under his breath and excused himself. I later found out that Rico DeSilva, our star but prima-donna developer, had just told a salesman to perform some unnatural acts on himself, announced to his cube mates that he was "out of here," and left the building in a huff.

I shook my head to myself, feeling that I had gained at least some of the understanding I had been seeking. Despite its central importance to MCCA's success, the development team was taken for granted, quite literally kept out of sight in the basement, buying its own coffee while the executives luxuriated in their offices upstairs. Its leader, Phillip, did the best he could to go along with what was thrown at him, while trying to maintain peace and deliver on what Sales had promised, while its star developer,

Rico, periodically went off like a volcano. I didn't like what I was seeing, but at least I was getting the unvarnished view. If I could build some trust and find a way to get the development team more into the game, I might have something going here.

TRANSFORMING OPERATIONS, INCLUDING THE RELATIONSHIP WITH SALES

The day after the Rico incident, my focus was on getting to know Connie Esposito, VP of Operations, and making a step forward in improving the integration of the sales force with product development. I knew we had a problem, and I hoped Connie might have the glimmer of an answer for me, since she had a head start—and from what I had seen, she also seemed to have more guts than I do!

As I waited outside Connie's office for her to finish a phone call, I thought about the week so far. MCCA's management was consumed by the changes that Connie was driving to our operations, about which Jack Langley was having a lot of heartburn. This had been the topic of my first meeting at MCCA when I had come to interview, and it was still going strong weeks later. Today, I was going to learn about the struggle from Connie. I had a dog in this fight also, as I had seen in my introduction to Phillip's team yesterday.

"Come on in, Wes," I heard from the door and saw Connie waving me into her office. Despite my "democratic" sympathies with the development group downstairs, I had to admit that I loved how the MCCA executive offices were furnished, with meeting tables and comfortable corners in which to talk. In contrast, Cremins had standardized on modular cubes and had mandated that everyone, from help desk to the Chief Executive Officer (CEO), reside in large mazes. Connie sat in her armchair, and I sat down across from her on the edge of the small couch.

"Welcome to MCCA, Wes. Interesting time to join, no?"

"I'll bet it's always been interesting around here."

"It has been since I got here, let's see, that's almost six months now. The company is kind of a mess; our customers are variously in love with and hate us, our operations are inefficient and uneven, and our people are hard working and dedicated but seriously underskilled. And everywhere I go to try to improve things—there stands Jack, smack-dab in my way."

"I noticed that last month. How did you two resolve the argument over your organizational announcement?" I asked.

"We added some paeans to Sales in the announcement memo and Jack's ego was stroked enough that he okay'd it. Lynn mostly supports what I'm trying to do, although she hedges her bets with Jack too much for my taste," Connie said. "Jack is trying to protect his commissions. He's had a very sweet deal—his sales team gets a percentage of the profits of every sale, and it's based on the profit projection. And Jack gets a cut, an override, on everything! The idea is that Sales can't control execution, so salesmen—and they are almost all men—shouldn't be subject to the vagaries of actual profitability.

"The beauty of it for Jack is that each region has been effectively its own business, with the salesman at the helm. Formally, the local operations groups used to roll up to the Operations Senior Vice President (SVP), but it was a weak roll-up, with weak controls on contracting and cost forecasting. In practice, the local operations leads were under the thumbs of the salesmen, and they've learned that they don't want to kill a deal by having cost projections that make us uncompetitive. So, Jack and his team get their commissions, our operations leads get stuck with cost forecasts they can't meet, and the company continually takes it on the chin. All made worse by the fact that our operational skills are weak. Not a pretty story!"

Connie's explanation was consistent with what I had heard from Lynn and observed for myself so far, and it explained the financial status of the firm. Individuals within the firm were thriving, but the firm itself limped along. I feared the application of this sales-driven culture to my product development area, especially after observing Phillip's travails yesterday. Would the behavior of the Sales Department derail what I was planning to do? Did I have a battle coming up like the ones Connie had been fighting? Given these questions, I had several things I wanted to accomplish in this meeting, and I laid them out for Connie. I wanted to hear about her operations, its relationships with Sales, and plans for change.

"All right, Wes," Connie agreed. "You'll need to understand the sales force dynamics for your role as well, since your success will depend on them supporting the new product development efforts instead of forcing you to spend all your resources chasing uneconomic deals that only benefit Jack and his cronies. Here, let me show you the organizational structure before we changed it three weeks ago."

Connie walked over to her desk, which was totally clean and neat, and opened a file drawer. She drew out a thin folder and brought it back with her to our corner.

"Here it is," she said, as she drew a single sheet of paper out of the folder. Before I turned to the diagram, I commented, "Well, I'm already impressed by your organizational skills. Your office is spotless, and you were able to go to your desk and find exactly what you wanted immediately. I'm going to be embarrassed to have you over to my office!"

"Just habit. You know I spent the last twenty years at Toyota? Actually, NUMMI?" I nodded; Lynn had told me how she had recruited Connie from the Toyota–General Motors joint venture outside of San Francisco, hoping to bring MCCA operations to something approaching Toyota's quality and efficiency. "One of the first things they taught us was the 'Five Ss.'[1] You know them? Sort, Straighten, Shine, Standardize, and Sustain. Keep only what you need, everything in its place, regular cleaning, and keep it that way! We'd get a lot of guff if we didn't practice what we preached, so I just got used to it. After a while, I stopped thinking about it, and now I can't imagine my office looking any other way."

"How did you get into manufacturing management? I'll bet there weren't a lot of women managers at Toyota," I asked.

"It's kind of a long story. Has anyone told you my real name yet? It's not Connie or Constance, as you might think. It's Contentment. My parents were 1960s hippies, and when I was born, they cursed me with a name only they could love. My rebellion was not to do drugs or run around with boys; it was to want to build things—especially cars, the epitome of the corrupt capitalist consumption-oriented system.

"My dad used to tease me about my last name too—apparently, in old Italy, Esposito was a surname often given to abandoned children. He would say that I didn't seem like a child of theirs, that maybe the hospital had switched me for his real daughter, and that maybe he should give me up for adoption to a truck driver or a plumber. I knew he was just kidding around and didn't really mean it—he just couldn't understand how he and my mother had failed so miserably as parents! Anyhow, I began working at the GM plant outside of Oakland right after high school, disappointing my parents once more, and I stayed on after Toyota took it over and installed the Toyota Production System (TPS).[2] I wasn't doing very well at GM, but Toyota management gave me a chance to think and drive improvement, and I kept getting promoted. TPS made sense to me."

"Are your parents still hippies?" I asked. "Sounds like an exciting childhood. Mine was so boring by comparison."

"To the extent sixty-five-year-old retired grandparents can be hippies, they still are," Connie said. "They've reconciled themselves to my success in the business world, at long last. But enough about me, let's talk about my operations.

"Take a look at this chart of the Sales and Operations groups as I found them, Wes (Figure 4.1). Before I could even begin to make the operational improvements needed, we had to break down the control that Jack had over operations. You can see in the chart, each Operations VP was linked to a Sales VP, and that's where the real control was, not in the formal reporting relationships of the Operations VPs to my predecessor. The Operations VPs are usually collocated with the regional Sales leads, and their careers

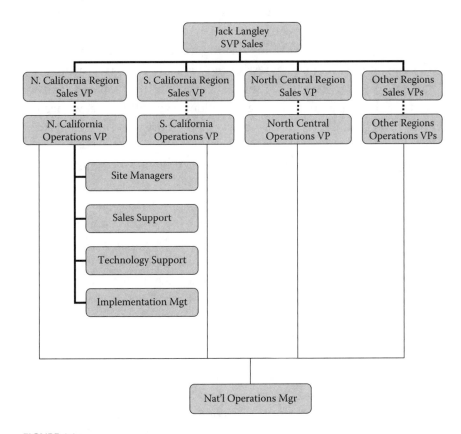

FIGURE 4.1
MCCA operations before reorganization.

depended more on how Jack and his team talked to Ernie about them than anything my predecessor did formally."

I had seen in Phillip's development team the control that Sales exercised over technology, and I could understand what that might feel like in Operations as well. But there had to be good things in the closeness of Operations to Sales: being driven by getting new deals and keeping existing customers didn't sound like a bad motivation to me. I asked Connie to elaborate: "Can you explain in a little more detail, Connie? Shouldn't Operations be focused on new deals and customer retention?"

Connie agreed. "Oh yes, indeed, Wes, that's what should drive Sales, but it's not solely what should drive Operations, and it's definitely not what should drive our entire company. Getting new deals and keeping existing customers is an outcome of the actions we take to build a great company. The company needs to be driven by profitable growth, not just revenue, and Operations—well, Operations needs to be driven by operational effectiveness and continual improvement. Lynn understands that our profitability and growth, at least in my sector, should depend on how good we are at Operations, not how aggressive and accommodating we are in Sales. We need to put more balance into our customer relationships, and we need to lead first with outstanding operational capabilities that we need to develop and tout, not by chasing every opportunity that Sales rustles out of the bushes."

"I can see why Jack wouldn't have been crazy about your plans. So, what exactly did you do?" I asked.

"I had to wrest control from Sales quickly so I could start changing Operations. I spent my first five months here traveling, seeing operations, talking with customers and salespeople, benchmarking competitors, and drawing up value stream maps[3] to determine just how much waste we have available to take out of our shops. I kept Lynn informed of what I was finding, and I was happy to see how much she agreed with what I saw and how I wanted to change things. I wasn't surprised, of course: she had specifically sought out someone with Lean operating experience, and especially someone with experience with Lean change. Anyhow, six weeks ago, I was ready to start in earnest, and I knew my first step had to be to clear the path of Jack and the control of his Sales group."

Connie took a sip of her soda and continued. "I worked with Human Resources (HR) and came up with a reorganization plan. We worked through it with Jack and Lynn, and you saw the result. Ultimately, Lynn

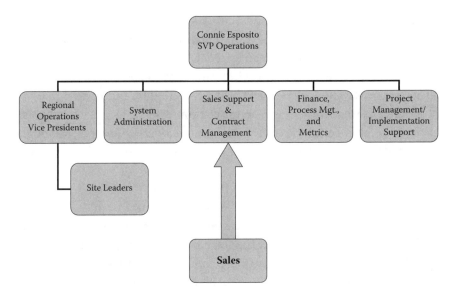

FIGURE 4.2
MCCA operations after reorganization.

had to force Jack to accept it, and so he seems to have done so. Here, take a look at what we did" (see Figure 4.2).

"As you can see, I've weakened the Operations leaders and the site leaders. They no longer control their own little empires. We made functional departments for System Administration; Finance, Process Management, and Metrics; and Project Management/Implementation Support. And the topper is we created a department for Sales Support and Contract Management, which is now the formal way into my group for Sales. It's been rocky, to say the least, and I don't have all the people and processes in place to make this work the way it should, but it's coming along. And now I have the levers to pull to install the TPS—or should I say the MPS—for MCCA Production System?"

As Connie explained the change she had just made, I thought of the change model that Mary and I had worked through with Neville. I thought that I was hearing a *drive people* model of change. I had a few more questions to ask to be sure.

"What are your next steps, Connie, now that you have the levers to pull?" I asked.

"I've got quite a few going on all at once," she answered. "I've hired several new managers who have TPS experience, and they are driving MPS into their own sites and regions. We are doing a lot of training—the new

TPSers are doing it themselves in their realms, and we've brought in some outside trainers to teach value stream mapping, continuous improvement, 5S, gemba walks, and visual management. All sites are expected to have their own plan to ensure that we implement MPS by year-end. The new TPS-experienced managers, a few of the consultants, and I travel to each of the sites as frequently as we can to see progress, teach, and evaluate the leaders. So far, most of the operations sites are doing quite well, although we've had a few managers quit, and a couple sites began to fall apart from all the change."

"And Jack? How is he taking all of this?" I asked.

Connie sat back in her chair and sighed. "It's hit and miss. I've been flexible about enforcing some of the changes. We aren't ready, on one day, to flip a switch and change all the formal and informal paths from the distributed sales force to the distributed operations managers. I've tried to start the transition with a small group in sales support, including building some higher-level skills around opportunity assessment and design, and that has been a benefit to the Sales group. Similarly, the Implementation group promises to add some reliability to new business setup, and Jack sees that and appreciates it. You should spend some time with those groups—perhaps we can make those functions common for operations and development."

"I like that idea," I said, and I mentally noted the need to get with the leaders of those groups and talk to some sales people in a month or so after they'd had an opportunity to live in the new regime for a while.

"As for my relationship with Jack, we are meeting weekly, with Cynthia, the VP of HR, as mediator and facilitator, and we have to jointly give status to Lynn's staff meeting, as you've seen. I think we'll make it."

At this, Cynthia herself poked her head in the door, announcing that Connie had a candidate waiting for an interview. My time with Connie up for now, I wandered back to my office by way of the coffee machine and spent a few minutes thinking through what I had just learned.

I took out the comparison sheet that Neville, Mary, and I had constructed last weekend, comparing the conditions at FinServia and MCCA that shaped our choices on the approach to change. Thinking over Connie's comments, I added a column for MCCA Operations (Figure 4.3).

Connie's situation seemed to argue as strongly as Mary's did for a *drive people* strategy, imposing a new system quickly and risking whatever disruption ensued. MCCA Operations has some good qualities, as our product development did, but all the other factors were more similar to

	People Driven	*?*	*Drive People*
Characteristic	MCCA: Product Development	MCCA: Operations	FinServia
Current Performance	Uneven	*Uneven*	Uniformly poor
Urgency of Change	Moderate	*High*	High
Technical Expertise of Leader	Low	*Very High*	High
Style of Leader	Participative	*Directive*	Directive
Support from Senior Executives	Supportive, but wary	*Very supportive and trusting*	Very supportive and trusting
Staff Trajectory	Growing	*Unknown*	Shrinking
Individuals Critical to Mission	Some of the technical leaders	*None in particular; willing to shake out nonbelievers*	Probably none
Ability of Organization to Reform Itself, Given Support and Change	Possible	*Impossible*	Unlikely

FIGURE 4.3
Comparing MCCA operations and product development conditions for change.

FinServia. Connie wanted to drive MCCA Operations to adopt the essentials of the Toyota Production System, to which she was accustomed and committed. She knew what had to be done, and she had lived through a successful transformation from a troubled operating environment at NUMMI. No sense wasting time or getting input; input would come later, within the feedback mechanisms of TPS. We just had to hope that any disruption would be modest and temporary.

Connie's plan was straightforward: wrest control from Sales and bring in enough new people and external support to help her drive her operations to the processes and tools of TPS, in the process building MPS (our version of TPS). She would go fast, and she would tolerate some disruption to existing operations. Once she had established MPS, she would build the focus on people that was demanded by TPS, but within the structure of that system.

The more I learned of Connie, the more I admired her, and also Lynn for having the vision and courage to bring her on board. I was grateful for the path Connie was blazing toward a new and better relationship with Sales, and planned to "hop on board that train." My newfound understanding of Operations and its relationship with Sales left me with one major remaining step in my exploration of MCCA: getting out to see some customers for myself.

WES VISITS SAN DIEGO NATIONAL INSURANCE

My opportunity to get to know our customers came after I had been at MCCA for a few weeks, mapping out the landscape and meeting the people. I had learned from Mary and Neville how important it was to "go see" for myself, and how critical it was to understand the value that we provided customers. Lean product development, after all, had a single purpose: building Lean customer value streams, providing customers what they valued and nothing else. I had to understand that purpose, what our customers needed, or I could well be moving MCCA efficiently in the wrong direction.

Fortunately, I wasn't starting from scratch. Fletcher, Wilkens, and Johnson (FWJ), our private equity fund owner, had done customer needs research as part of its decision to buy MCCA. Franklin McDonald, the FWJ partner who led the MCCA purchase, had become enamored with an approach to understanding customer needs that focused on what he called "important, unsatisfied job outcomes."[4] Rather than ask customers to tell us what solutions they wanted, this method sought out the jobs that customers needed done and metrics around the desired outcomes. After all, most customers are not qualified to design a solution to their information management needs in the way that MCCA presumably is, so MCCA shouldn't expect customers to order up specific solutions. Customers don't know about technological capabilities, the history of what has been tried and failed, or the state of the art, and most of them are not engineers. Frank's contention is that if we can understand the jobs that need doing and what a satisfying result looks like, we can figure out the best way to solve for it.

A brief aside on methodologies: Here in the realm of customer value, I found that Lean product development (LPD) thinking added much to

Agile software development methods. Agile methods, as I had learned them, typically assume that customers know what they want, and it's the project team's job to deliver it. The embodiment of this is the *Product Owner*, the person who can sit with developers and tell them precisely what is needed. My guess is this perspective is due to Agile's invention by software consultants, who normally begin a job not knowing much about "the business"; the idea of the "Product Owner" assumes away the difficulty of understanding customer needs and requirements. Lean, on the other hand, begins with the idea that the developer is at the core of the business, in the person of Chief Engineer. Understanding and delivering value is joined in LPD; in Agile, it can be subject to the vagaries of the customer giving the instructions and writing the user stories. Frank's focus on "unsatisfied customers" added a perspective that neither Lean nor Agile addresses.

As part of its due diligence of MCCA, FWJ had identified several jobs done or potentially done by MCCA customers, each with dozens of outcomes, and then determined which ones were most underserved. It then segmented the market by underserved need, and prioritized the development. For example, one of the jobs was "Enable viewing of data and related images." Another was "Get information to those who need it." Some of the outcomes desired for the latter were:

- Maximize likelihood of desired recipient to see relevant information.
- Minimize frequency of recipients wasting time on irrelevant information.
- Minimize time recipients spend to get to the information.
- Minimize delay time from information receipt to dissemination.

I was excited to hear for myself how FWJ's assessment applied to real customers.

PREPARING TO MEET SDNI

Lynn had given me guidance on how I should get out to visit some customers, especially San Diego National Insurance (SDNI), our lead customer for our new products. Sales, she warned me, behaved like a mother bear protecting her cubs when it came to our customers. Jack Langley and his team did not want any dissonant messages, and they certainly didn't want to create alternative sources of the customer's voice within MCCA. If I went directly to customers, I would bring the mother bear down on me. Better to try to partner with Jack, even if by doing that, I would get a filtered and controlled customer experience.

Thus it was that I found myself in Jack's BMW heading into downtown San Diego to the SDNI building, soaring thirty-five stories into the sky between the Gaslamp District and the harbor. Melissa Groves, a bright young woman who seemed to be a combination of Jack's protégé and assistant (and was scurrilously rumored to be even more), was in the spacious back seat updating us on the current situation and what to expect in the meeting.

"The relationship is on edge right now, Mr. Wesleyan," Melissa started as we headed out of our parking lot toward the freeway. "We met our first big deliverable two months ago when we delivered data extraction from the images we store, and storage of the data and documentation produced by SDNI's claims processing system. Mr. Milligan, the claims manager, was initially ecstatic with the new searching and reporting capabilities, and the fast turnaround he was able to provide with some fraud issues impressed his boss and peers and made him look like a hero. But as the volume of data grew and SDNI found new uses, we started to grow a long list of bugs and requests for new features. Our contract was not clear about how to handle either, and we are still working through that list."

"Please call me Wes, Melissa." I said, "It could be a lot worse—at least we've delivered some value and they want more."

"Very true," said Jack. "But we need to get our act together. Melissa has been drawn 100% into managing this list now, and she can't get Phillip and his team to commit to a schedule to complete it. He can't give us good estimates for how much some of the larger items will cost either, so we can't give good quotes. SDNI argues that some of the items should be standard product enhancements and they shouldn't pay for them at all, which makes sense in a way, but we haven't set any product strategy or development plan yet. Phillip has given us some of Hannah's time to take the list from Melissa and manage it in Phillip's group. We hope that will help."

"We really should hire someone to run product development, eh Jack?" I joked self-deprecatingly. He laughed also, and the tension lifted. "Are you finding that selling and supporting a software product is more difficult than the operational services we've done in the past?"

"We've always had some technical content," Jack agreed, "but it's much more intense now. When we sold the more predictable operational services, Finance knew how to estimate costs for an operation, and the pricing was usually a straightforward markup. Once we had an operation running, we could measure its costs and manage its profitability. With this software product, it seems like we can't estimate development costs or time frames, and once it's "done," it's still not "done" because of the bugs. Add to that the idea that once we build something, it's reusable by many customers, and the decision making around what to provide, to whom, and at what cost becomes a can of worms."

"Just what I was hired to make sense of, Jack. With your help, we'll figure this out. Melissa, could you tell me who we'll be meeting with, and what is on their minds?"

From the back seat came Melissa's clear voice. "We will be meeting with three people, Wes," she started. "Emilio Fernandez is SDNI's Records Manager, our primary contact. He owns the imaging operations, and he convinced Mr. Milligan, the claims manager, to take a chance with us. Mr. Milligan is scheduled to attend also, although he may have to leave early. Daphne Zellern from the Technology Department will also attend. She is responsible for managing the technology risk we present, and for integration of our technology with theirs."

"It would be great if all three are there," I said. "What have you led them to expect from the meeting? Do we have an agenda?"

"No formal agenda needed," said Jack. "I've known Emilio for ten years, I take him to the golf tournament at Torrey every year, and I send Christmas presents to his kids. I told them we've hired a new director of marketing and product development and that I want to introduce you to them. They are expecting to meet you, and maybe hear from you how you are going to help us better meet their demands."

"Perfect," I said. "How about you do introductions and set up the purpose, and I'll take it from there? If I get in trouble, feel free to kick me under the table and I'll shut up."

"I'm not too worried," Jack replied. "Melissa and I will take whatever help you can give us. It's not working now with Phillip, no matter how much he tries."

LISTENING FOR CUSTOMER VALUE

We parked in the underground lot, took one elevator to the lobby, presented our credentials in return for badges, and took another elevator to the eleventh floor. There we found a receptionist sitting behind a gleaming metal desk, under a similarly gleaming modern SDNI logo on the wall. She showed us into a brightly lit conference room, with a stainless steel and glass table surrounded by stainless steel and black leather chairs, black stone floors, and walls of steel, chrome, and black rock. We were offered water and soda, and then we waited a few minutes for the SDNI executives to join us.

Jack leaped up when our customers came into the room and walked over to Emilio Fernandez, giving him a quick man-hug and saying how glad he was to see him. Jack introduced us around, to Pervez Milligan, the claims manager, and Daphne Zellern, the technology staffer. Emilio was a large man, as tall as Jack, but older and rounder. He seemed voluble and friendly. Pervez was younger, more reserved, whereas Daphne was the youngest and quietest of all. We took our seats around the table.

"Emilio, Pervez," Jack began, seeming to willfully ignore Daphne, "Wes here has been dying to meet you, so thanks for taking the time. You remember what Lynn Hollander, our new president, explained to you about our commitment to you and our investment in our new product line that you are using?"

The SDNI representatives nodded in agreement.

"Well, Wes is part of that commitment. He has been hired to lead our product development efforts, coming to us from some excellent work leading a big project in Minnesota, and prior to that, a dozen years as a strategy consultant. I want you folks to meet Wes, and for Wes to get to know you, so he can direct our product development to satisfy your needs."

I took that as my license to proceed to conduct the meeting. "Thanks for the introduction, Jack," I said. "Can I suggest an agenda for our meeting?" No objection, so onward. "If you wouldn't mind, I'd like to hear from you why you chose us to help with your information management needs, your assessment of how we are doing, and what you'd like to see from us over the next few years. I'm mostly in listening mode now, but I'd be happy toward the end of the meeting to tell you some of my plans for our product and get your feedback. Does this work?" I asked.

Emilio was a large, voluble man; he didn't need much encouragement to start discoursing. "How about I talk about how we got into this deal, and then Pervez takes over and tells you how MCCA is doing for us, and what we want to come?" he asked, looking at Pervez Milligan for confirmation. "Wes," he continued, "our relationship goes way back, to when Ernie just started out. Wes, have you met Ernie—founder of the company? Yes? He is quite a guy."

Emilio was rolling now. He went on, "I was working in the print room at the time, and I remember like it was yesterday when he strolls in and tries to sell me on the idea of microfilming all the paper reports I was struggling with. I had never bought a thing for the company at the time, but it sounded like a good idea, so I pitched it to my boss. He liked it too, so we started having Ernie microfilm the reports we needed to retain. I looked good, my boss looked good, we saved some money and provided better access to our records. I think Ernie made some money, too! Ernie and then Jack and now Melissa have been helping us ever since.

"Over the years," Emilio reminisced, "as we grew and technology changed, Ernie, Jack, and I spent time talking about our growth and problems, and we continued to grow and change the relationship. I remember when we first put imaging in and we could see customer claim forms on computer screens—quite an accomplishment! We were one of the first in our industry to do that, and it paid off in lower processing costs and better customer service."

"Emilio, what was it about MCCA that kept bringing you back for more services over the years?" I asked. "It sounds like Ernie and Jack's ability to understand your business needs and propose solutions was important." It sounded to me like Emilio owed a lot of his success in business to the MCCA partnership, and probably vice versa.

"That's been a big part of it, Wes," Emilio answered. "Even though we are a big company, we don't have a lot of technical resources devoted to the documents area. For example, Daphne here has just a few people dedicated to my group, and it would take an act of Congress to get more. MCCA takes care of all that, providing ideas for new technologies, the technologies themselves, people to operate them, and all for straightforward payment of volume-based operating fees. Daphne's predecessor argued that we could do it less expensively ourselves, but once we added up all the cost and risks, it just didn't make sense. Over the years, we've been pitched by other companies who say they can do the same type of work, but even when things have been rocky between us—and they sure have been at times, eh Jack?—the cost and disruption to switch are so high that it's worth it for both of us to compromise and get things back on track."

I was encouraged by what I was hearing, and it validated what I had heard from Connie and Lynn on how our operations business could be a springboard for our new technology platform. The tricky balancing act Connie was running—to improve our operational consistency, cost effectiveness, and capabilities without undermining the foundational relationships between our customers and our sales force—was fundamental to the success of the new products on which I was focused.

UNDERSTANDING THE CUSTOMER'S NEEDS

I took a moment to write a few notes on what I was hearing in the framework of unmet customer needs and outcomes. I had just heard several hoped-for needs with respect to SDNI's information management requirements:

- Maximize the likelihood of applying the right technology at the right time to meet document management needs.
- Minimize customer technology and operational staffing needs.
- Minimize financial complexity for customers.
- Maximize financial flexibility for customers; volume-based costs.
- Maximize customer sponsor visibility for success within his/her company.

"Back to how we got into this latest deal," Emilio continued. "A few years ago, a young manager in our claims group came up with an idea and proposed it to Pervez. We had all this data about our claims in our claims management system and our data warehouse, and all these images of claims documents, photos, reports, and so forth, but they were separate, and as she called them, 'so nineties.' She started looking for a way to make our claim data available like the Internet tools she used every day. Can you take it from here, Pervez?"

Pervez Milligan appeared to be Emilio's opposite. He was younger than Emilio, thin, introverted, serious, a thinker rather than a relator. His insights, however, were equally compelling.

"Katie Flambeau—that's the woman who got us set on this path—wanted to make our data like Google and Facebook," Pervez said. "At the time, neither Emilio nor I knew what she was talking about, but as she showed us what we might be able to do, it became clear to me. Our capability to understand our claims was good, but it was limited to the coded data in our processing system. Each analyst and processer had to go out and look at reports, and our interactions between processors, analysts, and investigators were therefore slow and formal. Katie thought we could make it much better. I mentioned this to Emilio, who brought Jack in to talk with Katie and me."

Looking over at Jack, with what seemed like a mixture of admiration and chagrin, Pervez continued with his story. "Jack got excited about Kate's ideas, said that MCCA had been working on a new module for the imaging system that did this stuff. Katie was skeptical—she doesn't think much of any technology company over five years old—so we set up a test. Katie put together the data from our processing system, along with the output documents such as customer letters, e-mails, and investigator reports, for a group of claims for which MCCA already had images. We asked Jack to put it all together and show us what the new module could do."

Emilio laughed at this. "I don't think I've seen Jack go quite so pale," he said. "There wasn't really a new module yet, was there, Jack?"

Jack squirmed and laughed along with his clients. "It wasn't quite all the way to 'module' status yet, I must admit," he said. "But we had begun development, and your little test sped us up, didn't it?"

"Anyhow," Pervez went on, "we gave Jack a month, while we went out and looked at other products in the market. We weren't crazy about what we saw—a lot of great technologies, but in pieces that we would have to integrate and support, with companies that we didn't know. After six weeks, Jack and Melissa came back with your technology manager—Mr. Glass, I believe—and showed us what you'd come up with. It about knocked Katie's socks off, Wes."

"What was it she liked, Pervez?" I prodded.

"The data storage and searching was awesome. All of the text documents were fully indexed and searchable, to start with, and the data from our processing system was also available to drill down into," Pervez explained. "Searches brought up everything—the data from the system, the text documents, and the related images. Users could add index values and links to documents and cases; for example, if a repair estimate was found to be fraudulent, the investigator could click an attribute and mark it, and put in his own comments as well. The kicker in the whole thing, though, was the personal pages."

Here Daphne spoke up for the first time. She was young, probably under thirty, in comparison to the older Pervez Milligan and much older Emilio Fernandez, clearly the junior partner here. "I had worked with Katie and Melissa in laying out some ideas on the personal pages," Daphne said, "but Phillip's programmers took the ideas a lot further. Each user of the system has her own page, where she can indicate her expertise, knowledge, experiences, interests, and preferences. The interests and preferences are lined up with the imaging and document indexing values, and it's all linked in to the data in our processing system."

Daphne was on a roll, and it was great to see her enthusiasm for our joint work. "For example, if I am interested in auto insurance, fraud, and body shops, and my preference is a daily summary of body shops newly suspected of fraud, that's what I'd get—an e-mail each day, with summary statistics and links to the data and images. Or if I want to understand about the cost to repair hail damage in Tallahassee from the latest storm, I can get averages by home size from our processing system, find outliers, and go look at images of the submitted invoices along with photos of the damages. I can easily find the personal pages of our claim investigators there if I want to e-mail or talk with them. There is even a mapping feature so I can see where the homes are, which helps with claim evaluation."

I had heard in Daphne's summary many of the job objectives that FWJ had discovered in its research and several others that sounded difficult to achieve on a broad scale. These included:

- Maximize the integration of documents (images and text) with customers' line of business data.
- Maximize the ability of system users to know and leverage each other.
- Maximize the ability of users to customize the amount and method of information delivery to themselves.

Pervez took back the narration, saying, "Our people were very excited with the demonstration. We did several more demonstrations for our own department and related departments, and we did a business case of benefits for us if we had this tool. Wes, the numbers were compelling: not only would we save a lot of time and effort, we thought we could reduce losses and fraud, provide better customer service by making some of the data and images available to customers themselves over the Internet, and increase revenue through better customer retention."

Jack, who had been sitting back and enjoying the narration so far, interjected with a sigh, "And then the lawyers got involved."

We had returned to Emilio's province now, vendor management. He continued the story, "Indeed. With such a large benefit potential, and the visibility that had been generated, our corporate counsel became involved. We'd never had long, formal contracts with MCCA, defining our interactions and commitments; we'd always had simple agreements with simple pricing, and dealt with new items and disputes informally. Wes, I assume you've looked over the contract?" Emilio asked me.

I had indeed. I've been involved in a lot of contract work for services, coming from the consulting world, so the contract was familiar to me in form and concept. My impression was that MCCA had agreed to a lot of vaguely worded requirements, firm timelines, tough performance standards, and crippling penalties for failure to deliver—it seemed one-sided. I said so now, although in kinder, gentler words.

Emilio laughed. "Our lawyers put together a contract that, frankly, I don't think you had much of a chance of living up to," he said. "They were concerned that this being new software and all, and you being not exactly IBM, you wouldn't be able to deliver. They wanted us to have some rights of recourse just in case. Daphne and her management had a lot of input as well, around privacy, security, disaster recovery, and the like. We do seem to have you on the ropes a bit, don't we, Jack?"

"Emilio, you are a tough negotiator, no doubt about that," Jack fawned. "But we knew what we were doing. Partnering with you on this would give us a great company, right here in town, as our beta site for a whole new class of product. We think it's a good contract and we fully intend to live up to it, and we're not doing so bad right now, are we?"

Pervez took this question, as I noted for the group that we were moving on to the next topic in our agenda: How are we doing, and what does SDNI want next? Pervez gave his evaluation of our work so far, "Not at all, Jack. We implemented our first phase right on time, with some great features that have helped us a lot. We are happily paying you for the service, as we've agreed. However, once we hit production, we've been continually growing the list of bugs and new feature requests, even as we move into the future phases specified in the contract. We somehow need to get more alignment between what our users need with your release schedule, and improve the quality of the software so we aren't always fighting defects.

We also need to take some of the setup work—like drop-downs for new index values, interest types, preference types—and put them under our control, instead of having to continually go back to your programmers. We are being patient, and we're not enforcing some of our rights under the contract, but we have to start seeing improvement in these items or we'll need to get our lawyers back involved."

I could see Jack becoming defensive at this, and I didn't want him to take a hit for this state of affairs. I was impressed with what MCCA had been able to accomplish through Jack and Melissa's closeness to the customer and Phillip and Rico's technical brilliance and hard work. The need for the structure that I hoped to bring was clear, and it was my responsibility to answer Pervez's challenge. First, I needed to prove I was listening.

"Mr. Milligan," I began, becoming more formal on purpose. "I hear you saying that you need us to improve our ability to respond to your users' needs, to create the ability for you to administer your own system, to improve quality and predictability of our releases, while continuing to deliver the new features as specified in the contract. Is that a fair summary?"

"Yes it is, Wes, and I see some of the things you are doing to help. Melissa has told us that you are going to dedicate a project manager to our account, and your new role is encouraging."

"We have a lot more decked up for you," I promised. "As you know, we are being provided significant investment capital, and we will be spending it to grow our development and implementation teams. Making SDNI a big success is critical to our plans. I'd like to find a way to strengthen the relationships between our teams so we can do the best job we can. Would it be OK if I came back in a month or so, along with some of our development team, to watch your staff using our tools in production, and talk to some of the users about what they like and don't like? I'd also like to share with you how we are evolving our release planning and management, so you understand how your requests get slotted for development and release, and also our testing improvements."

Emilio liked what he'd heard, thankfully. He joked at Jack, saying, "Jack, you've finally found someone who's going to build product as well as you can sell it, eh?" Turning back to me, Emilio continued, "That sounds great, Wes. We've always had that close, multilevel relationship in our imaging operations, and we need to build the same with the software stuff. It seems so much more difficult, although I don't understand exactly why. We seem to lose in translation—we tell Melissa what we want, then she tells Phillip, who tells his programmers, and then when we get it back, it's not quite what we'd hoped. Sometimes it's much better, doing things we hadn't thought of, but often it's missing key pieces that we had specified. You think you can help?"

"I do," I said. "We're going to be implementing some new methods to make our processes more visible to you, and to provide better quality," I promised. "Would you be open to hosting some of our team members to come sit with some of the users of your system? I'd like to give our development team more direct experience of user needs and views. In fact, I'd like to come out again myself and spend time with your people."

"I think we could do that," Pervez agreed. "Just coordinate it through me; we'll give your guys an education!"

Fantastic. Now I could get our whole team to "go see" firsthand! I couldn't think of a better way to get Phillip, Rico, Hannah, and the rest of the group a better feel for what needed to be done, nor a better way to break the iron grip of the sales force on our priorities.

I wrapped up the meeting by thanking our hosts for their business so far and their patience as we improve, and promising to improve our delivery for them. With that set of promises, the meeting ended on a good note. I was now on the hook with Jack and our largest and most important customer to show some progress. I could see the beginnings of the transformation we needed; now I had to get it accelerating by getting our new roles in place and the team formed to drive improvement.

Signposts	Transforming MCCA
	• Wes meets with his developers, focusing on their relationship with Sales. Development is driven from crisis to crisis, with little long-term vision or control. The situation is at a breaking point, as we see in Rico's temper tantrum.
	• Wes learns about Connie Esposito, VP Operations, and her actions to reorient Operations and its interactions with Sales. He thinks Connie can provide a model for the Sales interaction, although not for the overall change model.
	• Along with the Sales VP Jack Langley, Wes visits customer San Diego National Insurance. He confirms the market research FWJ had provided and sees for himself the promise and challenges in MCCA's business plan.

Change Guides from Wes	• **In order to make change, you must understand the current situation.** How does product development work now, and what are its relationships to other groups such as Sales and Finance?
	• **Use the Lean and Agile model as a lens for understanding:** *People, process, tools*, with, as usual, a primary focus on *people*.
	• **Don't rely on reports or metrics or explanations.** Go see for yourself, and be sure your whole team does so as well!
Coming Up Next	We return to FinServia and hear about Mary's parallel work to understand and then change the GRI software development outsourcing arrangement.

ENDNOTES

1. Liker, *Toyota Way*, 150.
2. The NUMMI experience with learning TPS is briefly described in Liker, *Toyota Way*, 132–133.
3. A value stream map is a type of super flow chart that shows not only the process steps but the inventories and delays associated with each step. Mike Rother and John Shook, *Learning to See* (Cambridge, MA: Lean Enterprise Institute, 1999).
4. This approach to understanding customer wants is from Anthony Ulwick, *What Customers Want: Using Outcome-Driven Innovation to Create Breakthrough Products and Services* (New York: McGraw-Hill, 2005).

5

Reorienting FinServia's Relationship with GRI: March

Narrator: Mary

Several weeks ago at Neville's house, I made my list of priorities. Sitting right on top of the list was dealing with the GRI contract—taking development responsibility away from the company I called (to myself) Glacial Resources, and getting it back into the business where it belonged. Today was the day on which our planning and preparation would be tested, and the die cast for our movement ahead. Would Finservia succeed in our goals, would the companies reach an uneasy but workable accommodation, or would we be stuck in a stalemate?

Global Resources, Incorporated (GRI) was headquartered in an opulent campus north of Dallas, Texas. Tanisha Clark, our GRI vendor manager, and Josh Lambert, our legal counsel, joined me in an early morning flight from San Diego. GRI insisted on picking us up at the airport, in what turned out to be a luxurious limousine. What waste! They apparently did not understand what I was coming for—or such waste was such a part of GRI's routine that it simply no longer registered. As we drove, I reviewed what I had learned about GRI, and what I hoped to accomplish today.

GRI'S DEATH GRIP ON FINSERVIA'S TECHNOLOGY

Yesterday, Tanisha, Josh, and I had spent most of the afternoon getting ready for today. We met in my favorite conference room, mockingly called the "Sunshine Room," because, even though it was dark and depressing, it was one of our few meeting areas with a window. FinServia's new headquarters, designated as part of our spin-off from Cremins Corporation, was actually quite aged; the building was almost fifty years old, one of the four printing plants separated with us from Cremins. The Sunshine

Room wasn't as pleasant as its name implied; rather than having walls and expansive vistas, it was a dingy rectangular space, surrounded by free-standing divider walls, containing an old beat-up conference table and fifteen miscellaneous chairs. We had commandeered an unused section of the underutilized plant for our offices, putting up a mostly soundproof wall between the sections. We had only temporary furnishings, including stand-up lamps Greg had bought at Wal-Mart for us. Greg promised we would get nice office space once we had proven that FinServia would be profitable and grow.

I was a few minutes late because I was talking with our Human Resources Department about starting to recruit a new development team. I hoped that after the GRI meeting I would have a better idea about where I could go with development, and I wanted to be ready to build our own team when we could. When I walked into Sunshine, Tanisha was impatiently waiting for me. I asked that she come prepared to explain the nature of the services GRI provided and the interactions of FinServia staff with the vendor. I quickly and gratefully found Tanisha knowledgeable about the contract and the relationship, and she was interested in helping me do what I felt we needed to do. Her loyalty was clearly with FinServia, even though she had a good relationship with and trusted the GRI people with whom she regularly dealt.

The interaction between GRI and FinServia, Tanisha explained, was precisely prescribed in appendices to the contract that had been developed and refined over several years. The formal name was the Cremins Development and Risk Control Process, commonly referred to as The Process,[1] which specified all the steps, the procedures within and between steps, and all the "artifacts" or documents required throughout a development project. It went so far as to require project plans to look almost exactly alike, with the sole exception being the dates. I really hated this; to my way of thinking, it crippled communication and planning.

Tanisha described how The Process worked at FinServia now. She had a dedicated vendor management team of business requirements analysts, process/project managers, and user acceptance testers. Their responsibility was to take requests from The Business and document requirements in enough detail to get a "rough order of magnitude" estimate. (Note that I capitalize The Business to illustrate its use in this context. Somehow, Tanisha perceived herself as not part of The Business.)

If The Business wanted to pay for the project after that rough estimate, GRI analysts wrote the detailed business requirements, which the FinServia vendor team presented to The Business for sign-off. GRI then handed the approved requirements to its design team, which came back with a fixed-price bid, accompanied by a detailed functional specification and design for the work. At this point, the vendor management team worked with The Business to approve or reject the bid; if rejected, The Business had to pay only for the requirements and design work done so far. The amount of requirements and design costs paid, without going forward, had declined over the years, I supposed because the business units became more and more careful about asking for things. There was often an extended period of discussion about the functional specification and the design, although the business units tried to keep it short due to having to pay for GRI time even if they never agreed to proceed.

Once The Business accepted the bid, GRI handed off the specification and design to the developer pool. Because the flow of work was so uneven, it was impossible for GRI to keep a team of developers familiar with our business and the code, so there was often a start-up time, misunderstandings, and technical glitches that could have been avoided. As code began to flow, the vendor management team handled change controls, which typically added 20% to 50% to each project. The change controls would begin to arrive as the development team asked clarifying questions during development, but normally were concentrated in the user acceptance period. User acceptance was the first time FinServia team members got to actually see the software, after the GRI test team completed its set of tests in their QA environment. No surprise there—people, especially non-software professionals, were notoriously poor at specifying in great detail a system-to-be-built, and even worse at understanding what a system specified by others would look like and how it would perform from hundreds of pages of bulleted requirements, functional specifications, and design documents. Sad but true.

As I had expected to find, there was an astonishing amount of waste in the FinServia development process. In Lean terms,[2] we had handoffs, task switching, inventory becoming obsolete and never turning in finished products (such as requirements documents never coded), defects, overproduction (all the work that didn't lead to production code), duplication of effort (two groups testing the same things), and delays. It wouldn't be difficult to vastly improve this; in fact, I thought it would be difficult to make it worse! I kept this assessment to myself for now—Tanisha was proud of The Process and I needed her help. There would be time later to educate her and determine if she would bring her energy and commitment to a new way of doing things.

The last item Tanisha and I reviewed was the project results from the last three years. The typical time between project request and production was well over a year. Many projects were canceled prior to development beginning, and several were canceled during user acceptance testing. I calculated that less than half of all development spending resulted in anything going to production, and the cost of the ideas that actually made it to production grossly inflated due to inefficiencies and high GRI overhead costs. I already knew from my discussions with Lynn and others how dissatisfied the FinServia leaders were with results and the value that Tanisha and GRI were delivering, and the data certainly bore this out.

As we wrapped up our review of project results, Josh Lambert was shown into the conference room by my administrative assistant. Josh was a junior partner at an external law firm, new to this issue. The existing FinServia–GRI relationship was covered by the larger Cremins Corporation agreement that had been managed by Cremins' internal counsel. Now that we had spun out of Cremins, we had no internal counsel of our own, and had chosen Josh's firm to assist us.

Josh and Tanisha briefed me on the state of the contract. GRI contended that the contract was technically in default due to the spinout of FinServia, although GRI was not asking for anything unusual to resolve the issue. They proposed that we simply document the existing relationship, as governed by the Cremins contract, in a new FinServia contract, although the pricing would be increased by 10% because the volume discounts earned by Cremins would no longer apply. The Cremins contract was structured with rates per server managed, fixed rates negotiated for each major application we owned, and time and materials for application development and support. Help desk services—initially aimed at internal Cremins users, but later extended to cover FinServia's external customers as well—were priced per call, plus hourly fees for labor required to deal with new or changed services.

Tanisha ran me through our spending for software deliveries over the past three years. I had also reviewed the server support costs, the help desk costs, and the feedback provided from the help desk to our product development (almost none). Most of my hunches were borne out—we were spending a lot for very little in application development, and help desk costs for our external customers were high—not actually too high per call, but very little had been done to reduce call volume by feeding knowledge back into the product development process. I had seen that before: it's difficult for a provider getting paid on a per-piece basis, whether calls answered or paper processed, to get very excited about reducing its revenue. I was pleasantly surprised that the hosting costs appeared to be reasonable. I was also relieved when Josh confirmed that despite GRI doing the application development and hosting, Cremins, and by inheritance, FinServia, had total ownership of its own applications. However, there were some utility software elements that GRI owned, such as file transfer and security utilities.

The three of us wrapped up our trip preparation by laying out what we wanted with respect to GRI. My preliminary thoughts were:

- Take back application development immediately (not more than six weeks from now).
- Take back customer-facing help desk next.
- Have GRI continue to manage the server and network infrastructure, preferably at lower costs, but I'd accept it as is (prior to the 10% price increase).
- Make the transition smoothly, without operational disruption.
- Don't get into a big contract contretemps.
- Get personnel assistance—training, temporary assignments, or hire some of GRI's staff who know our systems.

The question I had been thinking about overnight, and again in the limousine, was how to make that happen. I wasn't seeing a win–win situation here, at least not yet. I knew what *I* wanted, but what did *they* want?

MEETING WITH GRI: BEING CLEAR ABOUT WHAT FINSERVIA NEEDS

We were being hosted by Wayne Mellinger, the GRI's relationship manager for Cremins Corporation. Wayne and I had talked a couple of times on the phone and exchanged some e-mails as I took on my new role. Wayne was concerned about my perception of GRI's role with Cremins Corporation, and by inheritance with FinServia. Wayne had consulted with Trevor McDonald, who had been the lead for GRI on the Cremins United project, and no doubt had learned about my distaste for the The Process. I was expecting defensiveness.

Tanisha, Josh, and I were escorted from the limousine to the grandiose entryway, where we were greeted by a guard. We got our badges and waited for a few minutes until Wayne's assistant came to escort us up to the conference room. The conference room was in GRI's Customer Center, a space designed to ooze solidity and professionalism. The room was dominated by a horseshoe-shaped table, with a dozen deep leather chairs surrounding it, and another ring of smaller chairs lining the walls. The front wall of the conference room was a screen on which was projected a welcome message. The facing wall had large windows overlooking what looked like a nature preserve. The far wall was smoky glass, which we later saw magically clear to reveal a perch overlooking the space-age data center.

Waiting for us in the intimidating room were Wayne, Trevor (to my surprise), and five or six others. The others included some of the people involved in the day-to-day operations and development, plus legal counsel. After introductions and some obligatory small talk, Wayne began the meeting.

"Welcome, and thank you for coming. How about we review the agenda and begin? I thought perhaps Mary could start by telling us about FinServia, some of your plans and strategies, and any thoughts on how GRI can help. Then, we can go from there, depending on what we need to do. We are prepared to dive deeper into what we do today for you, our capabilities, and so on, but we'll only do that if you'd like. Our only goal for this meeting is to see how we might be able to help you, and then to do the necessary formal legal work to clean up our contract now that you have split from Cremins Corp."

I appreciated how Wayne had brought this meeting right to the point. I didn't need to know more about GRI or the existing arrangements, so I jumped right into it. I gave the history of why, when, and how FinServia had been created, and then began on what I wanted to see.

"Our business strategy is centered on building on our printing relationships in the Financial Services sector, and extending the system that you have begun on our behalf to be a full communication portal among companies, their shareholders, and companies providing shareholder services. We have a beginning on this set of capabilities—such as shareholder signup, e-mail management, and document hosting—but we have a lot of new things to build out. We have a couple of competitors with a head start, so we have no time to waste. I'm focused on what is the fastest, lowest-cost approach to build out the highest-value items to first get us back in the game, and then get us ahead."

I paused here and checked for understanding. Wayne spoke up first.

"We can certainly help you in that, Mary. We currently have only a small team dedicated to development of your applications, since the workload is intermittent. We have the resources to staff out a larger dedicated team for you, and we can provide whatever you need in developers, analysts, testers, and project managers. Would you like us to put together a proposal for you? Do you have an idea of what you want to build, or what you might want to spend?"

"Wayne," I said, "I believe that the best way to build vendor partnerships is to be completely honest, and to seek and find win–win relationships. I'd like to lay out what I'd like from you, then you tell me what you want from us, and we can go from there and try to find an agreeable arrangement."

"Certainly, that would be excellent," Wayne replied.

"We would like your help in several areas. We'd like to continue to have you host our servers and network connections, and to do our internal desktop management and help desk services. And we'd like your help to move our application development and customer-facing help desk services in house." I just laid it out there for them.

It was silent for what seemed like forever, even though it was probably only thirty seconds.

Wayne was the first to speak. "Well, Mary, it's good to hear that you want to continue with some of our services, and I can't say that I'm surprised to hear that you want to take over some of the services we are now doing for you. Obviously, Trevor shared with me your background and expertise, and I couldn't imagine why Greg would have hired you other than to take over software development from us. Nevertheless, for the sake of clarity, can I ask why you want to take over application development and support? My understanding is that we have done a good job with your group. We've fulfilled all of our obligations, delivered a system that is reliable and performs well, and contributed the process and methods that have resulted in predictable, steady application delivery. And we saw in Cremins United how difficult it is for a business for which software is not a core competency to build complicated technology."

I didn't want to make the GRI team feel bad about their contributions; I needed them to be cooperative going forward, and hopefully to keep managing our servers, so I didn't need to waste cycles making a change there. As much I would have liked to tell them how much they sucked, I wasn't going to do that if I didn't have to. Assuming I could control myself.

"It's not about what kind of job you've done in the past. From what I know, I'm not dissatisfied with the quality of what you have done. It's about what we need to do going *forward* to succeed. Cremins outsourced its technology to you because it was not believed to be a core competency. With our spinout and our new strategy, software development *must* be a core competency. That is what Greg hired me for, and it's what I need to do. We need to lower costs and accelerate delivery, and bring more creativity and innovation to the game. This is a decision we have made, and it's not up for debate."

Trevor looked unhappy. He knew how much I disagreed with the processes he had conceived and imposed (with internal complicity) on Cremins, and I'm sure it was killing him that I was rejecting his proud work completely. But he remained calm and asked, "How do you propose to take over development? You don't have the people or skills do it. What kind of time frame are you looking at?"

"I'm thinking about six weeks. But that would depend on what kind of support you would be willing to provide for the transition," I replied.

"Six weeks!" Trevor exclaimed. "How can you do it that fast? What kind of help do you want from us to make that possible?"

"A couple of things," I said. "Documentation of the existing system, training and mentoring on the application for my new team, perhaps some ongoing assistance until my new team gets up to speed. But now that you've heard about what I'm looking for, I'm eager to hear about what *you* want. Is FinServia, without the application development and customer support activities, still a good business for you? Is it aligned with what you do well and with your ongoing focus?"

GRI GOALS AND THE WIN–WIN

Wayne Mellinger responded. "Well, actually, the application development business of FinServia alone, without the larger Cremins work, is smaller than our typical engagements. It has been difficult for us to keep it staffed effectively due to the intermittent nature of the work, and we've been seeing fewer requests for estimates and less pull-through over the last year. We knew that Cremins' focus was elsewhere for the last few years, but we had hoped to grow our business with you to support the spin out."

I was sympathetic to GRI's plight on this: on their scale, it wasn't getting much revenue from us; it had to keep people on stand-by; and there were ups and downs on staffing. I thought of another Lean manufacturing concept, *heijunka*,[3] which means "level flow." Leveling the flow of activities wherever possible is a great waste reducer, because over- and under-utilization of people, machines, and facilities causes waste at both peak and trough usage. I was planning on doing that with my new development staff—work to understand its capacity, keep it working at a steady output pace, and continually feed it the highest-priority items. Coming to understand the maximum steady-state output is one of the highest planes of Agile software development and Lean manufacturing: in Agile, we call it *velocity*[4] (whereas in Lean manufacturing it's called *takt time*[5]—the amount of time it takes to put out one unit of work). With all the rigmarole The Process imposed between idea and coding, it would be impossible to keep working at that steady state, even if The Process had any conception of takt time (which it did not). Lean requires understanding capacity and velocity and working at that pace steadily without waste; The Process did not have any focus on the whole development system; instead, it sought to reduce the risks in each particular development project by following supposed "best practices" at each step.

"I'm sorry, but GRI's growing its application development business at FinServia is not an option, ," I confirmed. "How about the other aspects of our business: the server and network support, the support for our internal desktop systems and users? Are we too small there also for you?"

"No, not at all," Wayne enthused. "Those are volume businesses, with little differentiation among our clients. You would actually be in the mid-range size of the spectrum of those businesses, although our delivery model for you would be somewhat less specialized than we've done for Cremins. We perform those services efficiently and well, especially if you have standard hardware and software, which you do since we've been supporting them for years. I think you could look long and hard and not find a better provider than GRI for those services."

I liked what I was hearing. The prospect of changing providers or taking these services in-house scared me: it would be a lot of work, cost, and attention that added little value to FinServia's new mission. It looked like we were getting closer to an understanding. I now probed for anything else that GRI might be after. Was there anything else FinServia could do that would make GRI not just accept this change, but continue to value FinServia as an important client?

I usually don't surprise easily, but GRI's response got me. It came from Trevor, of all people.

"Mary, there is an opportunity that might help you accelerate the migration of development into FinServia, and help us develop a consulting practice we are just starting to get underway," Trevor replied. "As you know, at Cremins Corporation, we established the Cremins Development and Risk Control Process, and that is what FinServia has been following in its work with us as well. The Cremins process was simply a customization of the overall GRI development process that we used with many of our clients."

"As our work at Cremins decreased, I was reassigned to lead our development methods group. That group establishes, trains, and audits process internally, and it provides development methods services to our customers. Our business has been steadily declining over the past three years because the interest of our customers and prospects has shifted— they want to learn about Agile software development, and we are not perceived as expert in that area. We wonder if you might partner with us to help us build out our Agile skills, both for our own use and to assist our customers."

Sometimes I don't do such a great job of controlling my emotions and my mouth, and this was one of those times. "Trevor, you are about the last person in the world I'd have thought to hear that from!" I exclaimed. "I always felt that you were completely opposed to Lean and Agile software, and that you did whatever you could to impede my group in the Cremins United project."

"I can see how you felt that way, Mary," Trevor said. "GRI was engaged from the very top of Cremins to ensure structure and control in the project. I do believe in The Process, but I understand that just following it does not ensure success. I saw how your team succeeded where other parts of the project that were religiously following The Process failed, and I admired what you did and how you did it. I'd like to learn about Agile and help GRI build an Agile practice, and I can't think of anyone who could help us do that better than you could."

"Why, thank you very much for that, Trevor. May I ask exactly what you have in mind? I see myself fully occupied in FinServia matters; I'm not sure how I could help you."

Wayne Mellinger, our relationship manager, answered. "We've thought hard about this, Mary, and here is our proposal. We give you a full-time transition manager, billable of course, to help you take over development on your own, as quickly as you can handle it. Once that is complete, we could do the same for the customer-facing help desk. You are going to need some help in implementing Lean and Agile processes, unless you are able to hire a fully qualified team ready to go, which is probably unrealistic. So, we propose to provide you at a discount several full-time Lean or Agile consultants, to do training, coaching, and support. We have some in-house now, and will add more. You work with Trevor to define the services you want, and to guide us in developing support services that are generalizable to the market. The consultants start out full time with you, and over six months, they wind down until they are no longer assigned to you; at that time, they are helping us build our practice. If you like what we develop, you say so publicly, you help us with published success stories, and you serve as a reference."

Here it was—our win–win proposition. How exciting! There was only one more item I had to insist upon, but it was a little ticklish.

I said, "It sounds very good in principle. I do need some training and coaching support, and if we can find the right people, this could work very well. I do have one request I will need to insist on, though, and Trevor, I hope this doesn't hurt your feelings. I don't want Trevor to be involved in the consulting with my team. I'm happy to work with him on the hiring, the service definition, and so on, but I think it will be a while before he'd be able to add value directly with our people." I looked over at Trevor while I was saying this, and I saw he was actually smiling.

"Mary," he said, "I couldn't agree with you more strongly. It takes time for an old dog to learn new tricks, so to speak. I'll be involved in the service definition and management function, and I will be learning from you and our other consultants. Shake on it?"

I reached out my hand, took Trevor's, and shook. With that, we got down to the detailed planning to get our contract back in decent shape, and we laid out some next steps. I had to admit that Trevor brought a certain structure to the planning, and I certainly didn't doubt that he would follow up reliably.

Signposts	FinServia Transformation
	• Mary learns about the GRI relationship from her vendor manager and legal counsel.
	• She establishes her goals, primary among them wresting back control of development.
	• Mary lays out her needs with GRI and seeks to understand its needs as well.
	• GRI is disappointed to lose some business, but it agrees to establish a new partnership with FinServia.

	• Trevor McDonald, one of the authors of The Process, is now charged with developing a Lean/Agile method and consulting practice. Mary agrees to partner with him in doing so, and the FinServia–GRI relationship is back on a promising track.
Change Guides from Mary	• **Try to integrate your vendors as partners.** Many organizations depend on vendors as part of their technology suites. Integrating these vendors as partners into a Lean and Agile process environment can be a critical success element.
	• **Consider all options for partnering with vendors.** There are several options for such partnership, ranging from termination of the uncooperative but disposable, accommodation of the necessary but immovable, and partnership with the able and willing. You must find the win–win, if it exists, in your own situation, and if no win–win is possible, be sure you win and the uncooperative vendor loses!
Coming Up Next	Wes tackles the Chief Engineer puzzle at MCCA. He identifies his potential talent pool and noodles over his options with Neville and Mary.

ENDNOTES

1. The Process is described in Chapter 2.
2. An exposition of waste in software development, seen through the perspective of lean, can be found in Tom and Mary Poppendieck, *Implementing Lean Software Development* (Upper Saddle River, NJ: Addison Wesley, 2007).
3. *Level out the workload* (*heijunka*) is one of the Toyota Production System's principles. See Liker, *Toyota Way*, Chapter 10.
4. For a discussion of the velocity concept in Agile, see Mike Cohen, *Agile Estimating and Planning* (Upper Saddle River, NJ: Prentice Hall, 2005), Chapter 4.
5. *Takt time* is the idea of synchronizing the rate of production to the rate of sales to customers, also associated with a steady but adjustable cadence of production. For a description in the manufacturing context, see James P. Womack and Daniel T. Jones, *Lean Thinking*, 2nd ed. (New York: Free Press, 2003).

6

Solving the Chief Engineer Puzzle at MCCA: March

Narrator: Wes

I was feeling a little better about being able to deal with the sales force after my joint visit to San Diego National Insurance (SDNI) with Jack last week and because of the alliance I had formed with Connie. The next major item on my priority list was to deal with the space between Sales and Development. In Lean Product Development, as practiced at Toyota, that space was filled by the Chief Engineer (CE), who worked to understand customer value and drive programs to engineer solutions that delivered that value better than competitors. In what I had read and otherwise learned, the Chief Engineer sounded like a superman—starting as an outstanding engineer, with innate leadership abilities, organizational talents, and an ability to empathize with customers. I had no one at MCCA who even approached that profile, and I was sure it would take years to develop someone who could fill those shoes. What was I to do in the meantime? I decided to look for other models that might work. But first, I wanted to see what raw material I had to work with.

FINDING A PROJECT MANAGER TO HANDLE PART OF THE CHIEF ENGINEER ROLE

Lynn had recommended that I check out several people, among them Hannah Hoffman, who was providing some structure for Phillip Glass's group, and Joan Dillingsworth, a master of business administration (MBA) in finance who was involved in new contract negotiations. I had asked their managers—respectively, Phillip Glass, our development manager, and Sasha Bilokov, our Vice President of Finance—and also Cynthia Evans-Goldenbogen, our Vice President of Human Resources, about them and other potential strong talent that we might aim at project, program, and/or product management. The sense was unanimous: if we had senior leadership potential in these areas in our firm today, Hannah and Joan were it.

I started with Hannah. It seemed easier to have my first session with someone who actually worked for me—well, she actually worked for Phillip, but he worked for me. I had my assistant set up an hour in my office, and labeled the session "getting to know you." I was working at my PC returning e-mails when I heard a knock at my open door. I got up from my desk and walked over to the door to greet Hannah Hoffman.

Hannah was tall, perhaps thirty-five years old, and dressed much more professionally than the usual style at MCCA. Her hair was plainly cut, her face slightly mottled as if by teenage acne, her eyes piercingly intelligent. She stuck her hand out toward me, smiled, and said in a slight German accent, "Hello Mr. Wesleyan. I'm Hannah Hoffman, where would you like me to sit?" She looked first at the chair by my desk, and then to the small table by my window. I gestured her toward the table, and she walked over and took a chair. I joined her.

"Please call me Wes, Hannah," I began. "Thanks for joining me. I've asked you here today because I'm trying to get to know our organization and business, and Phillip and Lynn both recommended that we talk. My current focus is on establishing a team that can build out our technology products into a full information suite, and my sense is that we need to put some structure around project and product management. I understand that you are doing project management in Phillip's group, and I wanted to get some of your thoughts."

She seemed a bit wary of me, so I tried to put her at ease. I asked her about herself—usually that is everyone's favorite topic.

"I'm a software engineer by training. I went to school in Austria, at the International School for Informatics in Hagenberg. I'm sure you've not heard of it?" I nodded that I had not. Hannah went on, "I was married there, to a computer scientist. Johannes, that's my husband, was transferred here to San Diego by his company four years ago. We thought it was a short assignment, perhaps just a year, so I decided to do some contract programming work. Four years later, Johannes is still on assignment, and I've become an employee. We have no plans to return home at this time."

"Phillip tells me that you have become the organizer for his department," I prompted.

"Yes, I have. I never thought I'd wind up in that role," Hannah said. "I was mathematical, not organizational, and I never thought I would be a leader, especially once we came to California. Also, it's such a cliché: the organized German, making and following rules. But after being in the department for several months, I just could not stand the disorder and chaos, and I began to put together lists of the things we had to do. It just grew from there."

"From what I've heard and seen so far, Hannah," I said, "It seems like there was not much structure in place. Phillip told me how the company grew, with Ernie or Jack working directly with programmers to get things done quickly. There's a certain attractiveness in that picture, but it doesn't seem to scale very well."

"That's for certain, Wes," Hannah agreed. "The first thing I did was build a way to log requests, without changing how we dealt with them. Once we had a list, the prioritization question arose, but we've never resolved that. Mr. Langley seems to believe that technology should do whatever he wants, whenever he wants it; when we sought to create a prioritization process, he intimidated Phillip into backing down. Perhaps with you here now, we could try again?" she asked, with a hopeful lilt in her voice.

"Perhaps," I said, and smiled at her. Phillip had given me the log of project requests when we met earlier this week. There were thirty or so requests, ranging from requests from our lead information management customer, SDNI, through new operational site creation to minor modifications to our capture and viewing software. I knew from our SDNI meeting that there were many items on the separate SDNI list, and I guessed that there were other lists floating around as well. Nevertheless, even though Hannah's "master" list was incomplete, I was glad to have it!

"How about methodology?" I continued. "It seems like we don't have any particular methods? Is that right?"

"Not entirely," Hannah replied. "I'd call what we do *developer's choice*. We have programmers, but not many analysts, and very few project managers. The programmers each specialize in some areas of the code, and Phillip juggles them around and ensures they get cross-trained. The operations staff in the field used to funnel all their requests to Phillip, but now they come to me instead, and I log them in. Then Phillip assigns them. If the programmers don't know exactly what to do, they ask the person who requested the work. Some of our more recent hires do more documentation of the requirements or the designs, depending on what they learned before they came here."

"And you, Hannah, do you have preferences? What are your thoughts on what we should be doing?" I queried.

"In school, I learned formal development methods, with a standard flow from requirements documents through design and development. I'm not sure how that could work here; we move too fast, and I don't think Phillip, Rico, and the rest of the programmers would go for it. I believe we need to do something more formal, though, especially with the San Diego National project."

I had seen that earlier on my visit to the company. Phillip told me earlier that Hannah was taking on a project manager role for the San Diego National project. The project had been floundering for quite a while, with the customer alternately excited with what Phillip, Rico, and team were delivering, and angry with what was not being delivered, or delivered in a way that failed to meet expectations. The MCCA side of the project had been driven by Sales—Jack Langley himself, our VP of Sales, and Melissa Groves, the young saleswoman operating as Jack's assistant. Melissa would work with the customer's staff and provide requirements and committed timelines to Phillip. As the project became rockier, though, Phillip had moved to insert Hannah between himself and the duo of Jack and Melissa.

"Tell me about that project, could you?" I asked. "I had the opportunity to visit the customer briefly, and I would like your perspective."

"I've just started to get involved," Hannah said. "I don't know much yet, other than what I've seen peripherally here. I was planning on going out to visit the customer with Melissa next week. The software that Rico has built is fantastic; it combines image, data, and text document management into one searchable virtual file, and merges all of that with Internet-like social networking features. The problems seem to be about aligning what the customer wants, in what order, with what the contract says, and expanding our development capacity beyond just Rico."

"And then hardening the features into products that we can sell to other customers," I added. "Sounds to me like you're on the right track."

By this time in the conversation, I had seen enough of Hannah to believe that she could fill at least part of the Chief Engineer role we needed. She was bright, energetic, organized, knew technology, knew our people and culture, and was unafraid. I launched into my explanation of who I was and where I wanted to take the company, including my top five priorities (which I had developed over dinner with Mary, Neville, and Cornelia[1]), and I asked if she was interested in joining me in making the changes we needed to grow this company. She seemed energized by the ideas and plans and eager to learn Lean and Agile if that could help her manage the SDNI project more effectively. In fact, she asked if I would join her on her visit to that customer—just before I asked her if I could do so myself.

As our conversation was winding down, Hannah seemed to be considering whether to bring up another topic—just a slight hesitation in her walk toward the door. I asked if there was anything more, and she came back to the table, sat down, and clasped her hands in front of her.

"Have you met Rico yet?" she asked.

"Just in passing. I understand he's a very talented developer." Phillip had introduced us at Rico's cubicle a few days ago. It was hard to find Rico in the middle of what seemed to be dozens of monitors, scanners, printers, papers, books, and the remnants of lunch. Rico had barely looked up from whatever he was intensely focused upon to acknowledge my presence.

"Indeed he is," Hannah stated. "Probably the most sophisticated, productive programmer I've ever met. He is the primary force behind our software, which in turn has been the moving force for the whole company. The problem is that Rico knows how important he is, and he thinks he can do whatever he wants. Over the years, he has threatened to walk out several times, and each time Ernie has calmed him down and ensured that he stayed. Now with Ernie gone, the growth in our operations, and the SDNI project, Rico is under more pressure than ever. We can't afford to lose him, but on the other hand, when he blows his top, it is very disruptive and scary. He's off on another of his little "sabbaticals" right now after getting into a fight with a salesman. You might want to take a look into the situation."

I thanked her for her warning, and I promised to keep the source of the information confidential. Her caution on Rico had thrown some wet noodles on my excitement at finding Hannah, but on the whole, it had been a promising meeting. With Hannah, I thought I had a bead on the project management dimension of my CE problem; next step, product management.

FINDING A PRODUCT MANAGER TO HANDLE PART OF THE CHIEF ENGINEER ROLE

Joan Dillingsworth was next on my list. She worked for Sasha Bilokov, Vice President of Finance, as a financial analyst. I had talked with Sasha a few days ago about Joan, and what I learned was encouraging. Joan had been with MCCA for four years, having joined right out of the University of California–San Diego (UCSD) MBA program, where she majored in finance. While an undergraduate at UCSD, she had worked part time at MCCA in operations, and she had continued to work part time through graduate school. Sasha, who had joined the company at the same time as CEO Lynn Hollander, assigned Joan to get control of the commitments we were making in new contracts. Sasha had two conflicting thoughts about the potential for Joan to become a product manager for me—she'd hate to lose her, but she'd love to have a partner outside of finance to help manage product vision and profitability. Sasha had given me her blessing and encouragement to talk with Joan to explore product management and Joan's interest in it. However, Sasha wanted to join in on the conversation; no problem here! We met in Sasha's office, which was adjacent to Lynn's. Sasha asked me to come a few minutes before Joan, so we could prepare for the meeting.

Sasha was a certified public accountant (CPA) by training and trade. Franklin McDonald, the Fletcher, Wilkens, and Johnson (FWJ) partner most deeply involved with MCCA, had met Sasha while working in Los Angeles at one of the companies FWJ had invested in perhaps ten years ago. Sasha had come to the United States from Russia as a teenager in the early 1970s, and she attended high school and college in California. She still had a noticeable Russian accent, which I enjoyed listening to. Franklin had found her an impressive talent, and he remembered her when he needed to restaff the management ranks at MCCA. I found her single-mindedly focused on profitably growing MCCA quickly, toward FWJ's "liquidity event."

"Joan will be here in ten minutes, Wes. Your plan?" Sasha was a woman of few words.

"We need to do better product management," I said. "We don't do a good job of setting product direction, prioritizing opportunities, understanding our competition, and pricing. In her current role, Joan spends her time trying to ensure that we don't enter into bad deals. I'd like to talk to her about taking her role to the next step, to keep her financial focus but also move into marketing."

"I've talked with her, and she is interested. However, she has some doubts about the role that you'll need to address," Sasha said. "Assuming you can overcome her doubts, and you find her qualified, what are you proposing?"

"I'm not entirely sure," I answered. "I've been studying product development models, especially Toyota's, which relies on a Chief Engineer who combines marketing, financial, engineering, and project leadership skills. I love that idea, but I don't understand where we would ever find someone like that. So I am investigating the talent we have here now in those areas and considering how we could put a team together to fill the CE role. For today, I'd like to get to know Joan a little, tell her about what I hope to do, and test her interest. Then I'll see where it goes. Does that sound okay to you?"

Sasha was a top-notch finance professional, and she had seen models of product management before. She asked if I was thinking of something like the Procter & Gamble model, where the product manager is responsible for the product profitability and direction, relying heavily on analytical tools to position the product versus the competition and grow profits. I said I wasn't sure, but something like that, yes. Sasha nodded that she understood and indicated that we should begin our conversation with Joan. At that, she walked out of her office and came back with Joan. She introduced us and laid out our agenda.

"Joan, as we talked about earlier, Wes was brought on board to drive our product development strategy and execution. He is considering how we should improve our product management and Lynn and I both suggested that he consider you for a position in that area. I am supportive of this idea, if you find it to your satisfaction. Today Wes would like to learn more about your current role and talk over some ideas with us. We'll end there today, and then circle back later and set next steps. Sound good?" Sasha asked.

Joan was young, no more than thirty, I thought. She was professionally dressed, like Hannah a cut above the office standard, and she seemed outgoing and confident. She had set a notebook in front of her, open to a legal pad, and had begun a page of notes; I could see that she'd written a date at the top of the page.

"Yes, sounds good," Joan said. "Shall I start by telling you about my current role?"

"Please," I agreed. "And if you give me some background on how you came to this role, I'd appreciate that also. Then I can reciprocate on what I am trying to accomplish and how you might help."

Joan began articulately. "I joined MCCA full time four years ago, after I completed my MBA in finance. At that time, we were growing rapidly, and the VP of Finance needed someone to do analysis. Prior to that time, there had been little financial analysis done by anyone but the VP himself—we'd been profitable, and Ernie had followed a simple model. Jobs and contracts were all bid at cost plus a comfortable margin, and the Finance Department—it was actually more of an Accounting Department—had kept score by job or operation. The salespeople were paid according to forecast profits for the first year of an operation, but after that, they got paid a percentage of actual profits. If a job was losing money, Finance informed the salespeople that they had to find a way to fix it, and they usually could, by raising prices, cutting costs, or finding a higher margin business to add to the mix. The problem came as we grew, and the model stopped working quite so well."

Sasha added, "There were several factors, in retrospect, that caused the problems, we think. The market became more competitive as the technology to do the work we do became more commoditized. Also, as we grew, Ernie couldn't be everywhere all the time as he seemed to be when MCCA was smaller. We also began to face offshore competition. The sales group seemed to become more short-term focused and began taking bigger risks. It didn't take many troubled projects to result in depressed overall profitability."

"I saw some of this myself," Joan continued. "During college, I worked in operations, and I saw the transition we were making from fairly straightforward imaging work into more sophisticated jobs, like optical character recognition, key-from-image, unusual size of originals, and the like. We had a couple of contracts that we really screwed up. The jobs were sold before we had the capability to do them, and it turned out much more difficult to deliver than had been estimated.

"My first two years here were focused on cost analysis. I was assigned to work on the biggest money-losing jobs, to assemble the cost data in more detail, and work with the sales and operations managers to figure out how to fix them. We had some success, but eventually, we realized it would be a lot easier if we could avoid taking on losing contracts instead of just trying to fix them after the fact. We tried to make that happen, but we didn't have much success until Ernie retired. We had a couple of debates early on with sales over the projected profitability—they'd argue down our cost models, saying we were being too conservative, and after we'd lost a few battles, we became discouraged and went back to after-the-fact troubleshooting. Until Sasha took over, that is."

"I joined soon after Lynn," Sasha took over the narration. "And Connie joined soon after that. Our early strategic planning identified the wide variation in operational profitability, especially the few large losing deals of the past few years, and we set a goal of putting better early-stage controls in place. With Lynn and Connie both strongly supporting the initiative, we've been much more successful. Connie has taken a leadership role in the cost projections and shown that, although she's willing to take some business risks, she'll draw the line when she needs to. Sales has lost a few deals because we've not been willing to take the risks in a deal, and there have been some bitter words as our decisions hit the Sales Department right in the wallet. Joan has done a wonderful job, both analytically and politically, in a tough spot."

"Thanks for the kind words, Sasha," Joan said to her boss. By this time, I was well along to being sold on Joan. She was insightful, experienced in our business and culture, analytical, a good communicator, and courageous. I wondered if she'd be interested in what I had in mind. Her next words were encouraging. "It's still not enough, though, is it?" she said. "We can usually stop bad deals, but we aren't doing much about getting good ones. If we could target our services at what we are good at, and where competitors have gaps, perhaps we could get more business with better margins."

"Ah," I exclaimed, "That is exactly what I have in mind—proactively understanding customer needs, and designing our services and products to add value and make us money." With that, I repeated, for what seemed like the hundredth time, my explanation of whom I was and where I wanted to take the company, including my five priorities.[2] Joan and Sasha were particularly interested in establishing a better relationship with the Sales Department (they wished me good luck), and determining the project management and product management regimes (which I hoped would address our problem of not having a single chief engineer). They asked me about my experiences with Lean and Agile software development, of which they had both heard but not seen in action. Joan had been exposed to Lean manufacturing ideas in business school, and she understood the typical roles played by product managers. I gave a quick summary of my experiences observing Mary's team at Cremins Corporation, but I noted that this situation is so different that I wasn't entirely sure how the concepts should be applied. That's why I was looking to build a strong team, to help set and execute direction.

With that, I asked Joan and Sasha their reaction to my plans and how they might like to contribute. Joan looked over at Sasha and must have seen a go-ahead nod, because she said, "Sasha and I have talked about this. I am interested in moving the cost–profit direction setting earlier in the sales process, so we can get ahead of the game. I am concerned about whether we could actually succeed, given how powerful the Sales

Department is in this company. We are so reactive, and so flexible, that it's going to be difficult to influence how the company works."

"I'm glad you are interested, Joan," I said. "I'm not entirely sure how we are going to do this, but we have a lot of the elements in place. Lynn, Connie, and certainly Sasha," I smiled at her boss, "are all supportive, so it's our game to lose. Can I make a proposal?" I tested. "How about I put some thoughts together, and run them past the two of you, on how we might approach this? I need to consider project and product management together, and I need to think through some options. Once I get some ideas down, we can talk over next steps. Deal?"

"Deal," said Sasha.

"Deal," said Joan. We shook hands, all feeling that we had begun an important change, but not knowing exactly where it was going. I felt good that I had now identified product management as well as project management talent, and that I certainly had the support of the finance people (always a good thing). Now I had to figure out how to fit this all together.

EXPLORING ALTERNATIVE DEVELOPMENT MODELS: POWERFUL INDIVIDUAL CHIEF ENGINEERS VERSUS DEVELOPMENT TEAMS OF PEERS

Believing that I had completed my survey of available talent and the project and product management cultures at MCCA, I was ready to reengage with my "sensei" Neville and Mary. This time, Neville suggested that Mary and I come over to his home Friday evening after work, a twenty-minute drive north to Carlsbad. We arrived at the Roberts' home, which was in a newer development where the homes and townhomes were arranged around a series of pools. We settled into comfortable, metal-framed, padded outdoor furniture on the deck overlooking one of the pools, while Cornelia delivered some fresh guacamole and chips and Neville's usual California Pinot Noir.

Neville started by asking how our weeks had gone. Mary began by relating her success dealing with GRI and how excited she was at how well it went. She had some trepidation on using them to help her build out her Lean and Agile development processes, and she was worried about how Trevor McDonald would adjust away from his beloved Process. But GRI's commitment to help her transition development and customer support from their clutches, and to continue to provide hosting and desktop management services for internal users, relieved a lot of her fears. Assuming GRI could deliver, Mary could focus on higher-priority items.

My story was less triumphant. I had focused primarily on the sales–development interface, and on resolving the Chief Engineer issue for MCCA. Cornelia and Neville were fascinated by Connie—the daughter of 1960s hippies rebelling by becoming a supervisor at an automobile plant! I kept that story short so I could get to the topic on which I sought guidance, how to configure the Chief Engineer role at MCCA.

"Oh great sensei," I joked, "Please guide me." Neville pretended to stroke his nonexistent beard, and he looked appropriately pensive. "Seriously, Neville, I could use some thoughts. I've read about Lean Product Development and the role of Chief Engineer, and I had a chance to see you in action on the TRIM project[3] at my old job. I really like the concept, but I don't see any chance of having someone like that at MCCA in any reasonable time frame. After all, Toyota develops these people over decades.[4] I don't have that much time, and even if I did, I'm not sure I could figure out how to hire and develop them."

Neville replied, "You have a great point, Wes. It took me a couple of years in my last job to be an effective CE. Although I had the technical and other skills and experience, I didn't know the business well. Even if you went out and hired the best people you could, they wouldn't know your business or your company, and they wouldn't be able to do the job effectively. And internally, if MCCA hasn't been focused on developing this type of person, it is extremely unlikely you have a near-term candidate."

"You could go down an Agile route, Wes," said Mary. "In a scrum,[5] the Chief Engineer role is split into several elements. The customer-focused role is the Product Owner, who speaks at a detailed level about what is needed, its relative priority, and details of requirements, including being in the development meetings every day. The project-focused role is the Scrum Master, who facilitates the creation of the backlog, the release plans, and the development sprints."

"But Mary," I said, "wouldn't you agree that a scrum simply assumes away the problem on which I am focused? Somehow we have an all-knowing Product Owner who can not only speak definitively on behalf of the entire business on priorities and requirements, but can also sit for hours and hours with developers specifying the minutest details of product design?"

Mary laughed. "I guess that's so, Wes. Scrum was conceived by developers and consultants to help them self-manage development projects, assuming a given set of requirements. It does provide some good ideas in that realm, but you're right, it doesn't provide you with much guidance on filling the gap of not having a Toyota-like CE."

"Maybe you could describe how you are planning on managing product and projects at FinServia, Mary," I asked. "That might be helpful."

"We have a similar problem to yours, Wes. I don't know a thing about printing or shareholder services, but I am pretty darn good at technology and project management. Greg knew this, and he knew he needed someone who knew a lot about the business in which we were choosing to compete. He found and recruited Mervin, who had been in the business as a buyer of these services, and he's smart, aggressive, and ambitious. Greg needs to be deeply involved in our new product development, so he has chosen to have Mervin and I both report to him, rather than have Mervin report to me. Also, I'm going to be fully occupied redesigning our whole technology organization, so I won't have time to focus on learning the customer space right away."

Neville summarized, "You are creating a two-headed chief engineer! That's certainly a viable approach. It sounds like Greg is having Mervin be a fairly traditional product manager, similar to what you might find in a consumer products company. Mervin focuses on customer needs, understanding competitors, profitability, and the business case for development, telling you what to build and how much it's worth to build it. He sets prices, approves major deals, and owns your budget. Right?"

"That's basically it," Mary said. "I just hope we get along well. I'll need to teach him how to participate in our development projects, and I'll gradually teach him about technology. We'll see how that goes."

I still had a question for Mary. "We've dealt with the *product* side of the equation, and I know you have the technology element. What about *project management*? What are you going to do there?"

"Didn't I tell you?" she asked. "I thought I did—I know Neville knows. I hired Alex Fuegos away from Neville. He's going to work for me and help build out a Lean and Agile environment, with a beginning focus on project management. The actual project management will be integrated under the development managers, leveraging Alex's mentorship. And the GRI consultants are going to do some teaching and mentoring as well."

"That's not very helpful," I complained. "Instead of choosing a general model for roles, you are just hiring people you know, and you lucked into the GRI deal. That doesn't help me very much, since I don't know anyone I could hire."

"Well," said Neville, "let's talk over your situation. You don't have a CE type. You want a collaborative, team-oriented environment, because that's who you are, and because you don't know enough to tell people what to do. Sounds like you need a team model that leverages the people you have, but provides them the structure they need. I've got just the thing for you, I think."

"Great! What is it?" I asked.

"It's the Microsoft team model.[6] The basic idea is a team of peers, all sharing a common goal of shipping a quality product. The team members all report up to BUMs—business unit managers—who ultimately are responsible for configuring and enabling the team's performance. There are several team members, with overlapping roles—everyone is encouraged to get into everyone else's business, so long as the goal is to ship a quality product on time. Want to go through the roles, and see if you have someone for each of them?"

"Yes, of course. Where do we start?" I questioned. This was sounding promising, and I grabbed a napkin to jot down what Neville said next (Figure 6.1).

FIGURE 6.1
MSF roles.

Neville began, "*Product Management*. This is pretty much the same as Mervin's role with Mary. Definitely not involved in every development meeting or design session; there are other roles for that. Customer and financial focus."

"Got it," I said. "Joan Dillingsworth."

"Next is *Program Management*. This is a fairly traditional role, owning the project plan, team communication, and driving decision making. The twist is that the program manager also owns the functional specification; that is, the transformation of the product vision, which is the responsibility of the product manager, into what the developers actually code. It's much better to have this responsibility in *program* management than in *product* management, because otherwise you get project managers who are empty-headed rule followers. Program management owns the solution and has to balance what product management says it needs with the cost and risks of development as provided by the development management."

"No problem there, either. That's Hannah." Two for two.

"The next one is also simple—*Development Management*. This job comprises technical design, development, estimating, posing design trade-offs, getting ready to deploy." Neville was rolling now.

"Also no problem—that's Phillip Glass. This is a perfect role for him. Right now, he's trying to do way too much, a lot of which he's really bad at. He'd love this job, especially if he's on a team with others helping him with the stuff he hates." Three for three.

Neville paused and took a sip of his Pinot. "Some would say that these three roles, which you just filled, are the three most important ones. But you need to be very careful of assuming that. The model is very explicit about this being *a team of peers*, a six-sided polyhedron, with all the complexity that implies. In practice, some of the team members will be more powerful than others, make more money, have more connections, and be more persuasive. But as a BUM, you need to reinforce the team-of-peers idea. Especially with this next role—*Testing Management*."

"Hmm," I fretted. "I don't have anyone in mind for that. I haven't seen much evidence of testing in my group yet. I'm sure it's done, but I'm not sure how, when, or by whom."

"This is also a fairly traditional role, except that in agile development, the importance of the testers is magnified. You need someone with strong technical skills, because you need to automate testing as much as you can. The test manager needs to be very detail oriented (because that's the nature of testing), yet also must be able to rise above the details to find new, faster ways to test, and has to be able to plan testing and recruit and manage other testers. The testing manager has to be collaborative; otherwise she'll be fighting with Development all the time about bugs, and with Program Management, which will always be trying to compress testing time. But she has to be strong and independent, so the team gets honest answers and a strong advocate for quality." Neville paused and took another sip. (Was talking about testing driving him to drink? I hoped not!)

At this point, Mary chimed in: "Testing Management is the hardest role of all fill, at least in my experience, Wes. The qualities that make a great tester almost disqualify one from being a great test manager—great testers often see trees but not forests, and they can be a huge pain in the rear. If you don't have an obvious candidate now, you should start looking right away. You'll probably have no idea what to look for, so how about I refer you to a recruiter I know—maybe she can help."

"I'd appreciate that," I said sincerely. One of the things I appreciated about Mary was her unvarnished, guileless honesty. She was completely right about me not knowing what to look for, although it did sting just a bit to hear her say it—again. "What are the two remaining roles?" I didn't even have a good guess.

"*User Experience* and *Release Management*," Neville explained. "Again, just because we are covering these last doesn't mean they are less important. *User Experience* is responsible for the details of the user interface, the user training, and help desk support. This should be someone who is passionate about the users themselves, focused on what they need and want in detail, whereas the product manager is focused at a higher level.

"*Release Management* worries about the migration of the software from Development to Production—servers, networks, security, disaster recovery, performance, and fault management. Mary and I can both tell you stories about projects where we didn't do a good job of filling the Release Management role."

"That makes a lot of sense. Off the top of my head, I don't know people for those roles either, but since I have identified three of the team, I'm sure they could help fill it out. Thank you so much, Neville; this should work well for us. Any other issues I need to be thinking about?"

"Indeed, just two more thoughts," Neville said as he wrapped up our business dialogue for the evening. "Although in your case I'd recommend one leader per Microsoft Solutions Framework (MSF) role, in some instances you can combine roles—just be careful that each focus area gets enough leadership bandwidth. And finally, just because you have an approach that you think fits you now, you shouldn't give up your quest to build Chief Engineers. That combination of engineering, customer focus, and leadership skills is extremely powerful and valuable, so keep building those skills with intensity. Even if you never implement a CE system like Toyota's, the people you build with that completeness of skill and knowledge will pay back your investments many times over however you deploy them."

I felt lucky to have the guidance of both Neville and Mary as I puzzled over my MCCA challenges. Tonight, I felt I had cracked the CE puzzle; tomorrow, I'd figure out how to implement this team model, along with other Lean and Agile concepts. In the meantime, I had some catching up to do with my own Pinot.

Signposts	MCCA Transformation
	• Wes seeks to fill MCCA's gap between the Sales and Development Departments.
	• He interviews Hannah and Joan, and finds both worthy candidates, one for project management and the other for product management.
	• Mary and Wes meet with Neville to explore a variety of product development leadership models. The pure Chief Engineer model fits neither of their current situations, but each finds an acceptable alternative.
Change Guides from Wes	• **Product, project, and engineering leadership are critical to Lean and Agile success.** The Toyota model, which uses a Chief Engineer, is not appropriate in all situations, and it's not possible in many.
	• **Alternative models to the Chief Engineer model can succeed.** For example, a marketing-centered product manager can pair up with a product- and engineering-focused development manager. Or a team of peers can be configured in a variety of ways to manage the six areas identified in the Microsoft Solutions Framework (MSF)—product, program, development, testing, user experience, and release management.
	• **When filling new roles, err on the side of giving bright and ambitious people already in your organization a chance to grow,** rather than always seeking "better" qualified people outside. This is why Wes chose Hannah and Joan. You may have to provide added support to ensure their success, but the benefit of continuity and the vote of confidence in the existing staff is more than worth it.

	• **Don't give up on developing people with CE skills** Even if you never implement that model completely, the integration of CE skills in your leaders will pay off.
Coming Up Next	Mary takes over storytelling, relating the six-week period in which she plans and executes her major organizational change. She designs the new structure, fills the key roles, and rolls it out.

ENDNOTES

1. Listed at the end of Chapter 3.
2. Listed at end of Chapter 3.
3. See, for example, Chapter 10 of Levine, *Tale of Two Systems.*
4. Chapter 7 of Morgan and Liker, *Toyota Product Development System.*
5. Scum is described in Ken Schwaber and Mike Beedle, *Agile Software Development with Scrum* (Upper Saddle River, NJ: Prentice Hall, 2002).
6. My favorite explanation of Microsoft's approach to software development is by Michael Cusumano, *Microsoft Secrets: How the World's Most Powerful Software Company Creates Technology, Shapes Markets and Manages People* (New York: Free Press, 1998). The book is getting a little dated now, but remains very fresh to those who have not been exposed to the ideas. The current material from Microsoft is at (as of September 2011): http://www.microsoft.com/download/en/details.aspx?id=3214. The team model itself is Microsoft Solutions Framework White Paper, MSF Team Model v. 3.1 (Redmond, WA: Microsoft, June 2002).

Section III

Beginning the Transformations
April–May

7

Six Weeks to Change the FinServia Organization: April

Narrator: Mary

It has been just six weeks since my momentous meeting with GRI that started to give my quest at FinServia shape. In the meantime, I've been frantically busy designing our new organizations. Back in February, when Wes, Neville, Cornelia, and I talked through possible approaches to making change, I said that I was comfortable creating disruption, and that is certainly what the last six weeks have been about.

In this chapter, I'll describe the activities of the last six weeks. They began with the GRI meeting in March (Chapter 5), and ended with Roberta Greely, our VP of Human Resources, and I looking back at what we'd wrought with satisfaction and hope. In between, Roberta, Greg, and I designed our new development organization, worked with GRI to plan the transition, selected and hired some of the key leaders, let some staff members go, and asked the remainder to recommit to a new future. Oh, and Wes and I set a date to get married, in the first week of January on the beach in Maui. Other than that, it was a quiet and peaceful period.

EARLY WEEK ONE: PLANNING THE FINSERVIA DEVELOPMENT ORGANIZATION

Greg Allenby, my boss and president of FinServia, Roberta Greeley, FinServia's VP of Human Resources, and I were sitting in the Sunshine room, a name better suited to earlier in the day. At 8:00 p.m. we had no sun, but thankfully neither did we have to suffer the room's usual background noise from the printing plant. Nor did we have any prying eyes and ears to interrupt us while we tossed around the ideas that would shape our company's future.

It was unusually quiet in our offices. During the day, sounds echo off the high ceiling and the concrete floors, but it was early evening and there were few others in the offices. Roberta had picked up some Chinese food, which was now spread out over half the table. While Roberta and Greg picked at the last of their moo shu, I walked up to the whiteboard covering one wall and reached for a marker.

"Wait a moment, Mary," Greg interrupted. "Let's talk over how we are going to approach this before you just start drawing on the board. What are you going to draw?"

"I thought I'd draw out the organizational structure I had in mind for you and Roberta to review," I said.

"Let's not start with your proposal," began Greg. "I'd like us to consider some options instead of jumping right to what you want to do. Roberta, you've seen technology development operations—how about you propose something?"

This was a typical interaction for Greg and me. He loved to consider options and fancied himself a teacher in the Aristotelian mold. I understood these characteristics contributed to his quality as a leader, but it nevertheless frustrated me no end. By the time I was ready to broach something with Greg, I usually had arrived at my conclusions and all I wanted was approval; I wasn't looking for help thinking it through. I should have learned that I had to frame my proposals with options to show I had considered them, and I did that sometimes, but other times, like tonight, I wanted to get right to the point. It was not to be.

Option 1: A Functional Organization

"I'm not an expert in technology," Roberta excused herself, "but I can help us construct some options. I like to think of three basic kinds of organizations: functional, divisional, and matrix.[1] I'll draw out what a functional organization might look like for you."

"That sounds like a good start," Greg agreed. "Why don't you divide the board into three areas, and we'll try all three."

Roberta drew two vertical lines on the board, and began drawing on the far left. The diagram she drew is shown in Figure 7.1.

As Roberta drew, she explained, "This is similar to how Cremins organized its technology groups. Each functional specialty is in its own department, and the departments work together either directly or through projects run by the project management department to accomplish goals.

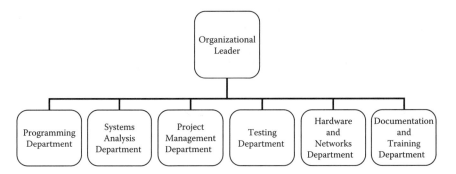

FIGURE 7.1
Functional style development organization.

The benefit is in expertise, uniformity, and control. The programming department can ensure that we don't duplicate systems and ensure that proper expertise is built and applied, and so on with the other groups."

Memories of the slow-moving, maddeningly frustrating, control-over-delivery bureaucracy at Cremins flooded over me, and I think I physically shivered. "We can't have that kind of structure, Roberta," I said. "Greg and I are both committed to the principle that the best product development is driven by chief engineers, who combine programming, project management, and marketing skills. Your structure makes it impossible to develop those people. It also makes focus on customer value very difficult, because the power is in the hands of functional specialists instead of leaders aligned with value."

"That's not necessarily true, Mary," Greg chided me. "The CEs could live in the project management department."

"Theoretically," I replied with a heavy dose of sarcasm.

"All right, Mary, then let's consider another option."

Option 2: A Divisional Organization

Greg was humoring me. "Roberta, can you draw out what a divisional structure might look like for Mary?"

"First, we have to decide what the division might be, Greg. Some options would be by product, by geography, or by customer segment," responded our HR chief.

"I can help with that," I said. "This is closer to what I am thinking about. I was thinking about dividing the group along customer value lines: a

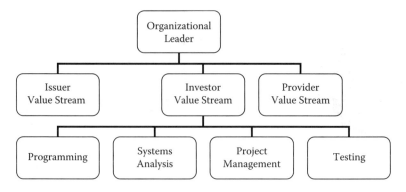

FIGURE 7.2
Divisional style development organization.

group devoted to providing value to security issuers, one to investors, and one to companies that provide services to issues or investors."

Roberta drew that out (Figure 7.2). As she did, she asked what was in each of the groups, and as I told her, she added that subtext to the investor group, noting that it would be replicated across the groups. That replication, she added, was one of the downsides of divisional organization.

"That may be," I agreed, "but that risk is more than offset by the focus on customers, ease of monitoring performance, and above all else, the development of leaders proficient in more than one specialty. Giving our customer-focused leaders direct control of the resources needed to deliver value will make us flexible and responsive to change."

"At the cost of duplication and lack of consistency," Roberta said. "And isn't there only one underlying set of technologies shared by these value streams? How does that get managed in this structure?"

"We would take the underlying technology components and allocate them, best fit, to the several value streams. But you're right, Roberta, a pure customer value stream organization, for this company, presents some real issues."

"Got it. Looks like neither a pure functional nor a pure customer-focused approach is without serious problems. So let's finish the options with a matrix organization," Greg asked. "What would that look like, Roberta?"

Option 3: A Matrix Organization

"It is simply a hybrid of the two we've already drawn," Roberta said. "We would create departments for both the value streams as Mary suggests, and the functional departments I drew in the first diagram. Employees would be assigned from the functional to the value stream organizations as long as they were needed there, and they'd move to another when they're needed elsewhere. Each employee has two loyalties, to their functional area and to the customer value stream to which they are assigned. In practice, almost all large organizations have some flavor of matrix management. For example, here at FinServia, our HR function is matrix, with all the HR generalists reporting to me formally, but they're also assigned to each VP area."

Roberta drew out a matrix organization of chief engineers for each value stream, leading people drawn from the functional areas (Figure 7.3).

"That's true, Roberta, we do use some matrix organizational structures," Greg interjected. "It can help with flexibility, and it gives some of the benefits of customer focus while still retaining the functional expertise and control. I worry about struggles between the functional and customer-focused managers, and I don't see where we grow our CE talent—where are the junior CEs? Also, Roberta, who are you thinking the CEs would report to? To Mary? That would put a lot of pressure on her, having to manage both the CEs and the functional areas and to ensure that the two differently focused leaders work effectively together."

Roberta knew that Greg and I were fans of Lean Product Development, and professional that she is, she had done her homework.

"From what I've read, Greg, that's how Toyota organizes its product development," she said. "They have the Chief Engineers and the functional leads

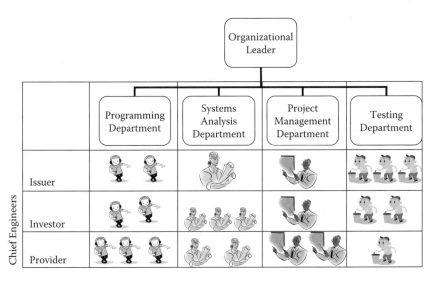

FIGURE 7.3
Matrix style development organization.

reporting to the overall product development center leader, and then they have dedicated cross-functional teams for each specific component area. They call these component-focused groups *module development teams*. For example, there would be a "doors" team, led by a junior CE, with people from the metals, glass, electronics, and other functional areas.[2]

There were many things I liked about the matrix Roberta was explaining, but I was concerned about the coordination burden it would put on me if all the CEs and all the functional areas converged functionally to me. I hoped Greg was ready now to listen to my proposal.

Option 4: Chief Engineers with Shared Support

"Greg," I said, "I have a proposal that combines the divisional and matrix ideas in a way that I think can work for us. Is it okay if I draw it now?" Seeing him nod, I quickly erased all three examples that Roberta had drawn (lest their vestiges pollute my plan), and I drew the structure I had been contemplating (Figure 7.4).

"You see that the primary structure is *divisional*: there are four customer value stream chief engineer organizations, much as Roberta drew in Option 2. Since we've agreed that the product management remains with Marketing, we'll need to work with Mervin to align his product managers to our CEs."

I continued, "We take the underlying technology components and allocate them to the CEs as best we can. By giving the customer-value-focused CEs as much ownership of the software and the resources to change it as we can, we improve accountability, flexibility, and decision making. Most of the technology is easy to allocate, such as the investor portal going to the investor CE, but some of the shared components get a bit tricky. I will continue to have an important role ensuring collaboration and teamwork."

I paused to check that Greg and Roberta were still with me; they were, so I continued.

"We deal with the overlaps, gaps, consistency, and the need to guarantee professional expertise by adding some critical structures that partner with the value stream groups. Here I call them development support, learning, and infrastructure. These areas become facilitative leaders across the teams, helping the CEs and their teams to create the standards, architectures, training programs, project methods, test environments, release procedures, and whatever else is needed. My senior team becomes the four CEs, a development support leader, a learning leader, and a data center/network leader."

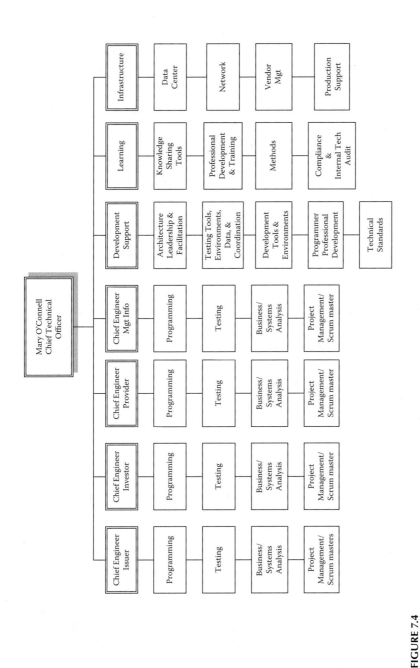

FIGURE 7.4
Mary O'Connell's organizational proposal.

"The alternative, I suppose," thought Greg out loud, "would be for the CEs to have the staff matrixed to them, as Roberta just diagrammed in Option 3 (Figure 7.3). Given how new this whole organization is, I think I have to agree with you that at least for now we need to give the CEs as much chance as possible to provide value. Having direct control over their more critical people will do that, and then we'll have to rely on the support groups to ensure we have the consistency, safety, and professional expertise we need."

"And don't forget, Greg, both the CEs and the support groups will report to me and will work together on my team. My management of the team will be critical to the success of the structure," I reminded him.

"Understood," he agreed. He had something else on his mind as well. "What happens to the technology to support Printing, and what happens to the administrative technology, like our finance and human resources systems?" Greg asked.

"My preference would be for printing technology to be distributed to the Printing Department, and for our VP of Finance to take the administrative systems. I don't know enough about their technology leadership skills to know if that is feasible or advisable, Greg." I hoped I wouldn't need to get distracted by non-product-development technology management, but if I had to take that on, I certainly would. Many functional managers are simply not equipped to manage their own technologies, even if all that means is selecting and managing a technology leader to do it for them.

"I'm not sure either," Greg responded. "My sense is that our VP of Printing could probably do it, but I doubt if our VP of Finance could." Turning to Roberta, he went on, "Roberta, can you make a note to talk with me on this topic in the next few days? It's not central to this discussion, but it's important that we resolve it soon." He paused for a moment, still looking at Roberta, and then asked her, "Are you okay with this structure?"

Roberta perused the org chart on the wall and gave her approval. "I see no reason this won't work, if we can find the right people to fill the critical roles. What do you think, Mary, do we have some of this talent?"

"Very little, Roberta," I said. "The technology group we have is a bureaucratic control group. Our project managers are rule followers and enforcers; our business analysts are scribes for what The Business tells them they want; and our testers couldn't automate a test if their lives depended on it. I have hired Alex Fuegos from Cremins Corporation, and I'm sure he can fill one of these roles, and perhaps some of the GRI staff we will be eliminating from our account might be interested. We've got some hiring to do, and we need to do it quickly."

"You've got your budget target, Mary. Does this plan fit within it?" asked Greg.

"It does, Greg, I planned it that way. We cut our GRI costs almost immediately by 50%, as we stop almost all development during the migration. We also cut much of our own existing team, as they were largely focused on managing the handoffs to GRI and back."

I wanted to wrap this up and get on with it. "Roberta, Greg, do I have your approval for the organizational plan? Can we get on with it now?"

"Yes, of course, Mary," Greg said. "Roberta, how do we do this? It's such a big change!"

Roberta thought for a moment and then said seriously, "The best way I know is to announce the plan and the organizational structure, including job descriptions of all positions that will be available. Make everyone apply for the new positions, and anyone who doesn't land one has their job eliminated. We'll have a stressful and disruptive period in which not much will get done, and we could lose some good people, either by their own choice or because we make some poor personnel decisions. But then we're over and done, and on a path that you two both like."

"Greg," I asked half jokingly, half pleadingly, "do we need to consider options to Roberta's suggestion also?"

He laughed. "No, Mary, unless you or Roberta want to. I can't think of a more efficient or fairer way to do it. We're going to have a heck of a few weeks ahead, aren't we? Let's knock off for the night, sleep on what we've decided, and hit it hard again tomorrow morning. We've got a lot to do!"

On the drive home, I talked with Wes. My car has built-in Bluetooth, which puts the cell phone conversation through the car's sound system and provides a microphone built into the ceiling just above the center console. I love the feature for its convenience, but it took a while to get used to hearing Wes's voice surrounding me in the small space. He was echoing now.

"You're doing the right thing, Mary," Wes reassured me. "Just as we discussed at Neville's, you need to move quickly and take the risks that entails. It's the fastest, most decisive approach, which fits you to a T."

"But you are going to do nothing like this," I protested. "If you don't drive the change, how can you be sure you'll get it? Don't you need to change your structure and your people also?"

"Of course I do," Wes agreed. "But I have to do it more slowly, and I need to have more of the decisions come from our people themselves. You have to build the capability of your team to be involved and share in leadership, whereas I already have some of that in place. Think of it this way—you are only going to have to do this once!"

"Thank goodness for that," I said. "You know, though, I am excited to do this. I know it will affect a lot of people, some for the better, some not so positively, but I don't think about that much. I know we'll make some great decisions and some bad ones while we're setting FinServia's future, but we are going to be as fair to everyone as we can be. These decisions will ultimately determine whether FinServia succeeds or fails. I hate to admit it, but this is going to be fun!"

"You are one odd duck, Mary," Wes said. "If I were doing what you're doing, I would be a wreck. So many decisions, so fast, with such limited information, affecting so many lives and careers—but there you are in the middle of it deciding and acting without it eating at you. Opposites do attract, don't they?"

"They sure do. Wes, is it too late for you to come over?" I asked. I needed some company.

LATER IN WEEK ONE: PLANNING THE TRANSITION WITH GRI

I couldn't do this particular meeting at the office. Causing even more gossip and speculation would serve no useful purpose, and in fact, it would be disrespectful to our employees to do so. Instead, I asked Trevor and his new Lean and Agile Software Group to stay at the Shelter Island Hotel, and I booked a meeting room there.

Shelter Island sits on the north side of the San Diego harbor, on the path of the big military ships traversing their way to their berths beyond the airport. It is narrow enough that from the south-facing hotel windows, the ships are visible going by, while from the north-facing windows, the vista is the yacht-filled lagoon to the north. Yet because its main road goes nowhere but to the end of the sandy island, traffic is light, and it has a feel of a vacation within the city. It is one of Wes's and my favorite places, and for me now, especially convenient because Wes is living there for a few more weeks before moving into his new sublet apartment.

My assistant had booked a meeting room above the lobby, with views to the north—the yacht basin. As I walked in from my car, I shivered a little. San Diego mornings, especially on the water, can be chilly, although after my stint traveling to Minnesota, I rarely complain anymore. I stopped in the lobby to get coffee and the key, and walked up the open stairway to the balcony and our room. I had planned to get here a half hour before the meeting was scheduled to begin so I could prepare the room, and I was glad to see I was alone.

The half hour of preparation passed quickly. Soon I was joined by the GRI team and Roberta Greeley, our VP of Human Resources. As they meandered over to the coffee and fruit, Alex Fuegos entered the room. Alex had been Neville's lead program manager in Cremins' Financial Services Division. He hadn't formally joined FinServia yet, but he had agreed to do so, and these were his last few days at Cremins. He'd been stunned when I had e-mailed him the news of our new partnership with GRI, and his amazement was capped off when he looked into the room and saw Trevor McDonald. He had met Trevor in his Process role at Cremins and had viewed him as a naïve and dangerous enemy—not to put too fine a point on it! Alex gestured me out of the room soon after he'd entered.

"Mary, what is *he* doing here? You've got to be kidding me!" Seeing Trevor present threw Alex into a tizzy. Alex enjoyed structure and organization, and to him, Lean and Agile concepts defined the status quo. He had never worked in an environment like the one defined by Trevor and The Process, and the prospect of having to deal with Trevor scared him. "I was surprised that you were going to have GRI involved with us, but Trevor—that's off the deep end!"

"Calm down, Alex," I tried to reassure him. "He's not such a bad guy. Once the Cremins project collapsed, he was brought back into GRI's methods group, and he became part of their Lean and Agile initiative. GRI's managers liked his familiarity with traditional methods and his enthusiasm for process, and they believe he has enough of an open mind to grapple with something new. They figure that if Trevor buys into Lean and Agile, he'll be able to sell it to anyone! He's going to be the lead for GRI to build what we are doing together into a formal practice for GRI, but we've agreed that he won't be involved in our work other than in managing the engagement. I also have assurances that if at any time we want him off our account, all we have to do is ask. So let's give him a chance."

If anyone could take a new look at Trevor, it would be Alex. He is an amazing people person: he naturally likes people and wants to help them, and he also wants others to like him—and they usually do. With his taste for order and practicality added in, Alex was a perfect complement to my own less people-focused, more immediate action-oriented predilections.

As I had hoped, Alex shrugged his shoulders and his eyebrows and said he'd give it a try.

As we walked back into the room, we found Trevor with his new Lean and Agile consulting team sitting patiently at the table waiting for us. Alex graciously welcomed Trevor, who stood up, shook hands, and proceeded to introduce us to his team. His team stood up for the introductions.

"Mary, Trevor, Roberta, let me introduce your new team. We have searched GRI globally for the right consultants to become the foundation of our new practice, and we're beginning by joining you in your build-out of the FinServia development team. First, Manish Jhawar," Trevor said, gesturing toward the man on his right, who was Indian, perhaps in his mid-thirties. "Manish began his GRI career in our India development operation ten years ago, where he became an early advocate of Agile. He led its implementation for one of our major clients, which we were in danger of losing due to dissatisfaction with the slow pace and poor fit of the results we had been delivering."

"Nice to meet you," Manish said. "Trevor has told me about your mission here, and I am very happy to join you." I later learned that Manish had attended university in England before returning to India and had been back and forth to the States over the past five years. His English was clear, with an accent that tended toward Neville's.

Trevor continued by introducing the older Japanese gentleman to his left. "We are very fortunate to have with us, at least part time, Masami Sato, here from Japan. Sato-san worked in Toyota's product development center in Toyota City for many years before becoming a consultant helping other companies to improve their own product development."

"I also have an MBA in marketing from Darden," Sato added. "I would like to help with the product planning to ensure that your Agile development is on track to solve customer needs."

"Interesting idea," I approved. "We can do some planning today, but then I'll need to get you with our marketing manager, Mervin Thomas. How long will you be here?" I asked, excited about the prospect of expert help for my critical partner.

"I have to catch the red-eye tomorrow evening for Boston," said Masami. "But I'm yours through end of day tomorrow."

"I'll see what I can arrange at our break," I said. "And finally," I turned toward the woman standing beside Manish.

"Last but not least, this is Margaret Olson, from our strategy practice. Margaret specializes in organizational design for technology groups. Her focus will be on how to make Agile scale across large companies. First, she needs to understand a lot more about Lean and Agile practice."

Margaret was a very professional-looking woman, probably about my age, beginning to gray and not hiding the fact. She smiled at me and said, "I hope you will share with me your thoughts and problems as you build your organization, Mary, and perhaps I can offer you some help. I've been assigned full time to the engagement, and I'd like you to consider me another pair of hands to help you and Roberta design and implement your changes."

Roberta liked that idea. "You are just in time, Margaret. We have so much to do—it's hard to know where to start!"

"I think I have some ideas on that," I said, and I directed the group's attention to the board, where I had jotted down an agenda early this morning. "Please, let's sit down and get going."

Once all were settled, I continued. "I suggest we start by my bringing you up to date on our status, and I'll share with you the organizational structure we've settled on. Then, we should talk about the transition plan, how we fill our leadership and other positions, and what changes we want to make to GRI staffing to help us while we build our own team. I'd like to then turn to the medium term and talk about concrete steps we will take to build our Lean culture and to begin Agile development. The last item on my list is to agree on communication of what we've decided and to set some firm dates."

The group reviewed and agreed on the agenda with a few additions from the GRI team, and we jumped right in. Margaret and Sato both approved of the organizational structure after some debate; Sato wasn't happy with Mervin reporting separately to Greg instead of being in my group, but after explaining the reasoning,[3] he understood and said he looked forward to meeting Mervin tomorrow.

We spent all day on our plan to change the organization. Margaret was helpful, as she was able to draw on more experience in this type of radical organizational change than Roberta, Alex, or me. By lunchtime, we had several flip-chart pages summarizing the steps we'd agreed to, as follows:

- *We would announce the decision to take application development in-house, the revised relationship with GRI, the new organizational structure, and the process by which FinServia employees would apply for new jobs.* Our target was one week from today, next Thursday. We would do so in writing and through a town hall meeting; thankfully, we had open space in our cavernous facility to do so.

- *Greg, Roberta, and I would share the communication duties at the meeting.*
- *Simultaneously, GRI would announce the same to their team members involved in supporting FinServia.* Trevor volunteered Wayne Mellinger, the relationship manager for the FinServia account, to lead this.
- *In the meantime, we had to prepare the communication material, and all the job postings and position descriptions.* The postings would go up internally at FinServia, be shared with the GRI support team in case any of them were interested in joining FinServia, and be advertised externally on the Internet and with a few select contract-to-hire and recruiting firms in San Diego.
- *Roberta and Margaret would orchestrate the interviewing and selection process,* and prepare for a major announcement five weeks from now. On the Thursday five weeks from now, we would announce our team and do whatever terminations were required; we would be laying the foundation for our new future, which would begin the following Monday. It would be a grand rebooting of FinServia's technology group.
- *Alex and Manish would be working to get our Agile development underway* while Roberta, Margaret, and I focused primarily on organizational, people, and budgetary issues. Since we'd chosen to use process and tools to shape our culture, we needed to establish our Agile management tools and have Sato work with Mervin to start planning the backlog and releases. I wanted to start our first sprint one week after the grand reboot, which meant we had to get ready.

At the end of the day, Trevor offered to take us out to dinner, but I needed to run back to the office and update Greg on our results. I was excited and exhausted at the same time, and I was so grateful for Greg's support. He was happy to participate in the communication events, he wanted to review budget forecasts as we developed them, and he asked to participate in interviews of the leadership group. We had a discussion about whether we should use the chief engineer title, since it wasn't broadly used in the software development community and could cause confusion, and eventually we agreed to do so in order to set clearer expectations on what kind of leadership we sought. If we're rebooting anyhow, I thought, may as well start with a clean and fast base.

WEEK FOUR: SELECTING THE PEOPLE

Creating, defining, advertising, and filling 40 positions in only 6 weeks is no easy task. We found out quickly that, in this objective, our eyes were bigger than our stomachs. In the first few weeks after we set the organization, we worked almost nonstop; my only significant break (besides taking the usual time for my children) was a weekend away with Wes in Cabo. (I'll let him tell you about that later, as he enjoys the sentimental dimensions of storytelling much more than I do.) The one new leader we already had on board, Alex, asserted on behalf of the new leaders that they would like to have at least some control over their own teams, instead of coming on board to a team fully selected by others. So Margaret, Roberta, and I lowered our sights, and we settled for trying to hire just enough people (including the organizational leaders and some thought leaders) to enable a good start come our first sprint.

Our hiring team comprised Roberta, our VP of HR; Alex Fuegos, who wanted to take the Learning Facilitation position; and our three GRI helpers, Margaret, Manish, and Sato. Sato was not going to be available full time to us as he had other demanding clients, so we tried to use him sparingly, initially focused on engaging Mervin, our VP of Marketing, into the Lean and Agile processes. As we got underway, I was increasingly grateful to have Margaret and Manish, who had some excellent ideas to contribute and were eager to listen to what I wanted as well.

By week four, we had filled several of our critical positions. I was ecstatic that one of GRI's lead developers, Jim Maxwell, had immediately expressed interest in joining us: he agreed to take the development support role. He was originally from Los Angeles and was eager to escape from Texas. In his new role, he would be accountable for overall architecture leadership, overall test leadership, our development and testing tools, and training/personal development for our programmers. I'd have to guide him to change his leadership style to become more facilitative than directive, a challenge at which I believed we could succeed. (I was also taken by the fact that Jim went by his nickname "Max," just as my own Jim went by "Wes.") Max would be spending his first few months helping the rest of the team learn the existing code base and development environments, but after that he'd have an opportunity to grow his leadership skills.

The chief engineers were a more difficult problem. Our hiring team, in writing the job descriptions, had specified that candidates had to be expert in one of our critical disciplines (software technology, testing, systems analysis, Agile leadership, or the business area), and demonstrably strong in at least one other discipline. We wanted to see some evidence of entre- preneurial leadership as well and experience in an environment some- thing like the one we wanted to build. Greg, Alex, Neville, and I reached out to friends and acquaintances, and I contacted several ex-colleagues who might be good fits. By the end of week four, we'd found one solid can- didate, through Mervin's contacts, and had several promising possibilities lined up for visits.

Today was tester day. I had claimed ownership of the tester hiring; the others didn't seem interested in contesting me for it. Although we hadn't announced any positions yet, we had brought Max out from Dallas to help us interview, since overall test leadership was in his realm. Margaret was here today as well; she wanted to observe how I went about hiring test leaders. I had emphasized to her how important testers were and how difficult it was to find good ones.

Max, Margaret, and I were sitting in the conference room. It was early morning and the office was just beginning to stir. We'd arranged to get together for coffee and to plan the day; our first candidates were arriving at 8:30 a.m.

"Why is it so hard to find good test managers?" Margaret asked me.

"It's a conundrum," I explained. "First of all, the qualities that result in being a great tester—fanatical attention to detail, process inflexibility, and willingness to defend their rights on the team—aren't the qualities that make a great test manager. Test leaders need to see the whole picture, be flexible and innovative on process, and collaborate and compromise to get product shipped. Second, the dominant testing model in the companies that comprise our hiring pool is not a good fit for us—test teams separated from development teams, testing in distinct and unconnected stages, lim- ited use of technical testing tools, and poor usage of test data beds. In my last job, we developed test managers over several years, but we don't have that luxury here."

"We have quite a few testers and two test managers on staff already," said Max. "Unfortunately, they have lived in the model you described, and they sound more like testers than test managers."

Margaret was puzzled. "Mary," she said, "let's say you're right, that finding a good test manager is a tough job. How do you propose we do that today? I'm not sure either Max or I would recognize what you are looking for."

"I have a tool that I hope you will both find useful," I replied. "I've been hiring technical staff for more years than I like to think of by now, and along the way I've created a combination interview guide/evaluation form that I use. You want to take a look?"

They did, so I gave them each a copy of my test manager interview guide (excerpt in Figure 7.5).

"Here's how it works," I started to explain. "It's a standard decision matrix, with the decision elements in the first column, with weighted scoring. The useful feature for us is that it includes the answers we are looking for, as well as the questions we are asking. For example, the first criterion is about experience. We are looking for someone who sees a project in terms of the business results, not solely in terms of the activities they do. We want someone with experience on project or system leadership teams who has helped to *guide* endeavors, not just *respond* to them. The leader we are looking for gets involved from the beginning of projects, to help make them efficiently testable, instead of taking the project shape and testing stage they are given and doing the best they can within those constraints. The final "desired answer" I've listed is that the candidate is honest, can talk about what went wrong, and will describe what part he or she played in both making mistakes and learning from and correcting them."

I could see Margaret become visibly excited by my matrix. "Mary," she said, "this is awesome! It defines what to look for in Lean/Agile leaders. Can I take this and use it in our new practice? If we had evaluation matrices like this for all the key roles, I'd have a critical centerpiece of my new practice."

"Of course, Margaret." I was surprised; I loved my matrices, but few who had seen them had been very interested in them. "I hadn't thought of it that way. I just built these matrices for myself over the last several years. But you're right, there is a lot of knowledge or at least opinions encapsulated in the spreadsheet, to be grown and shared. I'd hate for candidates to get hold of these and game me, but so long as you use them judiciously, that's fine."

Max had been studying his copy, and he asked a practical question on how to do the interview. "Do you just read the question, and then evaluate based on what is said, or do you probe around to give the candidate a chance to address the specific items? Also, how do you remember what the candidates say so you can rate them? I can't see typing their answers in real time into a spreadsheet."

"You'll have to figure out what works best for you, Max," I said. "I normally print out the spreadsheet and make notes by hand on it, and then go back and put in my numeric ratings and type in my notes summaries. As far as questions, I try to probe to get the best sense I can of the candidate, in the order that flows the best with the conversation.

Area/Question	Expected Answer	Candidate Name/Date			
		Notes on Answer	Weigh	Score 1–10	Wt Score
Tell about most recent testing projects • Your role • End to end test strategy? • Continuous build?	Results in bus terms; on leadership team; involved from req definition, into development, and at end—no bull—didn't go perfectly.				
Career Progression	Solid grounding in discipline; enough time in jobs; learning; change in roles; knows own mind & takes accountability.				
Testing tools– knowledge/ experience/attitude	Automation is critical; knows some market tools; loves test harnesses; knows unit test tools and role in overall testing. Doesn't believe in auto conversion from req to test scripts; focus on test data.				
Relationships; ask about a conflict and how resolved; her usual relationships with developers; a time she stood her ground.	OK with conflict, addresses, productivity; partners with developers but knows tension is/ should be present.				
Leadership/ Innovation. A new technique or tool she brought to team. A change in test strategy she introduced mid- project. A person she mentored and is proud of.	Introduced continuous testing; taught developer how to use j(n) unit; drove creation of data scrubber for test bed; convinced org to build additional test environments; wrote stress testing software.				

FIGURE 7.5

Test manager interview guide (excerpt).

"One thing to beware of," I cautioned. "The spreadsheet itself looks very scientific, but you have to be aware of that. It is a structure that can help you crystallize and weigh your opinions, but you still need to use your judgment. Let me show you what I mean."

With that, I drew a chart on the board (Figure 7.6). It took me a few moments to get the math right, and Max gave me a hard time while I struggled.

"Give me a break, Max. I wasn't prepared to do remedial training this morning," I joshed back. "Let's say we have two applicants, Joe and Elaine. If we just take the weights and the raw scores, Joe would be the winner, with 700 total points versus Elaine's 680. But perhaps it doesn't feel right, and when you think it over, you believe Elaine would do a better job than

Area/Question	Weight	Joe Tester		Elaine Quality/Assurer	
		Score 1–10	Wt Score	Score 1–10	Wt Score
Tell about most recent testing projects • Your role • End to end test strategy? • Continuous build?	30	7	210	5	150
Career Progression	10	5	50	7	70
Testing tools–knowledge/experience/attitude	20	9	180	6	120
Relationships; ask about a conflict and how resolved; her usual relationships with developers; a time she stood her ground	20	4	80	9	180
Leadership/Innovation. A new technique or tool she brought to team. A change in test strategy she introduced mid-project. A person she mentored and is proud of.	20	9	180	8	160
Total Score	100		700		680

FIGURE 7.6

Tester comparison matrix summary.

Joe. The matrix can help you think that through. In this case, Elaine is much stronger than Joe in relationships. Is Joe's low score a knockout? Is the weighting on that factor perhaps too low? You can then go back and adjust the weights and scores if you need to, or just make your decision and go on," I concluded. "Max, you understanding this?"

"Got it, Mary. I think I can handle it," Max replied.

It was now close to the time to start our interviews for test manager, so the three of us got up and went out to the reception area to begin sifting through our candidate pool. With the help of my handy-dandy evaluation matrix, we would find the right test managers, I was certain.

WEEK SIX: ANNOUNCEMENT DAY

We chose to announce the results of our organizational design and personnel work on a Tuesday. Wes had taken me out to dinner on Coronado Island Monday night, and as we sat under the gas lamps on the deck overlooking the bridge, I told him what we had planned for the next day. He professed amazement at my calm. I told him about the first time I had to deliver bad business news, when I had to shut down a development site in my first year as a manager. I found I could deliver the news calmly and without being personally upset; I even worried that maybe I was missing a compassion gene or something. Intellectually, I felt bad for the people we'd be letting go, but that feeling was overwhelmed by my knowing it was the right thing to do for the business. Wes would have been much more tormented—the old softie!

Roberta and Margaret put the plan together for the day. We wanted to communicate the job eliminations as humanely as possible, both for the sake of the people losing their jobs and for those remaining. When we began the selection process, we did not have a preconception of how many of the existing staff we would keep versus those we would not, and many of the decisions had been difficult. At the end of the day, however, we wound up displacing over half of our group; we decided to err on the side of a clean start, since creating the new culture we sought would be hampered by having too much of the old in place.

D-day, as this Tuesday had come to be widely called, began at 8:30 a.m. sharp. None of us—Roberta, Margaret, Greg, nor me—could think of any better way to proceed than just to proceed. At 8:30, Greg's assistant sent out e-mail invitations to two meetings, one for those being let go in the open space in our plant, the other for those being offered positions in a nearby hotel, both at 9:30. We hired a bus to transport anyone needing a ride, but few took us up on it, since most people drove to work. I led the meeting at the hotel, and Greg led the meeting at our office. I didn't come to the office but rather went directly to the hotel to prepare.

Later, Roberta told me about the scene at the office. As soon as the e-mail was sent, people began walking around and talking to each other, or e-mailing or instant messaging, to try to understand what was going on. The staff quickly figured out the scheme, that there were two meetings at 9:30, and it didn't take long before they guessed which was which, and what their fate might be. Roberta and some of her team patrolled the cube farms to answer questions up to a limit, and encouraged everyone, regardless of the group into which they had fallen, to attend the meetings. There was some nervous crying and anticipatory packing up of belongings, while an exodus to the cars and the hotel began as well. I was glad I was able to skip that!

Each meeting was meticulously planned. Each attendee had a package prepared expressly for them. At Greg's meeting, the package included the description of their exit package, the disposition of their benefits, an explanation of job seeking assistance provided, and a legal release form to sign if they chose. At my meeting, the package included a written job offer, a memorandum from Greg and me that described our company's vision and plans, and the organization into which we hoped they would consent to recommit. Those offered new positions would need the org chart in case they wanted to talk with their new boss prior to accepting the position.

Greg's job was to give a respectful explanation of what we were doing and why, to thank the departing staff for their contributions, and to wish them well in future endeavors. Roberta would then describe in detail the contents of their packages and how they could get any questions they might have answered. The meeting ended in less than an hour, with a request that they clear out their desks and leave as soon it was convenient, but certainly by the end of the day, and a reminder that they not take any confidential information with them. We had discussed how to do the clear-out, and we chose to treat the departing with the respect that they deserved, and did not have any visible security on hand. We also decided that we would not require them to clear out before the remaining staff returned, in case they wanted to stick around to say their goodbyes. As it turned out, many of those whose positions were eliminated left immediately, and a roughly equal number remained to commiserate and wish their remaining colleagues well.

My job was to recruit those we wanted to stay. I recapped the process we had just been through, and I affirmed that this group had been chosen to be the core of what we expected to be one of the best software product groups in the world. Unfortunately, I explained, we had to make major changes to our organization and skills, so many of their colleagues were faced with position elimination. We had tried to be as careful and fair as we could, I reassured them, and the departing were being treated generously and with respect. Our hope and expectation, I assured the anxious audience, was that this would be our one and only downsizing. Our prospects were bright, and with their commitment, we would create a profitable and growing business.

Roberta and Margaret had emphasized to me the need to help this group get over "survivors syndrome," in which those who did not lose their jobs feel guilty that they are still employed while their friends are gone. I hoped that Greg's meeting was going well, and that those who would no longer be with FinServia would not be bitter.

I introduced the leaders we had selected, including Max, Alex, and two of the CEs, who each said a few words about themselves and their vision for their groups. I described my vision for how we would work, how we would behave with each other, and what we would be building, and I described in general our new incentive plan, which was designed to share our success with our team members. The meeting concluded with a question-and-answer session that lasted for a half hour, and my request for new team members to sign the offer letters if they felt ready and hand them in on the way out, or to take to the end of the week if they needed to. Anyone with questions should go to their new managers, Roberta, or me.

By the end of the day Tuesday, FinServia's technology development group had been entirely recast. By week's end, we would know how many of our chosen had recommitted, and by the following Monday, we would start our new journey. An intense six-week period was coming to an end, but I doubted the next six weeks would be any less intense.

Signposts	FinServia Transformation
	• The FinServia leadership team designs its new organization, centered on chief engineers leading complete development teams and supported by functional specialties.

	• The transition is planned, including the specification of each position, hiring, communication, and initial implementation.
	• "D-Day" comes, many staff are let go, and the remaining are recruited to commit to FinServia's new journey.
Change Guides from Mary	• **The choice of direct ownership of resources by CEs vs. matrix management is a central one.** Either can work, as can a mix. Which is right for your culture? Mary tilted to direct control, seeing more upside in stronger accountability and nimbleness than risks in duplication and waste. She feels she can make the CEs work together, with the help of the functional peers.
	• **Respect for all people is foundational for Lean Product Development (LPD).** Demonstrating that respect—even when forced to make difficult choices, such as position eliminations and reorganizations—will help set the key cultural expectations.
	• **People really *are* the most valuable resource, so choosing them is among the most important management choices you can make.** Any tool that specifies in detail the characteristics you are seeking, like the hiring template, can assist in bringing rigor to the process.
Coming Up Next	It's Wes's turn to implement his organizational transformation at MCCA. Unlike Mary's *drive people* approach, with its high degree of top-down control and disruption, Wes is following the *people-driven* approach. How does Wes get his team involved, and how does he balance letting them own the change with ensuring that change happens?

ENDNOTES

1. There are several examples in the organizational theory literature of organizational types. For a handy summary of this one online, see CliffsNotes.com, Five Approaches to Organizational Design, April 18, 2009, http://www.cliffsnotes.com/WileyCDA/CliffsReviewTopic/topicArticleId-8944,articleId-8882.html. I've used this article as the basis for some of the discussion in this section.

2. Morgan and Liker, *Toyota Product Development System*, 155–156.

3. Described in Chapter 6.

8

Six Weeks to Start the MCCA Transformation: May

Narrator: Wes

Over the past few months, while Mary has been tearing her company apart and rebuilding it from scratch, I've been guiding my development group through a participative transformation process, using Lean and Agile ideas. The spark came from Neville, when he suggested that we use the Agile scrum mechanism to drive the transformation itself.[1]

In this chapter, I present the activities of the last six weeks. They began with a weekend getaway to Cabo San Lucas with Mary, where we formally got engaged, and she helped me think through how I might lead MCCA forward. Next came some broad training of our team members in Lean and Agile concepts, followed by the establishment of our management scrum (the Lean Team). The Lean Team then set the change agenda (in Agile terms, the *backlog*), and we managed it through two weekly cycles in scrum meetings.

WEEK ONE: PREPARING FOR THE MANAGEMENT SCRUM

Saturday afternoon, mid-April, Cabo San Lucas, Mexico. I had been able to peel Mary away from her work and her children for a weekend through a combination of begging, threats, and bribes. For the past month, it seemed I hadn't seen her any more than I did when I was living in St. Paul, and because we were no longer in the same company, on the same project, I may actually have talked to her less often. Ultimately, I think it was the guilt that did the trick, and maybe she missed me a little too.

The slowly setting sun was shining on the turquoise water of Cabo San Lucas Bay. Mary and I were watching the sparkles and remarking on the color from the deck of the San Lucas Reina, an immense catamaran populated by hundreds of sunburned touristas. We'd polished off one of the free margaritas already and were starting on our second when the captain announced that Lover's Beach was coming into view. Lover's Beach, he said, is the only beach in the world that faces two oceans. The beach we saw facing us on the Sea of Cortez is Lover's Beach, whereas the side facing the Pacific is called Divorce Beach. That seemed like a great time to ask Mary to set a date and plan for our wedding. By the time she agreed and we set the date (the first week in January), the place (the Wailea Marriott in Maui—I had lots of Marriott points), and the guest list (just a few friends and family; Mary after all had already done this once), the sun had set and the buffet dinner was being served.

With the truly important items settled, our plates filled, and an acceptable spot on the upper deck secured, we began to catch up on our work activities. Mary told me about her exciting week planning her organizational change, and how pleasantly surprised she had been at how helpful the GRI team had become. We talked about what was coming up next week for her, with the organization and personnel planning, which were giving her a chance to put into practice everything she'd learned in her career and shape her own group. I loved to see her so animated and enthusiastic about her job.

By the time dessert was being delivered, we turned to my story. The idea of blowing up MCCA and starting over, as Mary was doing with FinServia, was horrifying to me, and was definitely not going to happen. I was adopting a different approach.

"Events at MCCA are not quite as dramatic as at FinServia, Mary, but I am ready to start making the changes. I've identified my key leadership to help drive—you remember, I'm doing *people driven* instead of your *drive people*—and I want to start. But I'm having some trouble figuring out exactly how to get going," I said.

"What are you thinking about?" Mary asked.

"Besides how beautiful you look right now?" I smiled, probably stupidly, at her, and then returned to business. "I like Neville's idea of using Agile scrum itself to manage the transformation," I said. "It gives a nice participative, visible mechanism, and it teaches our team while we are doing it. My problem is that none of us know much about the techniques. It's scary to say that I am our resident expert now, just from having watched you and Neville and from reading a few books."

Mary is my opposite in several ways. Whereas I typically listen, probe, and get input, Mary likes to listen a little, then solve and act. In this situation, it was just what I needed.

"No offense, fiancée," she said, "but with you as the sole expert in this, you'll probably struggle unnecessarily. You're going to need to train your whole team, and also some adjacent teams like Finance and Operations, so they understand what you are doing and why. You'll need to find someone experienced in the area to help guide you. You personally need to ensure that your team understands the need to change and buys into the path you are setting. The risk is that if you share leadership of the change process with your team, and really let them get their fingerprints on the plan, they could go in a different direction than you'd like."

"So I need to let go without really letting go, right?" I said. "I think I've got them on the right general path. We've been talking among ourselves about the need for change, and I believe many feel the same needs that I do. I've been talking about Lean and Agile, and several have read books, blogs, and articles, and are generally receptive. The chaos in our development group, the tense relationship with Sales, and our need to get our customer relationship with SDNI under control has created the call to action we need. Now we need to turn it into executable plans, and then do it."

"You're not going to believe what I'm going to recommend, Wes," Mary smiled. "You should give Trevor McDonald a call. You've got some money to spend, don't you?"

I was stunned, and for a moment, speechless. Trevor McDonald? Mary's nemesis at Cremins Corporation? Maybe I had one too many margaritas, or Mary was suffering from sunstroke. I knew Mary had made amends with GRI, and that they were helping her with her work at FinServia, but to recommend Trevor to me was quite a surprise.

"Why yes, I do have a little bit of money, but Trevor?" I responded. "You're stuck with GRI and have to cooperate to get your code back, but I could choose anyone to help. Why GRI?"

"They have three consultants helping me out, here in San Diego," Mary said. "All three are top notch—a Lean product development specialist from Japan, an Agile development specialist, and a Lean/Agile cultural change expert. I won't be using them full time, and they want practice building their practice. They'll be taking what they know, combining it with what Greg and I teach them, and turning that into repeatable consulting offerings. You might be able to work out a deal with Trevor, who is leading the build-out of GRI Lean/Agile offerings, to get a reasonable price on these consultants."

"Interesting idea," I said pensively. "What kind of help would you suggest?"

It didn't take Mary long to tell me what to do. "From what you've told me so far," Mary began, "I'd say you need to start with Margaret, the human resource/culture specialist, and do some planning. Then, do some broad training with Sato on Lean product development, and then more focused training of the development team and your leadership group on scrum management. Pick someone on your new leadership team who can do the management scrum mastering, and have Manish provide mentoring and support until your person can stand alone. Then, once you are into your development scrums, you'll need some more help from Manish or someone like him. Finally, you'll need ongoing training and mentoring, depending on how quickly and well your people learn, and on whether you can hire some people with Lean or Agile experience."

I thought about Mary's suggestions, and they all seemed to make sense to me. If I could use the GRI consultants to help, I would get Greg and Mary's assistance in a sideways kind of way through them, and I could also get informal guidance from Mary during off-hours. The three consultants sounded like they were capable and experienced, were accustomed to working with each other, and covered a broad range of the topics we would need help with. Why not give it a shot?

"Mary, my dear," I said, "that sounds like great advice, as usual. I'll give Trevor a call first thing on Monday. How about a cup of coffee on the bow while we return to shore?"

WEEK TWO: ASSEMBLING AND TRAINING THE TEAM

After returning from Mexico last week, I was able to talk with Trevor, and then with Margaret and Manish. We reached an agreement for GRI to assist me, and as fortune would provide, we were able to get started almost immediately. Margaret and Manish were in San Diego all week, and they peeled off a few hours Tuesday morning to get to know MCCA and set a path forward. They liked the idea of facilitating our transformation to Lean and Agile using Lean and Agile techniques themselves, as Neville had suggested.

The first step would be to assemble the team members—the *scrummers*—to get them on board and educated on what we would be doing, in preparation for developing the backlog (our first Agile planning step) in the week following. Sato and Manish had been planning on returning to

Dallas on Friday, but said they could change plans and do overview training instead. I jumped on the opportunity.

The Team Assembles: Overview Training

Most of the team I had targeted was available on Friday, so we scheduled the development group's training room for the 9:00 a.m. to 4:00 p.m. meeting. I had chosen this simple, functional room purposely. It was a level below the executive floor, where the top dogs, Sales, Marketing, and Finance, were located in luxurious quarters. The development floor appeared like it was a different company: no mahogany walls or tables, few private offices, no secretaries perched behind counters outside executive enclaves. The environment spoke no-nonsense practicality, and we needed the symbolism of the company coming to Development's turf for a change.

The room was set up with scattered small tables, seating 4 to 6 people each. This setup allowed small group work and discussion at the tables, while still enabling larger-group interaction. We had made name tags and assigned seating to mix up the group: for example, developers would be talking with salespeople directly. Little things lead to bigger things.

Our objective for the day was to prepare for the management backlog development next week. We knew that we wouldn't be able to impart the full extent of Lean product development and Agile software methods in a single day; instead, we wanted to get an overview done, to provide context for the steps to come, and to gain enough support among our leaders so we wouldn't be derailed.

When I started working at MCCA, I had made myself a vow that I would try to make meetings efficient and effective. One aspect was to ensure we started on time. I had been doing this now for several months, and I could see the effect rippling through at least my group. Since it was now 9:00 a.m., I sounded a two-minute warning so participants could settle into their seats. While they did so, I surveyed the participants.

MCCA had never experienced a meeting like this. We assembled the key leaders from many of our disciplines to learn and discuss how we wanted to do business together going forward. I invited many members of the executive team, and with Lynn's encouragement, many were present: Connie, VP Operations; Cynthia, VP HR; Sasha, VP Finance; and Lynn herself, our president. Lynn also prevailed on Frank McDonald, the partner at our owner, Fletcher, Wilkens, and Johnson (FWJ) Capital, to attend; I had asked Lynn to play a role, but she thought Frank might do a better job. Not surprisingly, Jack Langley, our Sales VP, had a conflict and could not (would not?) attend, but he sent Melissa Grimes, who was working on the SDNI account, and a few other salesmen who were in town today. The other VPs each brought along a few colleagues, including a regional operations manager, an accountant, and an employee relations specialist.

The development team was well represented by Phillip Glass, Rico DeSilva, and three recent hires: Lincoln Felsing, our new test manager; Narish Marumen, our release manager; and Janet Livingston, our user experience manager. I was excited about all three, as I filled out the roles that Neville had helped me understand. Lincoln was new to the company, Narish merely got a new title and scope for what he already did, and Janet came from our help desk. Our new product manager, Joan Dillingsworth, was at one of the front tables, along with Hannah Hoffman, our lead project manager. In all, about 25 of MCCA's leaders were in attendance, along with Masami Sato (Lean product development), Margaret Oslon (Lean and Agile culture), and Manish Jhawar (Agile software development) from GRI.

The two-minute warning period expired, and I began the meeting by thanking everyone for attending and conducting a round of introductions. I then pointed to a flip chart posted on the wall and laid out the objectives and the agenda for the day.

"Our objective today is to begin to learn about some exciting improvements in product development and software development methods, and to lay the basis for our adoption which will begin next week. Lynn and I have been considering the best way to accelerate our product development and have agreed on this approach, so we won't be debating this general strategy versus others. However, one of the basic tenets of Lean and Agile development is employee involvement and continuous improvement, so your understanding, support, and commitment are fundamentally important to our success."

Not seeing any objections, I pointed to another flip chart on the wall, with our agenda on it. I had spent most of the previous week preparing for this day, working with each of the speakers and trainers to tailor their message to the needs of the day. It was a lot to cover in seven hours, but I didn't have any more time, and had to make it work. I hoped I had it right!

I continued, "Our day will be divided into four segments. The first will deal with value and purpose: what are we seeking to develop, why are we doing it, and who will we benefit? We are very fortunate to have two guests with us today, Franklin McDonald from FWJ, representing the owners of our company, and Pervez Milligan from one of our most valued customers, San Diego National Insurance Company, to talk with us this morning. Mr. Milligan will be joining us in a half hour, so we'll need to stay on schedule to honor his time.

"Once we are solid in understanding our purpose, we will then turn to two segments of learning. In talking with many of you over the past weeks and months, I've found no lack of interest in improving our product development and software creation processes, so we are not going to dwell on our various gaps and needs for improvement; we are just going to assume a desire on our part to learn and improve, and move on from there." I paused for a moment, and surveyed the audience. I could tell they were with me, so I went on.

"We are very fortunate to have with us today experts on two exciting advances in product development and software creation. The first, Mr. Masami Sato, spent 15 years at Toyota in automobile development. He has also been consulting with other firms in Lean product development for the last 6 years, helping them improve their product development performance. The second is Mr. Manish Jhawar, a pioneer in Agile software development. Agile is a set of ideas and techniques developed by a community of software developers in response to frustration with the formal, process-centric, handoff-oriented methods that were contributing to so many project failures. Now, overformality hasn't been a serious problem here," I said, and received the expected laughs from the audience, "but Agile can provide us techniques to put valuable methods and metrics into our development process."

I took a breath and a sip of water and finished up. "We will end the day planning next steps—where we go from here. Some are already roughed out, and some you will have an opportunity to influence. The primary upcoming activity will be to establish the *product development scrum,* which will be how we will guide our progress. I know that might not make any sense yet, but stick with us through the day, and I promise that it will. Any questions on the agenda?"

There were a couple of questions, but they were on topics that were going to be covered by our speakers, so I asked them to hold on, and I introduced Franklin McDonald to start our discussion of value and purpose. After he talked about himself and FWJ for a few minutes, he turned to the question of value.

MCCA Value Defined by Owners, Customers

Frank, as he asked me to call him, was a caricature of himself. Tall, fit, sixty-ish, with short gray hair, inside a fitted suit that probably cost more than my car. His shoes were beautiful, as were his cuff links and tie. He definitely stood out from the crowd.

"I am so glad to be here," he started, "and I'm happy to contribute to your Lean and Agile voyage. I see a lot of companies, and from a financial standpoint, it seems to me that organizations adopting Lean principles are doing well. We've invested in your success, and we would like the opportunity to invest more, so go to it, with my support.

"Let's talk about value. How we can help customers succeed, in a way that they are willing to pay us well for? FWJ's guiding strategy is to find these value-producing opportunities, which we call *unmet needs*, and then find companies that are best suited to grow to meet those needs. If we do a good job of finding large-scale unmet needs, finding companies that can grow to meet them, and then execute well, FWJ succeeds along with our companies and their customers. Simple, yes?"

It was refreshing to see a New York investment firm so focused on building value instead of "financial engineering." Frank had the group's rapt attention. He continued, linking FWJ's general approach to why they bought MCCA.

"Obviously, we think MCCA is well-positioned to meet a set of underserved needs. But what are those needs? Come on, speak up!"

"Information management!"

"Document management!"

"Archive and retrieval!"

Frank was pleased. "Very good, I can see that you've all embraced your larger purpose. A decade ago, I would have heard, 'micrographics!' and last year, probably 'image outsourcing!' Those markets are respectable, but information management—now that is a whopper of a market! And when we started poking around, wow, did we find underserved needs.

"It's not that products and services don't exist to manage information. There are excellent database technologies, business intelligence tools, image storage and retrieval systems, mapping services—I could go on and on. But when you stop and look at any particular business situation, the ability to apply these tools in a meaningful way—a way that connects to the users with the power that is available free to Internet users every day—is simply not present."

Frank was getting excited now. "When we looked at the market and saw how difficult it was for organizations to marshal their information resources effectively for their people, at first, we thought it was a problem for small and medium-sized organizations that didn't have the technical resources to integrate their own solutions. We were surprised that the problem is nearly universal—big companies are often collections of smaller groups, and they have at least as much difficulty assembling the tools, techniques, and skills to manage their information well.

"There are thousands of organizations, in your market, who need help making sense of the overwhelming volume of information. It's worth a lot of money to many of these organizations, and MCCA has a great start on being one of the winners, helping these organizations succeed."

My cell phone vibrated with a message from our receptionist: the SDNI executives were here. I excused myself while Frank finished up his talk, showing some more detail on what customers needed, some more information on competitors, and some market size estimates.

Pervez Milligan and Emilio Fernandez had been tickled to be invited to speak to our group, and the group was equally interested to hear what they had to say. I had asked them to spend a half hour talking about the business problems they faced, how we had helped them in the past, and what they wanted from us in the future. There was little new for me in the conversation, as I had just had a similar conversation with them a few weeks ago.[2] Pervez did tell one new story, about his company's quest to find a fraudulent automobile damage adjuster in Portland, and how difficult it had been for the fraud unit to sift through the data in the data warehouse and the images that we captured and served up for them, even after suspicion had been raised through a tip-off. In the coming months, this story would be told many times as our product development team struggled to build the capabilities that would make our company great.

At my prodding, Pervez and Emilio ended the segment on value by elaborating where we could improve. Neither wanted to sound insulting or ungrateful for what we had already provided, so it took some encouragement to pull out their ideas. They began with product features—better alerting to new data, enhanced mapping, integration of reporting from the data warehouse with images, full-text search results faster, multiwindowing—the list seemed endless. They continued with requests not related to the product itself, such as higher initial quality on releases, faster turnaround of development requests, more predictability of release dates and contents to help them plan, better documentation and training, and better support for doing configuration themselves. Our group was curious and open to hearing this, which was encouraging to me. We had no shortage of areas in which to improve, and it seemed like our people were excited about doing so.

Lean Product Development Introduced

We took a short break after Pervez and Emilio's challenging discussion, and then Masami Sato took the floor to provide the group with an introduction to Lean product development as practiced at Toyota and other manufacturing companies. Sato began with some facts about Toyota's performance—its profitability and growth compared to other car manufacturers, its quality rankings, its speed to market, and its innovation, which he illustrated with the creation of its Lexus division and the Prius hybrid.[3] Given the turmoil in the U.S. auto industry, it didn't take much selling to get the audience interested in Toyota's product development processes. Connie, our VP of Operations who had grown up in Toyota's manufacturing operations at NUMMI, added her testimony and support of the ideas as well.

Sato proceeded to give a high-level overview of Lean product development (LPD), focusing on *people, process,* and *tools.*[4] For each of the principles he highlighted, he told stories from his experience at, and knowledge of, Toyota and other companies, which brought the principles to life. He began with *process,* because he found that groups new to LPD often found that most compelling. Our group found the idea of front-loading the development process compelling, especially the developers, who were typically given a problem (or more likely a contractual commitment) to solve quickly with very little time to consider alternatives. The idea of creating a steady flow of product development work, instead of the chaotic series of panics we usually found ourselves in, was also latched onto by the developers. Our Sales representatives objected that their flow of contracts was unpredictable by nature; they feared a loss of flexibility if these two principles were adopted too strongly.

Sato moved on to the *people* principles, where he presented several of the principles in combination: the chief engineer, towering technical competence, and build-in learning and continuous improvement. Once again, these were supported vocally by the developers, including Phillip and especially Rico, our lead engineer.

A brief aside on Rico DeSilva: Of all the people at MCCA I had been briefed on, warned about, or alerted to, Rico was the one most often mentioned. Critical to our software, but always holding himself apart, he was somewhat of an enigma. Rico had an extraordinarily strong software development background, having spent the last twenty years at some of the leading software organizations in the world. He had initially come to MCCA as an independent contractor to help with some particularly knotty problems. Ernie Gatherington, MCCA's prior owner, had recognized Rico's talent and convinced him to come on board, agreeing to Rico's lofty compensation demands to close the deal.

I had spent some quality time with Rico and found him smart, engaging, and wanting to please. My take was that, although he loved being the "big cheese" programmer, he would ideally enjoy being part of a team. But even after years here at MCCA, he wasn't sure this was the team for him, which left him somewhat of a tormented soul. He had doubts about whether he could build truly great software here, and he felt he had made a deal with the devil by accepting high compensation as the reward for putting up with the dysfunctional relationship with Sales, the lack of skilled testers and requirements analysts, and the constant demands for more vaguely specified software, faster. Everything at MCCA seemed to be a crisis, and Rico was usually at the center of it.

As I planned our change strategy, I came to believe that Rico had to be a big part of it. Lean and Agile software puts the software engineers into a critical role, unlike other methods in which the engineers are simply mechanical transformers of requirements into architectures, architectures into designs, and designs into code. And Rico was the center of our engineering. Others—Hannah, Cynthia, even his manager Phillip—warned me of the risk involved in depending on Rico to play a constructive role, but I felt I had to take the risk, and I was very pleased to see Rico so engaged in this training.

Sato's emphasis on towering technical expertise drew comments from our engineers. Phillip noted that, in the past, he could rarely get money for training or for hiring top people, while Rico expressed his frustrations with the lack of technical expertise in our sales group, which resulted in selling things that we couldn't deliver effectively. The idea of chief engineer was batted around for some time and threatened to throw us off our schedule; it was so at odds with how we operated now, with our sales–technology interactions largely unmediated by product or program management, that it intrigued and concerned almost everyone. I finally put a fork in the discussion by relaying some of the conclusions I had already reached on the roles we would use, which because they'd already been socialized with most of our leaders, were well enough accepted.

Sato wrapped up by talking through some of the *tools* that could help with product development, mostly around knowledge creation and management. He showed an example of a Toyota trade-off curve, a checklist, and an A3 (the simple one-page report widely used at Toyota)[5]. The idea of a standard one-page report that could cover problems, opportunities, status, competitive updates, and other topics was of great interest, and Rico seized on the idea, along with the need for knowledge sharing, to propose that we could take our own product and use it for A3 creation and sharing. Sounded like an excellent idea!

Agile Software Development: An Implementation of Lean Product Development

We took a break for lunch and then reconvened. Frank McDonald had left to catch a plane. I was grateful he had come to the morning, at least. Over lunch, Sato, Manish, and I had planned the transition from talking about LPD into the details of Agile software, and this is where we started.

"Sato-san," I began, as the group refocused, "do you see software development more akin to Lean product development, to which you've introduced us, or to Lean manufacturing?"

"Excellent question, Wes. We have so little time to introduce you to so many powerful ideas. In practice, software development seems to have some elements of each; it depends on whether the activities are routine or not. We need to balance the LPD elements that encourage learning, with Lean manufacturing elements that demand standardized work as the basis for continuous improvement."

Sato elaborated, "I'm afraid I skipped over an important principle in *process:* utilize rigorous standardization to reduce variation, and create flexibility and predictable outcomes. This is a principle right out of Lean manufacturing, but with a somewhat different focus. We need to reduce variation and enable predictability, without stifling creativity. We can do so by standardizing lower-level tasks, leaving flexibility and creativity at higher levels. For example, in your company, is there a standard way for a new employee to be given access to your systems and e-mails? Yes? Can you imagine if there were not? You would be spending all your time

1. Standardize
2. Takt
3. Pull
4. One-piece flow
5. Minimize handoffs
6. Visual management

FIGURE 8.1
Lean manufacturing concepts in Scrum.

being "creative" on routine tasks. Standardizing whatever we can, without stifling creativity, is critical to enabling that very creativity.

"There are some other Lean manufacturing principles that apply directly to software development, some of which are encapsulated in the Agile approach that Manish will describe for you." Sato-san approached the flip chart (Figure 8.1) and wrote a list as he talked:

"We just talked about standardization," Sato explained. "So let's go on to the second item, *takt*, which is the Japanese word for pace.[6] It means providing a steady, sustainable rate of output, matched to demand. In Agile, this is called *velocity*. Measurement of software output is much more challenging than simply counting cars coming off an assembly line, but it's absolutely necessary. We must be able to predict and plan our output.

"The third item is *pull*, which in manufacturing means that each assembly step pulls parts when needed, instead of having parts pushed to them; this enables simpler management and a natural pace, not a forced one. In Agile, you accomplish this by building a backlog and pulling items when ready to begin.

"Wes, Manish, shall I continue? I don't want to steal Manish's whole lesson," Sato asked.

Connie Esposito, our VP of Operations and Lean manufacturing expert, answered for the group. "Please continue, Sato-san, this is very helpful," she said. "Those of us not familiar with software development, but who are dependent on it, need this insight."

"Certainly, then. The fourth item is *one-piece flow*, which is a foundation of Toyota's manufacturing methods. Toyota seeks to build or deliver one piece at a time, just when needed by the next operation, and consume it as quickly as it can. This avoids building inventory, which costs money to hold, deteriorates over time, and can hide flaws that won't be discovered until use. Agile software is similar. Requirements are done when they are needed for design or build; building is done when testing is ready to consume it; and we go as quickly as we can from requirements to production, feature by feature. We don't build inventory of undesigned requirements, unbuilt designs, untested code, or software waiting to go to production."

Sato paused, looked for understanding and questions, and went on, writing as he spoke. "The next item is the *minimization of handoffs*. Each handoff poses risks for continuity and understanding and has switching costs. We seek to minimize these by how the teams are formed and by finishing items instead of continually juggling too many items.

"The final item is *visual management*, which in manufacturing is done through plant setup, display boards, and white boards. Visual management is more difficult in software, because the code isn't as visual as an engine or seats are in a manufacturing environment. So Agile software development uses the sprint-end demonstrations, burndown charts, and other techniques.

"Wes," Sato asked, "does that answer your question?"

"I think so, yes, Sato-san, thank you very much. I'll leave the flip chart up on the wall while Manish gives us the Agile overview, so you can check back with it. Any questions before we proceed?" I asked the group.

Phillip Glass, our development manager, spoke up. He didn't do so often in public, but when he did, people tended to listen. "I'm sure our developers will embrace these ideas—a steady flow of development work, finish one thing before starting another—it sounds like a dream. But how could we accomplish these things when we are so driven by each next sale?"

Phillip had hit at least one of our critical nails right on the head. I wish I had a good answer; all I had was an idea, at least for now. "That is a crucial question, Phillip, which we'll need to address as we seek to adopt these ideas. We're going to talk over implementation following Manish's session; can we hold that thought until then?" Phillip gave me a dubious look, but he resigned himself to wait, so I handed the floor to Manish.

Agile Introduced

Manish began his exposition in his hybrid British English and Indian accent, clear and pleasing to the ear. "Today," he said, "we are going to focus on a specific implementation of Agile software development called *scrum*. But before we go there, we need to set the broad framework. Agile means many things to many people, beginning with the Agile Manifesto and Agile Principles, which were created and publicized by a group of software consultants several years ago.[7]

"By its nature, Agile thinking is aimed at enabling teams to deliver quality software quickly and effectively. One of its key ideas is respecting the people involved and enabling them to learn and adjust to the uncertainties of software development and the specifics of their situation. So even though we are going to talk about a particular process today, it's important that you understand the top-level principles, so you understand the context in which you, as team members, are empowered."

Manish continued, ticking off values on his fingers. "Agile thinking begins with these values:

- "We value individuals and interactions (*people*) over *processes* and *tools*
- "We value working software over comprehensive documentation
- "We value customer collaboration over contract negotiation, and
- "We value responding to change over following a plan.

"It's not that we don't value processes and tools," he went on, "it's just that we value individuals and interactions more highly. Does this make sense? How do these values compare to those in your group today?"

No one spoke up, so Manish asked Hannah to respond. "Maybe we are already too Agile," she said. "We have only very minimal software process or tools, and we do almost no formal documentation or planning. We seem to value the working code almost exclusively."

"That's not all bad, Hannah," Manish replied. "It's probably easier to change the *software development process*, upon which we will focus today, than to change *organizational values*. It may be that some of the Agile Principles are more relevant to your organization; perhaps our scrum implementation will be more about aligning with those principles than aligning with the values."

Manish rustled through a stack of papers in front of him and pulled out a single sheet, looked it over for a moment, and said, "I have here the list of the 12 Agile Principles, which take the Agile values to the next level of detail (Figure 8.2).[7] Scrum seeks to implement many of these principles. How about if I read a few of these and get your reaction to them? If improving along these lines sounds attractive to you, scrum should help you improve. If not, well, maybe we are going in the wrong direction."

I was getting a little nervous now. Was Manish opening our whole approach to question? I hoped Manish knew what he was doing. On the positive side of the ledger, Manish certainly had the room's attention.

"From what Hannah said, you seem to already embrace many of the principles, since you have little formality in your process. But let's try some other principles and see how you are doing.

"The first Agile principle is that *business people and developers must work together daily throughout the project.* Do you do that today?"

"Not very well," responded Narish, our new release manager. "Most of the time we have a one-line requirement and we have to guess on the details, and we don't find out that we've guessed wrong until the users get it in production."

Agile Principles

We follow these principles:

1. Our highest priority is to satisfy the customer through early and continuous delivery of valuable software.
2. Welcome changing requirements, even late in development. Agile processes harness change for the customer's competitive advantage.
3. Deliver working software frequently, from a couple of weeks to a couple of months, with a preference to the shorter timescale.
4. Business people and developers must work together daily throughout the project.
5. Build projects around motivated individuals. Give them the environment and support they need, and trust them to get the job done.
6. The most efficient and effective method of conveying information to and within a development team is face-to-face conversation.
7. Working software is the primary measure of progress.
8. Agile processes promote sustainable development. The sponsors, developers, and users should be able to maintain a constant pace indefinitely.
9. Continuous attention to technical excellence and good design enhances agility.
10. Simplicity—the art of maximizing the amount of work not done—is essential.
11. The best architectures, requirements, and designs emerge from self-organizing teams.
12. At regular intervals, the team reflects on how to become more effective, then tunes and adjusts its behavior accordingly.

FIGURE 8.2
Twelve Agile Principles.

"How about the second Agile principle," continued Manish. "*Build projects around motivated individuals. Give them the environment and support they need, and trust them to get the job done.* Do you do that?"

There was an awkward silence, until Hannah answered for the development team. "We certainly have motivated individuals who get the projects done," she said. "But we have some gaps around having the environment and support we need. We didn't even get free coffee until a few months ago!"

Manish proceeded. "How about the third Agile principle: *Agile processes promote sustainable development. The sponsors, developers, and users should be able to maintain a constant pace indefinitely.* How do you think you do there?"

This one drew some twitters. Phillip stepped up to answer. "Sure, if a constant pace means working all the time," he said jokingly, but not in a funny way.

Manish marched onward: "How about this Agile principle? *At regular intervals, the team reflects on how to become more effective, then tunes and adjusts its behavior accordingly.*"

At this, the room fell awkwardly silent again. Finally, Janet Livingston, our new user experience manager fresh from the help desk, said, "I don't think we've ever actually discussed together how we work at all. We're so busy just trying to keep up!"

"That's probably enough, then," said Manish. "We've seen how your company embraces some of the Agile values and principles, and falls short of others. What we'd like to do now is provide a structure that brings more processes, tools, and documentation in line with these principles, without undermining those values of yours that are already Agile. This structure would also bring better support for the development team; it would provide routine interaction between business partners and users; it would offer a sustainable pace; and it would provide a mechanism for the team to continually examine how it's working and make improvements. If we could do that, would you be interested?" The room murmured its assent, and Manish moved on toward the specific Agile technique we had chosen, scrum.

Scrum Explained

"Now, let's move on to the specific implementation of Agile, called *scrum*,[8] which is what we'll base our initial development approach on. As Sato-san notes, scrum is a method that incorporates many of the valuable attributes of LPD and Lean manufacturing. How many of you have heard of scrum?" Manish asked. "Not in the rugby way," he joked.

Of the 25 or so people in the room, only about 10 raised their hands. "What have you heard?" Manish asked.

One of Phillip's developers answered. "I have friends at other companies using it," he said. "They like it. They say they get better requirements than before, have better testing support, and the schedules are more realistic and in tune with the customers. They also like the short meetings."

"Others?" asked Manish, and when no one responded, he continued: "That is a fairly typical response. Scrum is becoming quite popular now, much as Toyota's Lean manufacturing swept around the world and was adopted in one way or another by most of the leading companies. I believe that scrum, or some variant of it, is most definitely superior to how most software organizations used to work. It recognizes the basic nature of software development, its inherent unpredictability, and it takes out much waste while putting in much discipline and risk control. Wes, could you hand out my diagram, and we will start with planning?"

I handed out the scrum diagram Manish had prepared (Figure 8.3),[9]

Manish began with a broad-brush overview. "Please look at the upper left corner, labeled *scrum planning*. In this step, we create what we call the *backlog*, which is simply a list of the things we want to do or build. We try to define the backlog items in enough detail that we have a rough estimate of how big they are and so we can understand any dependencies or long-lead-time items. The backlog becomes the foundation for everything we do."

At this point, I interjected. "Let's be clear that prior to scrum planning, there is significant effort to be ready to create the backlog. We've already heard from Frank about the work to identify what he called *unmet needs*, which gives us a broad brush at our target market. We then have our corporate planning and budgeting process and our sales and customer engagement processes. These all are inputs to the team doing the scrum planning."

"Astute observation, Wes," Manish agreed. "In fact, there is an iterative loop between the up-front processes that Wes is referring to and the backlog formation done in scrum planning. Sometimes, inputs to the scrum planning are determined to be too vague or not of value, and they can be sent back upstream; other times, the plan coming out of the scrum planning will be reviewed by up-front participants and adjusted. Reality isn't quite so clean as my picture here."

My diversion over, Manish continued with his elucidation of scrum.

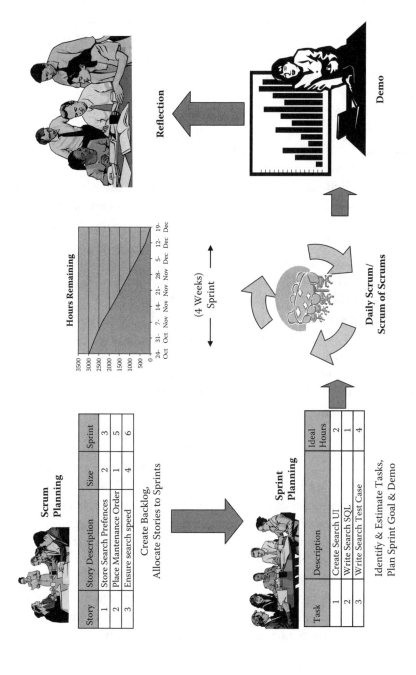

FIGURE 8.3
Scrum overview.

"Also in scrum planning, we want to set a release date and do a rough allocation of backlog items to what we call *sprints*. The *release* is defined as the date at which the software is released for use. *Sprints* are the development periods—i.e., the time between now (when we are doing planning) and the release date. Typically, sprints are between one and four weeks; we strive to keep them short, but long enough to enable useful pieces of software to go from requirements through build to test in the period."

Sato got up from his perch by the wall and chimed in. "I hope you can see what Manish is setting up here. We have a backlog from which we *pull*," pointing to his chart on the wall (see Figure 8.3). "And we have *one piece flow* within the sprint, with low handoffs."

"Thank you, Sato-san," said Manish. "Now, follow the arrow down, to sprint planning. Here, we dive more deeply into the items in the next sprint, breaking down the backlog items, often called *user stories*, into more finite tasks. The amount of work is balanced to the resources, and the sprint-end demonstration is set. If there is too much work, some of the items need to be returned to the backlog, or resources added. Note the identification of the sprint-end demonstration: we want to have something to show, usually working software. It focuses the mind and the effort, and it ensures regular communication with a broad audience; in this case, for example, Pervez Milligan at SDNI.

"Come with me to the middle now, where we have the sprint underway and we are doing the scrums. This diagram shows a four-week sprint. There are several items we will discuss. First, the scrum itself, a structured 15-minute meeting of the team members to update task status, communicate accomplishments and needs for assistance, and set up other meetings. You'll also see the *scrum of scrums*, for projects where there are multiple teams working together. Finally, look at the chart in the top middle—we call this a *burndown chart*, which shows, day by day, how many hours we have left to finish what we set out to do, versus the projection at the beginning of the sprint. Sato-san, I suppose you'd like to refer back to your chart?"

"I would," said Sato. "Note here the rigorous standardization of planning method, estimation, meetings, and tracking. This standardization of the *lower-level* tasks frees up the mind to be creative on the *higher-level* tasks, especially team collaboration. Also note the visual tracking, every day, of team progress, and the visual demonstration at the end of the sprint. Very Lean!"

Manish took back the floor and finished up his overview. "In the far right column, we have the *sprint-end demonstration*, in which the team shows its results to its partners and managers, and a *reflection event*. In reflection, the team reviews what went well and what needs improvement, and it focuses routinely on its *velocity*. Velocity stabilization and improvement is a holy grail of Agile development. If you look at the scrum planning diagram, you will note a *size* estimate, whereas in sprint planning, you can see a column for *ideal hours*. These are two methods of estimating how much time a backlog item will require to complete, which culminate in the burndown chart in the middle. In this example, the team is using hours to estimate and track at the task level; in reflection, the team will determine if its estimating is accurate and if its velocity is increasing, as it should over time. Sato-san, do you want to add anything?"

"Of course, Manish-san. Velocity in Agile is the same concept as *takt* in Lean manufacturing. What is the sustainable cadence? If we can figure this out, we can estimate more accurately, addressing one of the perennial problems in software," Sato concluded.

"We'll talk over each of these stages in more depth," Manish said, "but Sato-san is correct. Getting to a stable velocity means that a team is getting better—it knows its software, it knows the business, and it knows its capabilities. This will take time, so we measure the variance of velocity from sprint to sprint. Sometimes it stabilizes, sometimes it doesn't, but both results give us hints on where focus is required."

With the overview complete, Manish began to dive more deeply into each element of scrum, while the audience began to open up with questions. I was encouraged to see both my peers and my new development team engaging with the material, comparing it to how we did things today, identifying barriers and discussing animatedly with Manish and Sato.

Next Steps

By 3:30 p.m., at the beginning of our last break, between the Introduction to Agile and Next Steps Planning, I could tell the audience was both energized and overwhelmed. This had been a lot to pack into one day, probably too much. During the break, I strategized with Margaret, our culture consultant from GRI, on how to wind up the day. We agreed that we needed to end quickly, with some simple go-forward steps, rather than detailed plans. It seemed to us that our audience was fried! With that in mind, I called the group back to gather at 4:00 p.m., for a quick wrap up.

"I can see that you are all getting tired," I started, "so we aren't going to keep you much longer. Many of you may be thinking, 'Gee, cool stuff, but how do we do it at MCCA? What are the concrete next steps? Where do we go from here? It seems so much to do, and we are already so busy!'

"A wise friend of mine made what seems like an excellent suggestion for us: use scrum as the mechanism to manage the introduction of Lean and Agile itself.[10] That's what we are going to try—Thursday and Friday, week after next, when we will start scrum planning, beginning with creating the backlog. I'm going to take the role of the product owner, with overall responsibility for the team, since its focus is improving how we do product development. Hannah has volunteered to be the scrum master, and other volunteers from my group include Phillip, Rico, Joan, Lincoln, Narish, and Janet. I'd like to get representatives from Sales, Operations, Human Resources, and Finance as well, if you are interested in participating."

Connie Esposito spoke up first, with strong endorsement. "Wes, I'd be honored to have Operations participate. Can I get back to you Monday with a candidate?"

"Of course, Connie, thank you. Melissa," I said, to Melissa Groves, Jack's mentee and primary workhorse on the SDNI account, "would you like to join our scrum team on behalf of Sales?"

"I'll have to ask Jack," Melissa responded, "but I think he'll be supportive. Count me in unless you hear from me by Monday."

Sasha and Cynthia, our VPs for Finance and Human Resources, both agreed to provide representation as well; in fact, both were contemplating joining the team themselves.

Mission accomplished. I promised to keep this group informed of what the new Lean Team (my name) come up with, and I handed out an evaluation form for people to complete before they would be allowed out of the room. (I didn't enforce this rule; the threat was enough to get most people to comply.)

The day had gone as well as I could have hoped: a foundation had been created that gave the Lean Team legitimacy and space. Next step: form that team, and get scrumming!

WEEK FOUR: CREATING THE MANAGEMENT BACKLOG AND THE RELEASE PLAN

I wanted our kickoff of the Lean Team to be special, a big event, something to remember. I wanted us to begin to form as a team. This called for something extra—a junket! Very few luxurious off-sites were ever held at MCCA for any group but Sales, which held them regularly—in Vegas, Florida, Cabo, even once in Anchorage. I wouldn't go that far, but I did talk Lynn into letting us go off-site, to a resort north of the city. It was off-peak, and my assistant scoured the area for a decent deal, so it wasn't quite as extravagant as it appeared.

Our first official event was dinner Wednesday evening, after optional activities—golf or spa. Unfortunately, I had to complete preparations for the meetings, along with Hannah (our program manager), Joan (our product manager), Manish, Margaret, Sato-san, and Phillip Glass. The seven of us huddled in a conference room Wednesday afternoon at the resort, juggling the schedule, preparing props and charts, and planning the course of the next few days. We joined the rest of the group at dinner, which we kept low key and mostly social in nature. I was pleased to learn that several of the participants had taken it upon themselves to learn more about Lean product development and Agile software since our training two weeks ago; that would help as we began our work the next day.

Thursday dawned a typical beautiful north San Diego day, although it promised to heat up. In addition to the seven of us who'd done the planning, the group included Rico DeSilva and his protégé Jasna Pikula from Phillip's development group; our new test, user experience, and release managers; Melissa Groves from the SDNI account; an up-and-coming operations manager from Connie; Sasha Bilokov, VP of Finance; and Cynthia Evans-Goldenbogen, VP of HR. Sasha and Cynthia had both been excited to participate on this team: in fact, Sasha had commented that this was the first time she'd ever been in a meeting directly with our software developers. Indeed, the inclusion of not only Rico but also the more junior Jasna has been a topic of some surprise, since no one considered them "management." If we are going to focus on code, I reminded questioners, we need to involve some of the people who actually create it, don't we?

Our first order of business was to marvel at the pastries—quite a spread! We all got coffee and took our places. Our 16 people were spread across 4 tables, spaciously arranged around the conference room. Once the room had settled, I kicked off the meeting by going over the objectives and the agenda; then I handed off control to Cynthia. We had done enough pre-work and communication that the agenda and objective were no surprise: to build the Lean Team backlog and plan the next sprint or two. With no confusion to clear up, Cynthia led us through a get-to-know-you HR-type exercise, a little fun, a little warm-up, and a little useful.

With introductions complete, Manish took over the facilitation. He had hoped to be able to have participants come to the meeting with their own lists of candidate backlog items, but we had compressed the learning and the doing so tightly, there just wasn't time. So we were going to try to get the backlog built, dynamically, in one day. I understood it would be rough and need refinement, which would be my job as product owner of this effort. I much preferred to have the input and buy-in that this day would give me as opposed to just writing up and presenting my own views.

Manish began by explaining that the backlog is the foundation for the work we were going to do. The backlog is simply the list of "stories" we intended to take on over the planning horizon, which we had set for six months. The stories would be things that our staff members and customers would be able to do. We would elaborate on the stories, prioritize them, and then allocate them over six one-month sprints to come. But because we were laying out management tasks, we wouldn't estimate in any detail, just identify which tasks were small, medium, or large, so we could plan effectively.

To help with the backlog creation, I handed out to everyone their very own laminated version of the Lean and Agile "cheat sheet" that Mary had given me for the first time over two years ago (see Figure 8.4). Sato and Manish did a quick review of the principles, tools, and techniques to refresh the team on the training we did recently, and to frame the backlog creation. Manish followed this up with instructions on how to create user stories—the simple requirements statements that provide a common unit of granularity for backlogs.[11]

Once the group seemed conversant in the mission in front of them and in the Lean and Agile model we planned on using, we began the hard work in earnest. We split the team into three groups, one for *people*, one for *process*, and one for *tools*. We had preassigned the groups to have a mixture of skills and experiences on each team, and had Manish, Sato, and Margaret join the *process, tools,* and *people* teams, respectively.

The first session went for two hours, and then we rotated tables; actually, we had the teams get up and switch, for instance, from the *process* table to the *people* table. After the rotation, the new group was presented the results from the prior group, and they had one hour to modify them. After lunch, we did one more half-hour rotation, and then began the consolidation and prioritization exercise.

Lean & Agile Development

- Towering technical competence
- Chief engineers
- Managers as teachers
- "Module development teams"
- Culture: value, eliminate waste, continuous improvement, reflection, problem solving

People *Process*

Purpose:
Lean operational value streams

Tools

- Light project mgt: milestones/ responsibilities/"Go See"
- "Study" phase
- Integrating events
- Concurrent engineering
- Continuous Integration
- Agile development (sprints, scrum, agile planning, user stories)
  - One-piece flow/small batches
  - Test-driven development
  - Cadence & pull
  - Backlogs
  - Product owners
  - Enables "go see"
  - Eliminate handoffs

- Communication: one-page "A3's"
- Strategic alignment via "policy deployment"
- "Go See"
- Value stream mapping => Appropriate Process standardization
- Supplier partnerships
- Error proofing
- Team rooms

FIGURE 8.4

Lean and Agile development. (Adapted from Morgan, J. M. and J. K. Liker, *The Toyota Product Development System* (New York: Productivity Press, 2006), 18.)

One person from each of the teams was asked to present the results for their area to the larger group. Cynthia went first, presenting the *people* items: "Our team has a lot of items to add to the backlog. It was difficult to identify and agree on concrete items to do, and I think we probably didn't quite understand the user story idea completely. But here goes."

With that, Cynthia began taping 4-by-6 index cards up on the wall, under the *People* sign we'd prepared. "We've organized our cards by the items on the cheat sheet, and we worked with the other teams to be sure that all of them did the same. For towering technical competence, our first card is *Team Members Have Clear Definition of Competencies and How to Gain Them*. We believe that team members have to take some responsibility for their own development, but if we don't give them guidance and encouragement, we are playing roulette with what we'll get.

"The next is *Team Members Have Access to Documented Knowledge of Others*. Our dialogue on this was that we have a lot of knowledge in our company, but it's bottled up in people and not accessible.

"Here we have *Our Development Team Has Expert Test Lead.* We think this is solved now, since we hired Lincoln, but we still put it up to recognize the need and so that we might have one done already.

"Here is a big one: *We Have a Product Strategy with Names, Market Positions, Pricing, and Roadmaps,*" Cynthia said as she posted the next card. "We weren't sure how or whether to break this one up, or even if it belongs in *people,* but we all agreed we need this. We know generally where we are going, the market needs we are servicing, and so on, but we need more definition.

"And this one is related: *Sales Has a Defined Process to Interact with Product Development for New Opportunities.* Connie has already done this for Operations," Cynthia said, noting by a glance that Connie was on her card-writing team, "and we need to do the same for Development. We might think about combining the interaction with both Operations and Development into a single process."

Cynthia went on for almost an hour, taking questions and comments, discussing the estimated amount of work for each, and putting the cards in order. I thought she was confusing people items with *process* and *tools* items, but I didn't want to be picky. In one case, the rest of the afternoon was consumed with elaborating for *process* and *tools,* and those groups intermixed some *people* items themselves. At the end of the day, Lynn joined us for a wrap up, and I summarized the results for the group and set the stage for the next day.

"Lynn," I began, "today we created the backlog for our Lean Team. The backlog is simply a list of things we believe we need to do, along with some rough estimates of effort for each. The items are of two basic types: items related to our group or company in general, such as *Team Members Have Clear Definition of Competencies and How to Gain Them,* and items related tightly to specific projects, product, or departments, such as *Create the Backlog for the SDNI Customer Project.*"

Lynn walked up to the wall, perused the backlog items, and made some comments and inquiries. She then asked, "This seems like an awful lot to accomplish, especially considering that we need to run and grow our business at the same time. How are you going to take this huge list and turn it into something we can execute?"

Manish, our scrum expert, responded on our behalf. "That's exactly what we turn to tomorrow, Ms. Hollander. We begin by picking a release target and a theme, and then split the time between now and release into sprints. Then, we prioritize the items—"

As Manish was talking, Lynn's face lit up as she connected what we were doing with the training we had done last week. She interrupted Manish, politely, by saying, "Aha! That's just what we learned in your training class last week, isn't it? Using Lean and Agile techniques to make the company Lean and Agile—it only makes sense! We have what, another half hour? How about we talk over some more of these backlog items together, maybe I can give you my two cents on how to prioritize them?"

We ended a productive day explaining our backlog items to Lynn and getting her views on many of them. We even added a few more items to backlog at her request. We left the evening free of planned activities. I was pleased to see the group arranging dinner and other rendezvous among themselves, across our organizational boundaries. My evening was spoken for, however, planning tomorrow with our leadership group.

Friday morning, the room began filling with people who came early to elaborate on their favorite backlog items. We had left enough room on the cards to add some detail on what the outcome would look like, and on the back of the cards, we had put a label "Estimate and Approach." When we broke yesterday, Manish had warned the group that we were going to start by prioritizing the items, and he had suggested that more detail could lead to higher priority. We had some competitors in the room that needed to "win" the prioritization contest.

At 8:30 a.m., the group was called to order and Manish continued his facilitation. The next step, he explained, was to prioritize the items. [An aside before I continue: last night the seven of us who had planned this session had a hearty discussion on how to do the prioritization. Phillip and Hannah had pushed for a completely democratic approach: sort out the items, they argued, and vote; that way, the people who will have to do the work will get to choose what to work on. They felt that approach would be most effective. Surprisingly, Manish took the opposite tack: This is not a democracy, he said, and Agile is not meant to substitute the opinions of the development team for business leadership. Prioritization is the prerogative of the product owner—in this case, me! We ended up with a compromise, which Manish presented.]

Now that the backlog items have been clarified, elaborated to some extent, de-duped, and grouped, Manish explained, we were ready to go. Each of us would be given 10 sticky dots, and we could vote on what we thought were the highest-priority items. In accordance with our discussion the prior evening, each person could place up to 5 votes on any particular item—that way, if something was very important to someone, they could likely give it some priority by spending 5 dots directly. This was balanced by the fact that to reach the top part of the priority list, an item would take more than only one person's dots.

As product owner, Manish pressed me to give some guidance for the voting. I also needed to explain why I would be voting with 5 red dots, whereas everyone else had green ones.

"Last night, several of us planning this session had a bit of an argument over how to do the prioritization," I said. "The debate was whether I choose the priorities, as product owner, or you choose the priorities, as the team that will have to implement them. We agreed that I would give some guidance on how you should choose priorities, and that I would get these special red dots." I held up the dots and showed them off.

"Let's start with the choosing of priorities. We can't change our whole culture and processes overnight, and even once we've spent years on this path, we'll be continuously improving. Therefore, we need to pick those items that will have the most impact on our success and those that are necessary predecessors to other items that we will attack later. We also need to pick a balanced set of priorities, because different people in this room and outside of it will be working on different types of items. Finally, I'd suggest using your votes on those items that you in particular have a passion for and are willing to commit your own time and effort to, and the time of your teams and peers."

No problem there from the team, so I moved on to the dots. "How many of you play bridge?" A smattering of hands. "Then you'll know what I mean when I say these are trump dots—each one enables me to choose a priority and move it to the top of the list if I think it necessary. I will not vote until after you all have finished and we have tallied the numbers, and I might not cast any, or I might cast them all. This gives us a nice mix of you (the team) driving the agenda, and management (represented by me) having significant input as well. Does that sound fair?"

No one was opposed, or at least no one wanted to say to my face that they thought I shouldn't have my special voting tokens. So we took ten minutes, in which the attendees got out of their chairs, walked around the room perusing the backlog item cards on the walls, and placing their votes on the cards. We declared a ten-minute break while Hannah and I added up the votes, and I looked over the items to see if I wanted to use any of my trump dots. Most of the items I had to have on the list were there, such as *Prepare marketing concept document*,[12] which would give us the product names, market segmentation, and general roadmap, which we needed to have for our late July User Conference.

However, I did have to use a few of my superdots—there were not sufficient votes on two items I was adamant about, both related to the strategic advancement of our product line: *Create a separate team for product hardening*, and *Create backlog for product hardening*.

We had mentioned these hardening items yesterday and there were enough votes on them to get into the top 15 or so items, but given our strategy, I felt these had to be top priorities in the next month. Our strategic product (we really had to name it soon) was advancing steadily through the SDNI work, and there were plenty of votes for the tasks to get SDNI working more effectively through scrum and product management work. But just having SDNI happy would not give MCCA the growth we sought; we had to make (product name to come soon) deployable easily to hundreds of customers. That would mean building setup utilities, self-administration functions, integration capabilities, scaling, security—it was a long list that hadn't been established formally yet.

The group in the room evidently felt we weren't ready to take this on yet, and I was sympathetic to that belief, but I also had vision and possible options that weren't available to the others. I could make a case to hire more people, use consultants and contractors, create new positions. So it was up to me to bring the proper focus to these items. I was grateful that there were at least a few priority votes on my items so my trump card wasn't in obvious contradiction to what the group had chosen.

The group gathered to review the priorities; my selection was approved, with a few jokes around my using only two of my trump dots. Was I saving more for later? This gave Manish the opportunity to talk about my role as product owner and that I always had trump dots to use; I tried to soften that somewhat because I wanted to ensure that our team continued to feel ownership for the backlog. It's a tricky balancing act to both trust your team and to provide the leadership and vision expected of you as a leader!

Our final mission was to go through the backlog items in priority order, to ensure we had enough elaboration that we fully understood the next steps and outcomes, to estimate them, and to assign at least enough of them to fill up the first two sprints. We chose to split into two groups to work through the items, and then we got back together to share results. By the end of the day, we had filled up two sprints with well-defined items, assigned leaders to each of the items in the first sprint, scheduled the first two demo days when we would get together to review results and plan the next sprint, and agreed on how we would do scrums and reporting.

The discussion on scrums confirmed for me Manish's rather rigid perspective on Agile. He insisted that we have a daily scrum meeting. He also insisted we take the backlog items from the first sprint, break them into smaller tasks, and estimate them in story points. After a heated discussion, our group rebelled against these strictures. They didn't want to meet every day on this; weekly, or twice a week, seemed enough. They also didn't want to do time estimates; they just wanted to leave things assigned to leaders to manage. Finally, I wanted to be both scrum master and product owner for the Lean Team, a definite no-no according to the method. Manish made a final set of protests at our ill-advised decisions and then gave up, a little pouty. It seemed to me that Manish was as narrow-minded and rigid in his own way as Trevor McDonald, the true believer in Cremins' The Process, had been. Knowing this would help me understand how to deploy Manish going forward. One of the key things Neville and Mary had taught me was that it's not the specifics of the scrum method that matters; it's the Lean and Agile principles behind them.

The critical elements of our conclusions and our agenda for the next 60 days were the plans for the first two sprints (Figure 8.5).

Sprint 1 was to focus on beginning scrum for SDNI and on laying the foundation for broad adoption of LPD and Agile. The backlog started with two very big items: getting a start on our product roadmap—the Lean product development concept document—and on improving the Sales–Development interaction. We also decided to attack A3 management immediately, because the perception that we had serious communication gaps was widespread, and the idea of using the one-page, structured communication vehicle had resonated with the group.[13] I was excited about one of Rico's several contributions—the idea to use our own technology to create a searchable repository for the A3s we create. This could help us manage knowledge more effectively, get our team using our own products, and maybe result in a new market for our tools. Several items related to product hardening, and others pertained to improving our testing and continuous integration. The final items were training and physical facilities for our teams. Sprint 2 was taking the same items farther along, including looping in SDNI if they would.

We did a final check to ensure that there were important items that we were *not* tackling as well. If we tried to do too much, we'd overload ourselves and risk not accomplishing the really critical items. There were

Sprint	One	Two
Theme	SDNI scrum inception & prepare broad foundation	SDNI scrum implementation & begin broad foundation
Begin	May 15	June 20
End	June 15	July 20 (week before DocWorld)
Critical Backlog Items and Owners	• Write outline of concept document; candidate product names & positions (Joan, Melissa) • Generate options for Sales/Development interaction (Cynthia) • Build SDNI backlog (Joan) • Select SDNI scrum team (Wes) • Begin SDNI scrums (Hannah) • A3 training: Problems, opportunities, knowledge (Sato) • Create A3 management facility (Rico) • Hardening backlog (Joan) • Select hardening team (Wes) • Create Master Test Plan (Tester) • Plan for continuous integration (Rico & Phillip) • Find team rooms (SDNI, product name, product hardening) • Training: Plan & schedule LPD and Agile (Wes)	• Concept document first draft complete; product names & positions reviewed; pricing strategy created but not approved (Joan, Melissa) • Decide on Sales/Development interaction model; begin implementation (Cynthia) • Include SDNI in backlog management (Joan) • Do first SDNI demo (with SDNI if interested) (Hannah/ Phillip) • Begin insisting on A3s (Wes, Hannah, Phillip, Joan) • Implement A3s management facility (Rico/Phillip) • Begin hardening work (Phillip) • Set target for next customer (after SDNI) (Wes, Phillip) • Implement first test automation (tester) • Hardening scrums (Wes to appoint) • Training: Continuous integration and testing (Tester)

FIGURE 8.5
MCCA Lean Team Sprints 1 and 2.

some important but not urgent items we had left out for now, such as the item on ensuring team members know what competencies are needed and have guidance on how to gain them. That, and many other items, would have to wait.

We left the resort tired but energized, generally aligned and ready to move forward together.

WEEK SIX: LEAN TEAM SCRUM MEETING

Our second weekly Lean Team scrum meeting is about to begin. I'm hoping to do better than we did—I guess, to be honest, how *I* did—last week at our first meeting. I was committed to keeping to the 15-minute duration to limit the discussion to the prescribed "what did I do yesterday, what am I doing today, where do I need help."[14] The problem seemed to be that the backlog items hadn't been broken down effectively enough into well-understood items, so it wasn't so much that we *couldn't* keep to the format and time limits, we *didn't want* to keep to the format and time limit. When the team had agreed to extend the meeting to an hour, once a week, Manish was so dismayed that he asked to not participate; he'd rather, he said, focus on the Agile implementation for the software elements (SDNI and hardening). That was fine with me; he was causing more disruption than help in the Lean Team for now, and he had plenty to contribute hands-on in the development scrums.

Today's discussion began at 10:00 a.m. sharp with my first question, to Joan, regarding building the SDNI backlog. She had broken down that user story into smaller tasks and spread those across the four-week sprint; she had some of those tasks, whereas others were given to Melissa (sales), Hannah (project management), and Phillip (development).

"This week, I completed assembling the first draft of the SDNI backlog," she began. "I got input from Melissa, Hannah, Phillip, and Rico, and Manish helped me structure the list into a passable user story format. Melissa had most of it already done; I just had to add some technical scalability, performance, and maintainability items from Philip and Rico. Yesterday, Melissa and I met with the SDNI people, who prioritized the list and adjusted some items; they also promised to review the list internally with others to be sure it's valid. Next week, I'll work with Phillip to get estimates on the highest-priority items, while Melissa works with Jack Langley to examine any contractual implications."

"Joan, could you explain that? What is the contractual issue?" I asked. Here is where our modification of the scrum standard seemed valuable to me. We could have elaboration on the task right here in this meeting, instead of having to take them offline for later. For this type of management scrum, the hour length was working a lot better than the short time frame. In fact, I was thinking that now that we didn't have Manish's resistance, we might extend the meeting another hour.

"The current SDNI contract is vague as to what precisely we need to deliver as part of our initial contract, and how ongoing development requests and enhancements should be handled," Joan said. "This is important both for our direct SDNI work, as well as for the broader concept document and product roadmap. We need to understand both the written details and any informal agreements or understandings we might have."

"Other items?" I prompted.

Joan moved to her next backlog item. "I have a general outline of a product concept document and some samples from Sato. Frank of FWJ has provided all of the material he and his market researchers had produced at the time of their purchase of MCCA. Next week, I plan on updating the competitive research; I'm not sure exactly how to do that yet and I could use some ideas if anyone has some, especially around competitive features and pricing."

Sasha Bilokov, our VP of Finance, did indeed have some ideas. "I know someone at one of the IT research firms," she said. "Perhaps we could phone her together and get some direction."

Melissa Groves, the salesperson on our team, also had a suggestion. "I could put together a questionnaire for our sales force," she said. "They usually have a lot of information on our competitors, and are always complaining that they don't get listened to."

"Can I help with that, Melissa?" Rico added. "If we ask the questions in the right way, we can standardize the responses and put the knowledge directly into the repository I am creating."

"Great ideas," replied Joan. "I'll set up a half hour later this week for us to work on that. I'm excited about the work I've begun on product positioning and naming, but I'm not ready to spring anything on this group yet. I need to review it with Wes first."

"I appreciate that, Joan," I said, with a laugh.

Joan gave me a wry smile and then finished up her recitation. "The last thing on my list is to do the hardening backlog—the list of items we need to do the SDNI code to make it deployable to other companies. I've just begun this. I've taken some of the items from the SDNI backlog, plus some new items from Melissa, Phillip, Jasna on Phillip's team, and some ideas Janet brought from our help desk. I need to dive deeper into this next week; I don't know enough to ask for any help on this yet."

"Cynthia?" I prompted next, for our VP of Human Resources.

"This week, I spent time with Connie and two of her regional operations managers, understanding the Sales–Operations interactions, especially the results of the changes that Connie made a few months ago. For those of you not familiar with this area, Operations created a formal Sales Support and Contract Management Group through which all major new sales opportunities were to funnel. From the perspective of Operations, this change has been largely successful; there is more control and structure in the consideration and pricing of new deals, although there have been some gaps revealed especially in the Northern California region. Next week I have time scheduled with Sales and Finance and a phone interview with Frank at FWJ. I've started to lay out a few options to hang my findings on."

"Can you give us a preview of the options, Cynthia?" I asked.

"Of course, Wes," Cynthia answered. "Forgive me for how rough these are—I've just started to assemble them. My first option is to build on the role that Connie has created, making the Sales Support Department responsible for both Operational and Development opportunities. That poses some challenges in team member skill sets and in organizational design: if Sales Support is dealing with both areas, it probably shouldn't report to Operations, should it?

"My second option is to build a parallel Sales Support function within Development, and let Sales navigate between the two as they need. That has some advantages, because opportunities will often be one or the other. But where we have combined opportunities, we might create confusion, and we might cause some redundant "expediting" positions we don't need.

"Finally, option three is to have Joan (as product manager) directly own all the new development opportunities, and to give her (as Wes's representative) profit and loss (P&L) ownership for our new software products."

This was the first I had heard these three options, and I was impressed with where Cynthia was going with this. I said so, but added a cautionary note.

"Cynthia, regarding your third option, on P&L ownership, Lynn and I talked about this as an eventual direction, which she generally liked, but she was cautious on what pace we might move at. If that looks like a realistic contender, you should probably put the idea on the agenda for our staff meeting, so we can get a read from Lynn, Jack, and Sasha on acceptability."

"I'll do that, Wes," Cynthia said. "I see a lot of complications on that front, but on the other hand, that is a model others have used successfully, and it brings a lot of clarity to the structure, quickly. That's it for me," she concluded.

"Would you mind using the A3 format?" I asked. "We may as well get started using a common communication format and ensuring that we consider well the various options."

I called on Rico next. Rico was making an encouraging transition himself, along with the overall product development group. A few months ago, he had been on the edge of quitting (actually, he had been on that edge for quite some time). We had a couple of long talks, beginning during my first week, when he had walked off the job. He felt taken for granted, dumped on, continually committed by others to making impossible dates, compromised into writing bad software, and poorly supported by a great coder's usual partners: project managers, analysts, and testers. He had now become one of my greatest supporters and the clear leader of our new Agile movement among the developers. His eagerness to prove to the rest of us the usefulness of his software (still to be named) was great to see.

Rico reported on his week. "I worked on two items this week for this team: documenting some items for the product hardening backlog, and creating the knowledge management repository. First, the backlog: I just spent a half hour on it, listing out the major things I'm concerned about and giving rough estimates and approaches on how to do them. One example: our integration with databases, as opposed to documents, is now custom-coded for SDNI. We need to generalize that interface so it can be set up easily, and we need to integrate a better report-generation tool and interface to future clients' own reporting environments. I listed a dozen or so of this type of thing, with a couple labor-years of work to complete. We're going to need at least a few new developers to get this done."

Joan, our new product manager, responded, "I've been gathering items from others as well, so we're on track to complete this item this month as we planned. Thanks, Rico."

"No problem; it's nice to be asked! Moving on, I have set up a new instance of the information repository, and I configured it to handle A3 information. I created a schema to classify the A3s, by type, subtype, product, component, author, date, name, and a few more, and I set up the system to do full-text indexing as well. I grabbed an A3 template, in

Excel, from a site on the Internet, and I put drop-down list boxes in it for the typing and a macro to save it to our system. I also implemented a security and A3 versioning model, so once the A3 is finalized, it can't be edited except by its author or someone with a high security level. It's ready to go—in fact, maybe we'll use it for the first time to store the information on competitors we gather from Sales. Would you like to see it?"

I looked to the Lean Team for interest; it was definitely there. So we extended the meeting by a half hour to see our new management system. Manish may well object, but it was hard to argue with the energy in the room.

Signposts	MCCA Transformation
	• Wes, with Mary's advice and the help of the GRI consultants, plans out the MCCA organizational transformation.
	• The first step is a broad training initiative to familiarize team members with Lean and Agile concepts.
	• Next, Wes establishes a Lean Team, a leadership scrum, using an Agile technique to derive the Lean/Agile change.
	• The Lean Team establishes its backlog and conducts its first two weekly scrum meetings.
Change Guides from Wes	• If you are doing a people driven change process, be sure that the people know enough to make good decisions.
	• You can use Agile techniques to drive Agile change. Why not?
	• Mix team self-sufficiency and consensus decision making with decisive top-down leadership. If there are firm absolutes, let the team know; there are always boundaries; set them firmly, wisely, and clearly.
	• If you are going to measure progress primarily by working code, you should have someone close to the code in the leadership group.
Coming Up Next	About the same time as Wes's second scrum meeting, the FinServia management team is dealing with Mervin's frustration with Mary's unwillingness to commit to firm dates and costs for feature delivery. Does Agile development preclude fixed cost and time commitments? Mary takes over narration of a milestone FinServia event.

ENDNOTES

1. This idea is drawn from Schwaber, *Enterprise and Scrum*.
2. As described at the end of Chapter 4.
3. On Toyota's success, see for example, pages 11–12 in Morgan and Liker, *Toyota Product Development System*, and pages 13–18 in Michael N. Kennedy, *Product Development for the Lean Enterprise* (Richmond, VA: Oaklea Press, 2003).
4. This section is not meant to provide a comprehensive overview of Lean product development; rather, it is to show the kind of training that might be useful in a situation like Wes's. Sato's summary draws from Morgan and Liker, *The Toyota Product Development System*, especially Chapter 2, which summarizes the concepts. *Product Development for the Lean Enterprise* by Michael Kennedy is another good overview of LPD, as are some chapters in Liker, *Toyota Way*.
5. A3 thinking and usage is described in Liker, *Toyota Way*, pages 244–248.
6. Takt time, pull, and other Lean manufacturing principles are described in the classic *Lean Thinking*, James P. Womack and Daniel T. Jones, Free Press, 2003.
7. Agilemanifesto.org.
8. This section draws on Chapter 10 of Levine, *Tale of Two Systems*, which in turn draws on other publications, most importantly Schwaber and Beedle, *Agile Software Development with Scrum*.
9. Diagram is from Levine, *Tale of Two Systems*, Figure 14, page 93.
10. As noted, although in the book the wise man is Neville, in real life it is Ken Schwaber in his *Enterprise and Scrum*.
11. Cohen, *User Stories Applied* is a good overview.
12. Concept Documents are described in Morgan and Liker, *Toyota Product Development System*, pages 30–31.
13. An A3 is simply a one-page communication vehicle used at Toyota and other companies. It is named for a paper size used in Japan. For an explanation of the vehicle and its use, see Liker, *Toyota Way*, pages 244–248.
14. Scrum "rules" are available in Schwaber and Beedle, *Agile Development with Scrum*, page 43.

Section IV

Transformations Take Hold
May–September

9

Making Delivery Commitments at FinServia: May

Narrator: Mary

In my mind, today marks a milestone for my tenure at FinServia—the end of the beginning (but I certainly hope not the beginning of the end!). The last two months have been intensely internally focused. With a lot of help from my peers and my boss, Greg Allenby, I've assessed the situation, laid out a plan, and dealt with our top priority of rebuilding our own internal development capability. FinServia now has its own development group, and our attention is turning to delivery of software products. The questions we are all seeking to answer today are: What can this new group accomplish? How should the business move ahead with product plans and commitments based on those expectations? And what will be the nature of the Marketing and Development partnership in delivering value to our customers?

THE CLASSIC STRUGGLE: SETTING DATES AND COSTS

Before I tell about the meeting Greg called to air the argument between Mervin and me about making delivery commitments, I need to set some context. One of the fundamental conflicts in software development is the setting of dates and costs in conditions of uncertainty. The "waterfall" approach seeks to incrementally eliminate uncertainty by first doing all the requirements to fix scope; then completing design, to solidify approach; and then by estimating build cost and time. Once the estimate is complete, change is rigorously controlled, with adjustments to cost and time made as change is parsimoniously allowed.

Although this approach makes logical sense, in practice, we Lean/Agile practitioners believe with all our hearts that it is riddled with waste. The alternative approach sets the broad shape of a project and then gets going immediately on delivering value, in the smallest possible useful chunks along the drawn path. But in an Agile approach, how can the business plan? How can it know when a project will be done, how much it will cost, whether something is even worth doing? The answer is far from satisfying: the Agile team needs to do as much up-front requirements, design, and estimating as needed to generate the minimum information the business needs for immediate decision making, and no more. In some cases, this up-front work can succeed in bringing reliable planning information; in others, only the process of actually building software can bring the team the knowledge it needs to generate reliable planning information.

To business leaders who view new software development as something they should be able to simply order up and buy (like a can of soda, for example), the Agile approach can be frustrating. Who wouldn't rather have a firm cost and time commitment? The problem is that in many situations, insistence on an early "commitment" cannot be reliable and cannot help but result in waste. However, understanding the degree to which the development can reasonably "commit" requires knowledge of software dynamics—which many senior business leaders simply don't have.

Which brings us to today's meeting. Mervin is a software neophyte but a smart and aggressive businessman, and he has been pushing me to give him committed dates and times. I've pushed back, and the pushing has become evident to Greg, who has chosen to bring this push–push out into the open for our whole management team to observe and push a little also if they choose. Greg thinks this is a "learning opportunity"; privately, I think it's torture.

THE DATE/COST COMMITMENT STRUGGLE AT FINSERVIA

We're back at the Shelter Island Hotel, my favorite meeting place. Meeting rooms were free or cheap here as long as we consumed a certain number of nights of hotel rooms, and the GRI consultants were seeing to that for us. Greg, Ethel Jackson (VP Finance), Mervin Thomas (VP Marketing), Roberta Greeley (VP Human Resources), and I had lunch at Neptune's, a little farther down the point, while we waited for Manish's and Sato's plane to land from Dallas.

Over lunch, we caught up with each other. I related to Greg's team the latest on the reorganization of our development group and the progress of bringing application development back from GRI. Mervin gave us all a view of happenings in the market, which he thought favorable to us. The stock and bond markets' collapse had diverted attention from technological progress, as market participants hunkered down trying to survive, which gave us time to get our act together and be ready when the market came back to life. Ethel also credited the collapse with slowing migration from our print products and driving some limited new business from the major bankruptcies, reorganizations, and investigations. Greg was satisfied that we were on track so far, with the world cooperating to give us the most precious gift of time.

No one talked directly about the purpose of this afternoon's meeting, preferring to keep the premeeting lunch casual and comfortable. We knew we'd be struggling with some difficult issues this afternoon, and we all preferred to wait until we could do so in a structured context, and with the GRI experts, especially Sato, present. Mervin and Greg had both spent quality time with Sato, and both were wowed. Sato spoke with the confidence and authority of someone who had lived through the demanding wringer of Toyota's product development processes, for which especially Mervin felt awe.

As I walked from Neptune's to the hotel, I mentally reviewed the problem facing us. Mervin was working to revise the product plan. Under Sato's guidance, he was writing the concept document,[1] laying out the customer value propositions, the target audiences, and the financial targets. In order to do his plan, he asked me for time and cost to build the features he thought we needed. I pulled my new leadership together and we'd done the best we could, laying rough time and cost estimates for some of the highest-priority items. Mervin objected to language I had used to describe the estimates; he didn't want projections with future adjustment points, he said; he needed *commitments* on dates and costs. I told him that was impossible now, he'd have to pick his highest-priority items based on the rough estimates of size I had given him, and we would start on those, see what our velocity looked like and how our team performed, and then give him more information on which to plan in a few months.

After hitting a brick wall with me, Mervin went to Greg to complain, which led to this meeting. Greg hoped he could turn this impasse into a learning event for our whole team and lay some protocols and expectations down for the future. Since Mervin had grown to respect Sato, and to a lesser degree, Manish, Greg asked them to come along. The topic on the invitation was "Product Delivery Planning." Greg and I had worked out an agenda, and I had put together a few diagrams to use if need be.

We entered the Coronado room right on time and took our seats around the oblong table. Coronado was one of the larger meeting rooms at Shelter Island, so we gathered around the end of the table closest to the white board. From my seat facing the window, I could see the yacht basin—actually just the tips of the sails going back and forth across the window. Mervin, Sato, and Ethel looked over the table at Manish, Roberta, and me, while Greg started the meeting from his seat at the table head.

"Let's get going; we have a lot to talk about this afternoon," Greg began. "I want to start with the difficult problem Mervin and Mary are struggling with. Mervin, with Sato-san's help, is driving the product concept document as part of our study phase.[2] We are modeling this work on Toyota's product development process, part of our evolving adoption of Lean product development and Agile software. Mervin has done an outstanding job of understanding our customers, our competitors, and unmet needs in the market that we are in good position to fulfill. However, he's become stuck on the financial analysis and projections."

"Just to be clear, Greg," Ethel, our VP of Finance interjected, "it's not so much the analysis and projections as the *input to* the projections. We think we have identified what the target market needs and what it would pay for the services, but we can't get a good bead on when the services and features will be ready, which drives revenue, and what it will cost to build and service the products."

"Why is that?" Greg asked. He knew darn well the answer.

"Mary says it's not yet knowable," said Mervin, looking over at me.

"Mary?" prompted Greg.

"That's right, Greg," I started. "I can give some rough estimates based on GRI's experience, adjusted for the disruption we've just caused and the improvements we are making in delivery capability, but we do not have the capability to take a list of features from Mervin, with just a skeleton of details, and provide firm time and cost estimates. We've laid out a series of quarterly releases over the next 18 months and begun to allocate features in priority order to them, but past the first quarter, it gets murky. We did fix cost at the budgets we've agreed on, but getting the delivery dates on track is too much to ask of this new team right now."

Mervin finally joined the conversation. "I don't understand that at all, Mary," he said. "Sato-san described to me Toyota's development of the Prius,[3] where Toyota set a date, a cost to develop, and a cost to produce:

Toyota met all three, even though no one had ever built a hybrid car before." The frustration in Mervin's voice was almost palpable as he continued, "I'm not asking you to develop a whole new propulsion system, Mary. All we're doing is building some new software features in a system that already exists. I don't understand how you can get away with not committing to results, when sales and marketing have to commit to sales and profitability numbers!"

This was getting a bit personal now, and I let my frustration get the better of me. "Mervin, I am as committed to the sales and profitability goals as you are. We have exactly the same incentives, remember? So don't give me that line about you and Sales being The Business and I just need to deliver what you order, on time and budget. Without me and my team, you have nothing to sell. I'm telling you the truth about what we can expect in product delivery. You'll just have to build your plans around an uncertain reality that will emerge in the next several months. If you think someone can provide you with a better result—go ahead and replace me."

Greg had let it go this far in order to get the issues and feelings on the table, but this was far enough. "Let's be careful how we say things, you two. We need to have this discussion, but let's not get personal about it, OK? I have total confidence in both of you, and we are going to work through this together. No one is replacing anyone!" He looked first at me, and then at Mervin; Mervin responded first.

"Mary, I have no doubt that you're good at what you do. I just can't understand why you won't give commitments. In my previous jobs, if I needed technology developed, I asked our internal technology group and external vendors for bids, and they always provided them. Why can't you?" said Mervin.

I thought of several possible answers in a few seconds, but they were all questions challenging Mervin's previous experiences: How often did those bids get completed as bid? How much time and cost slack did the bids include? How complex were the requests? How similar were the requests to things the bidders had done already? While I sought a less confrontational reply, I was interrupted by our Lean product development expert.

Sato chose this time to attempt to provide some perspective. He occupied the silence left by my taking time to try to formulate an answer that might have a chance of getting through Mervin's thick head (after all, I had explained Agile principles to him several times already, why didn't he get it?) by saying, "Excuse me, Mervin, may I ask a question here?"

Mervin nodded.

"Mervin," asked Sato quietly, "how long do you suppose the engineers who gave the cost and times estimate in the Prius study phase worked together at Toyota, designing new cars?"

"I don't know," Mervin replied. "I understand that Toyota values longevity in position, so I guess five years or more?"

"Right, much more than five years. And how long do you suppose the study phase lasted, examining the customer needs, investigating technologies, and making trade-offs?"

"Six months?" Mervin guessed.

"Much more than that, Mervin," Sato corrected. "The formal study phase began in September 1993, and Prius didn't become an official project until June 1995—almost two full years![4] In addition, the Prius team was able to draw on a deep well of accumulated and evolving knowledge, including work on the hybrid power plant and batteries, which had been going on for years. You see, Mervin, Toyota takes a long view of its product development, and it nurtures its people, its expertise, and it partners' network to enable it to do something like create the Prius. It does not appear to me that you have yet built similar capabilities in this company?"

It was stated as a question, but it was instead a statement of fact. Mervin had no trouble drawing the conclusions, much as he might not like them. If you want to be able to develop software fast and reliably, you have to build the capabilities: people, teams, knowledge, partners. He thought for a moment, and said, "Thank you Sato-san, I think I see what you are saying. Any commitment or promise Mary gives me now is only as good as her team's knowledge of the business requirements, their technologies, and her team members. Unfortunately, she and her team do not have the capability of committing in anything other than intent."

"Much as I hate to admit it, Mervin, that's right," I said. "We'll give you our best educated estimate on delivery of your whole list, by quarter, based on our fixed budget and the limited understanding of my team. That will become a *goal* for us to meet or beat, but not a *commitment*. My challenge is to build our capabilities as quickly as possible, and while doing so deliver the highest priorities on your list. We will improve and learn from that work, and then be able to forecast and plan better while we do the next-highest-priority work. You need to develop our marketing and product plans around a set of delivery goals with increasing accuracy over time, but in a context of uncertainty. I know that isn't easy, but it's better to understand the reality of the situation and deal with it than to kid ourselves that we're better than we are."

CONFIGURING AGILE RELEASES: DISTRIBUTING TO AND MANAGING MULTIPLE BACKLOGS

Greg had been sitting back, listening to us, happy with his team's discussion. He saw we had now reached a basic understanding, and he wanted us to go deeper: How would we start working the high priorities? How would we build understanding of our capabilities and begin to improve our skills at forecasting and making delivery commitments? When would we know more?

Up to this point, I had not described our Agile approach in any detail to Mervin; I hadn't thought him ready to listen. He had taken anything other than commitment as excuses. Mervin had been so stuck on the idea that he would specify the features needed by the market, and my accountability would be to give him a date and a cost, that he had shut himself off from learning. He was used to being "the smartest guy in the room," and when he found that he wasn't that when dealing with technology, he tried to avoid engagement completely. I hoped we were now beginning to get past that.

"Mervin, would it be okay if I took some time and described our approach to development management?" I asked. "I've prepared a diagram that shows it on one page, and I think once you see and understand it, you'll be able to work with it comfortably."

"Let's see it," Mervin replied. Once he had accepted that he needed to understand our capabilities, not just date and cost forecasts, he had become curious. How would we manage the flow of development? How would we improve our forecasting?

I handed out the diagram I had prepared and vetted with Greg (Figure 9.1).

I began to explain. "Take a look in the middle—you see the three value stream teams, each with their own backlogs?" These are the Issuer, Investor, and Service Provider teams. Mervin and the others showed they were following, so I continued. "Each team populates its back¬log with a variety of inputs: requests from your team, Mervin, bug-fix can be populated in a coordinated or directed way from higher-level management, whether through the planning processes, strategy, or whatever.

"Each team prioritizes its own backlog into synchronized sprints and product releases. See the down arrows and the cross-arrow at the bottom of the diagram? We're planning on monthly releases for small and urgent

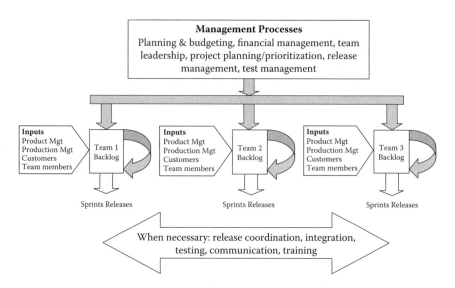

FIGURE 9.1
Coordinating multiple module teams.

items and major quarterly releases for significant new functions. Someday, we'll be good enough to do monthly releases that don't distinguish between size of release, but we're not good enough to do that yet. Each team must end a sprint on a schedule that enables integration and testing for each release; they can do shorter sprints if they wish, off-cycle, as well.

"The magic is on the top of the diagram: our management and leadership processes, which provide the guidance for each of our teams to prioritize their backlogs and size their teams—their development velocity—in alignment with our overall strategy. The team leaders, who are Chief Engineers, report to me, so I have direct influence through reporting relationships and my leadership team. Mervin, you and your people get input directly as members of each value stream team, and you also get higher-level input through product planning, the project approval and project management processes, and budgeting and forecasting."

Mervin had been following closely; I could see from the thoughtful look on his face that he was digesting. I paused for him to ask clarifying questions. Sure enough, he had a few.

"I think I get it, Mary. Can I test a few things with you?" Mervin asked. I nodded, so he tried out his ideas.

"Resources are fixed, at least for now," he said. I confirmed that, so did Greg.

"Given fixed resources, at least until we can ramp up revenues, our challenge is to get the most we can out of our team, by reducing waste and prioritizing effectively." Right, I said.

"How do we go about planning at least the first major salable set of enhancements? I'd like to start selling as soon we can, and I need to have a target date to give to existing and especially new customers." This question called for more than a simple acknowledgment.

"It's straightforward, at least in concept," I explained. "I've got each of my new chief engineers, for each of our groups, preparing the existing backlogs for their teams as best they can, and with each other. I know you have some broad goals for the products you want to sell. We need to work together to configure the minimum set of features those products need—we call them *user stories* because they are written from the point of view of system users. The user stories are kept as simple as possible while still being informative enough to start the estimation process.

"Our value stream teams, including your staff, Mervin, then break down the user stories into the elements of software that go into each of the value stream teams' backlogs. Then we prioritize each of the backlogs and estimate the size of the work for each, so we can allocate work to the work periods. Finally, if we have unevenness (for example, one team might take 3 months, another 6), we see if we can rebalance teams to move more velocity capability to the 'long pole in the tent.' After all of this, we have an estimate for code complete. At the end of the first sprint period—we're starting at one month—we would have more information on the accuracy of our estimates, so we can readjust the projected delivery date, reconfigure the feature list, or if it's worth it, potentially add resources."

"Very logical," Mervin nodded. "My problem is, when do I tell Sales to start selling the new stuff? At the beginning of the first sprint, at the end of it, or later? This method has too much uncertainty in it."

"It's not that the method has too much uncertainty," Greg helped me out. "It's that *reality* has too much uncertainty in it. This method *recognizes* the uncertainty and gives us a way to measure and monitor progress as quickly as possible. As time goes on, and as the team grows in knowledge and experience, our estimating will get better while our production velocity increases. In the meantime, we need to make a choice on when to sell what, based on full knowledge of the uncertainty involved. What are the implications of selling something in the case that delivery is delayed a few months? Is it better to overpromise, or is it better to be conservative?

Those are choices we need to make with Mervin, Mary, Sales, and Finance together, in full knowledge of the degree of uncertainty we have at hand."

I added, "Let me show an alternative, Mervin, and see if that works better for you. In order to give you a firm estimate, which would provide you with a high degree of certainty, I would need to have complete requirements and a complete design, and I would need to plan enough to allocate people to the major tasks. I could then—maybe two or three months from now—give you an estimate that would appear to be confident. However, as we began development, we would likely find out that requirements weren't perfect, and since I was being held to the estimate, I would push back on change requests or move the date as requirements were modified. We would also begin to find design decisions that didn't work as we had hoped, and we would find gaps in our designs. To deal with that, I would have to put some slack, or padding, into the estimate that would make it longer than might be really needed. As we get near the end of the development period, the requirements (which were done months earlier) would probably be getting stale and might have to be revised, causing waste.

"You see, unfortunately, Mervin, you don't get to choose between the Agile method Greg and I prefer and an imaginary world where you can get firm, realistic estimates now that you can hold someone accountable for. The world we actually live in gives us a different set of choices, and we prefer to live in that world."

Mervin sighed and shook his head, and then pursed his lips and licked them. He had an expressive face that didn't leave us guessing on his reaction: disappointment, a little anger, but resignation.

"I have to admit that what you say is consistent with the limited experience I have with development projects," Mervin sighed. "I was hoping it would be different here, and I understand that we are just beginning and it will take some time to improve. So let's try it your way. I'll put together a few options for what I want in my first two product releases, and you do your best to estimate delivery. Then we can solidify my release plan. Could we aim at having an estimate for my first release by end of next week?"

"That's fine," I said, "under one condition. You stop calling it 'your first release' and call it 'our first release,' and we'll get us that estimate." I knew this might annoy Mervin, but we had to start out this relationship on the right foot. Either we were a team, or I wasn't going to play. I could see I had annoyed Mervin, but he quickly apologized for his poor choice of words, and I was sure he got my point. Mervin wasn't ill-intentioned or territorial; he was just new to product managing software.

We were now positioned to move productively ahead. We had to help Mervin get his user stories done quickly, update the backlogs in our management tool, reprioritize, and estimate Release One all by the end of next week. Once we started performing, I was sure any lingering relationship issues between Mervin and me would soon be forgotten.

Signposts	FinServia Transformation
	• The FinServia management team gathers to discuss a conflict between Mary (in development) and Mervin (in product management). Should Mary be held accountable for firm time and cost commitments?
	• The team comes to understand that Mary's reluctance to commit isn't about *will*; it's about *reality*. Her team simply isn't capable yet of providing the detailed information Mervin wants.
	• The best possible solution, according to Mary and endorsed by Greg, is an Agile approach that delivers value steadily while building the knowledge to better forecast future delivery as well. Mary explains how her multiteam structure will coordinate development and prioritize work to succeed.
Change Guides from Mary	• **Be aware of readiness to listen and learn.** If someone isn't open (e.g., Mervin prior to this chapter), it does little good to lecture; instead, work to create conditions that are more conducive to learning.
	• **If you are confident you are doing the best that can be done, don't apologize to your partners.** Acknowledge the desire for more certainty or more rapid delivery, and give options if there are any (e.g., add more people). As leaders, our job is to take reality as it comes, together, and make improvements as quickly as we can.
Coming Up Next	We see MCCA's evolving Lean and Agile approach through the eyes of the sales force and customers, as Wes describes the events at the DocWorld conference.

ENDNOTES

1. The concept document in Toyota's product development system is described in Morgan and Liker, *Toyota Product Development System*, pages 30–31.
2. Morgan and Liker, *Toyota Product Development System*, page 51.
3. Liker, *Toyota Way*, Chapter 6.
4. Liker, *Toyota Way*, pages 56–57.

10

MCCA Engages with Its Sales Force and Customers at DocWorld: Late July

Narrator: Wes

As at any sales-driven company worthy of the epithet, our annual presence at DocWorld was an elaborate, even extravagant effort. This year, its San Diego venue was propitious, and Lynn, our president, wanted to take full advantage of the opportunity to announce to our market that we were becoming a much bigger player. Many of our existing customers routinely attended this conference; they could get some training, talk to vendors, look at new products, and participate in user advisory groups. This year, they had the added bonus of enjoying the seaside air and perhaps playing some golf on our dime. I need to learn that game someday!

WES'S SIX-MONTH RETROSPECTIVE

I had been aiming at this event since my first meeting with Lynn in February. As our team prepared for the various events and meetings, I took a moment to pull out the list of top five priorities that I had made at Neville's house that month,[1] and I was generally pleased with our progress. Much of it had come in the last two months in the framework of the Lean Team, which was working well. I took a few minutes to write down the list and my assessments, both for myself and to share with Lynn and my peers.

- **Priority 1:** Establish better linkage from sales and customer interest to our ability and intent to deliver.
  Done. We have adopted the model that Connie established for Operations (for a reminder, refer back to Figure 4.1 in Chapter 4). Both Connie and I will have a Sales Engineer role for new

opportunities; Sales will have a Sales Support function to work with salespeople on complex requests and work with the Sales Engineers. Joan, as Product Manager for the technology-based products, and Connie's designate as business lead for Operations, will "own" profitability and establish standard prices as much as possible. They will also establish exception pricing processes with ultimate appeals to Lynn and the senior team. Jack opposed this structure, as expected, preferring a much stronger role for Sales, but seemed resigned to it. I doubt we've heard the end of his opposition.

- **Priority 2:** Resolve the Chief Engineer issue. How would we configure leadership of project, product, and engineering management functions?

  Done. I chose the Microsoft Solutions Framework (MSF) model (shown in Figure 6.1 in Chapter 6) and put Hannah (as program manager), Joan (as product manager), and Phillip (as development manager) into their roles. I also added the test manager, release manager, and user experience managers for good measure.

- **Priority 3:** Deliver for our customer, San Diego National Insurance (SDNI).

  Promising. During the last two Lean Team sprints, we established the SDNI scrum team, built its backlog cooperatively with the customer, and completed our first sprint development cycle. We hadn't done the sprint demo yet (because of our absorption in getting ready for the DocWorld conference), but it was scheduled.

- **Priority 4:** Implement release management, including product vision, schedules, and planning processes.

  Promising. Joan finished the first draft of our product concept document, a 45-page Word document (yeah! substance, instead of a showy PowerPoint). We agreed on new product segmentation and tentative names (legal was vetting, although we were using them at this conference anyhow), and we had a first draft of product pricing. We now knew more about our competition than ever before, and we had a great sense of what our customers liked, thanks to Fletcher, Wilkens, and Johnson (FWJ)'s work[2] and our follow-up customer and prospect interviews. We had a very rough outline of releases for the next year that we are going to share with—and vet with—customers and prospects this week.

- **Priority 5:** Gain broad alignment about problems we faced and how we were going to solve them; build support for Lean and Agile management.

  Mostly Done. Almost all of my peers (Sasha in Finance, Cynthia in HR, Connie in Operations) and my boss Lynn are aligned and supportive. Jack Langley, in Sales, is not openly oppositional, but he certainly isn't a big supporter.

Overall, I was proud of myself and my team as we got ready for the big show.

USER CONFERENCE PREPARATION: THE PRODUCT ROADMAP AND CUSTOMER ENGAGEMENT PLANNING

It was two days before the conference was to begin, and Lynn's staff meeting was underway in her office. We were gathered around her desk early on Wednesday morning—her very strange desk/table combination, which she had inherited from her predecessor Ernie Gatherington. I had never seen such a piece of furniture before, shaped like a "T" with a short crossbar, which was the desk. Lynn sat comfortably in her usual desk chair at the top of the T, separated from the rest of us by the expanse of her desk, with us, but not completely. Ernie had reportedly loved the imperial touch; Lynn sometimes leveraged the power of the position behind the desk, and sometimes she joined the rest of us around the narrower part of the table. She even mixed it up sometimes during the same meeting, coming over and taking a table slot to increase her connection to her team. She had a bit of the imperial standoffishness that apparently Ernie had mastered, as well.

I looked around the table and surveyed my peers, including Jack Langley, Sales; Sasha Bilokov, Finance; Connie Esposito, Operations; Cynthia Evans-Goldenbogen, Human Resources. A good team, mostly. Lynn thought so too, and she said so as she moved the meeting on to deal with the upcoming conference.

"I'm excited about the conference," she said. "This team is developing into the best around, and I'm proud to show you all off. We have a great opportunity to reintroduce MCCA to our customers and the market. Let's do a great job! Jack, can you give us the highlights?"

When I joined MCCA, into an entirely new role leading product development, Lynn and Jack left "marketing" to Jack. At MCCA, Jack's "marketing" was now limited to just the promotion of the 4 Ps of marketing, with product, price, and place being my new domain. I was content with this division of responsibility, and I liked seeing Jack's enthusiasm for the job.

Jack handed out a packet of materials to each of us. He asked us to look inside and find the schedule.

"The conference begins Wednesday evening at 5:00 p.m. with a cocktail reception on the back deck of the convention center. Connie, Wes, and Sasha are attending. Then we have customer dinners: see the list for assignments, and see me if you want a change. Thursday morning, your people have booth duty; see the list and be sure they are there. Melissa is managing the booth, so let her know of any changes to schedules. Thursday at 3:00 p.m. is our customer and prospect main session, at the convention center. Lynn, Connie, and Wes all have performing parts; we run through it Wednesday at 4:00 just before the party.

"Also in your packet are the golf tee times and foursomes for Friday afternoon, the customer and prospect meetings that have been arranged, and a cell phone contact list. Questions?"

"Wes, would you go over the product strategy and messaging?" Lynn asked.

"I'd love to. We're going with the theme, *A Growing Investment: Your MCCA Partnership*. Our basic message is that our customers have made an investment in partnering with us, primarily in outsourced document-management services—image storage, image capture operations, document keying. That investment is now capable of added return due to our improving operational capabilities, thanks to Connie and her team, and our new product lines. The thought is that these days, few investments are actually growing, so this might catch some attention.

"We are using a 'money tree' motif to bring the message home. You've all seen the logo, I hope," I said, as I held up a display (Figure 10.1). "The tree has dollars for leaves, with our primary products labeled within the money leaves. You each have a pin in your package, so please wear it on your jacket lapel during the conference.

"Now I'd like to cover the product strategy and sales goals for the week. Your packet has a sheet summarizing the products shown on the tree. Sorry we don't have more details, but the segmentation of our capabilities into specific products, and their naming, was just completed last week. You're all familiar with our document capture, document storage, and data keying capabilities. We've now named them and have some tentative

FIGURE 10.1
MCCA's product line money tree.

standard pricing available. Our new capabilities, many of which have been implemented at SDNI and are ready to begin selling to others, we've named Info Linker and the MCCA Viewer. These new tools enable the integration of documents of all types, whether images, text, pdfs, or word processing, with structured information in databases. Plus, the Linker includes the user profiles and preferences, which will magnify the value of all our products."

None of this was new for this group, but it was nevertheless valuable to summarize as we went into a marathon of meeting with customers and prospects. The critical message came next.

"The product strategy is all well and good," I said, "but what matters for this week is what we want to do about it. There are several goals:

- "First, we want to position MCCA in a new way: get our market to think about us as a possible solution for a bigger set of problems than they have in the past. We want to start seeing new opportunities and have a chance to sell into them.
- "Second, by showing our innovation, we want to cast a beneficial shadow over our existing capabilities, potentially accelerating sales growth in those areas.

- "Lastly, we would like to start finding our follow-on customers to SDNI for Info Linker and MCCA Viewer. We believe we can handle two or three new customers, but they have to be the right type: in the sweet spot of the capabilities we've already built, needing no significant new capabilities beyond the generalization of what we've already done, and with implementation volumes and time frames that don't put our development path at risk."

Lynn chose to emphasize this last point. "I want to walk away from DocWorld with five or six potential clients for Info Linker," she said. "This is about finding the right customers for what we have to sell, not selling something we don't have. We are here to build this business over the next few years, and we need the right customers to help us do that. Jack, and the rest of you, as you engage with prospects, keep in mind that walking away from the wrong deal is just as important as listening closely to needs and finding the right deal."

"Thank you, Lynn," I said. "To help in your dialogues, many of the Info Linker team members will be available for meetings, including of course myself, plus Hannah, Joan, and if it gets technical, Phillip, Rico, and Jasna. Feel free to try the standard pricing, but leave open the possibility of negotiating special deals."

"And I'd like to remind everyone," Connie spoke up, "we are ready to handle new Operations business in a big way. Hosted document storage and retrieval, document imaging, data keying, and optical recognition—these are our bread and butter, we are good at these services and getting better. Our costs are coming down so the margins are good, and we have a great quality story and some strong customer testimonials to offer. As Wes said, use the standard prices, but leave open the possibility of custom pricing to close deals."

"Thanks, Connie, for keeping focus on our Operations business," said Lynn. "I'd like to see a dozen or more new prospects for Connie. With all the hype on our new product lines, we need to keep focus on what's brought us here and is paying the bills. Every new customer we get for Connie is a prospect for Wes's new products as well."

"One last item before we break," I said. "Friday morning, we are having a working session on Info Linker and MCCA Viewer. We've sent invitations to many of our existing customers, and we would welcome any prospects you find by then. We are going to do a demo of the current product in production at SDNI plus some new functionality we have built in the past few months, and we'll go over our backlog of new features to get input."

"Don't worry, Wes, I'll find you some attendees," said Jack. "Don't forget the sales group prep meeting Wednesday at 2:00 p.m. Hope to see you all there."

The stage was being set for an exciting kickoff, now we had to play our parts.

CONNIE AND WES AGREE ON SALES GUIDANCE

After Lynn's meeting, I scheduled time with Connie. I wanted to talk over our approach to working with customers, prospects, and the sales force over the next few days. To entice her, I'd promised to take her out for coffee—a surefire winner to get her off premises, since she was seriously addicted to three-shot skim lattes.

Connie and I drove about a mile down the road to the coffee shop, where I bought a caffeine fix for her and a simple decaf for myself. We settled into a wrought-iron table and two uncomfortable heavy black wrought-iron chairs on the patio outside the front door, on the sidewalk facing the parking lot. It was great to be outside on this beautiful morning.

"Connie," I started, "I wanted to review the new sales processes with you, to ensure we're on the same page. I also want to run an idea past you on how we can start to change the way we sell, from *hard* selling to *strategic* selling. You have anything you want to cover?"

"As a matter of fact, Wes, I do," Connie answered. "You're putting a lot of energy into productizing our offerings, which I appreciate. My team has followed your lead and has been productizing our operational offerings as well, and implementing the standard and exception-based pricing mechanisms, which we'll talk about. The gap I see is in product management and development plans for our bread-and-butter products, what are you calling them? DocKeeper, DocGrabber, and DocDataGrabber? These technologies are the heart of our operational offerings, and we don't have any clear vision around if we would, or how we would, sell without our operational services or a development path forward."

"Excellent point, Connie. Should we start there?" I asked.

"Since you're buying, how about you choose?" Connie replied.

"Your topic first. You're absolutely right, Connie. I've been focusing the Lean Team on our new products, not our existing ones, because that seemed to be the most pressing area. But now I see we need to have a similar focus on existing products and services. Do you have a sense of how you'd like to proceed? Seems like figuring this out is inevitably a partnership between you and me, since you have the operations and the knowledge of the products, whereas I manage the development teams."

"Actually, Wes, I do have a proposal. If you're amenable, I'd like to provide the product management for these three products, with you providing oversight and integration into the broader suite. I don't have any experience in marketing or sales and would like to learn, and this seems like the right time. Would you help me?" Connie queried.

I loved the idea and said so. My plate was full, I had little knowledge of these three core products, and I had little need to build that knowledge at the moment. So Connie volunteering to product manage the operations offering was a real gift. I promised to provide Connie and her team a framework that would fit with the rest of the product management my team was doing, Connie promised to put some next steps together, and we moved on to talk about our joint interface with Sales.

Connie's sales support and contract management function (which was also being called Sales Engineer) had started to reach its stride. The leader of that group had begun to standardize new engagements using Lean tools (including value stream mapping, checklists, and trade-off matrices) and had recently shown interest in our scrum methods.

Since I now had to create a similar function, and since our two Sales Engineers would need to work closely together on any engagement that included both a technology product and operational outsourcing (which we hoped would be most of them), I wanted to align my new role as closely as I could with Connie's, and to learn from her implementation struggles.

We came to the last topic we hoped to cover as our coffee was down to the last cooling inches in our cups. I introduced it.

"Connie, we know that one of our biggest challenges is ensuring that we make sales that are consistent with our capability to deliver. We also know that traditionally, our growth has come from selling things we didn't have, and that customer opportunities directly drove our development. We still want customer needs to drive our development, but we want that to be better planned and to be weighted more toward our marketing and product development activities, instead of simply reactively to commission-driven sales. Would you agree?"

Connie took a sip of her coffee, grimaced at how cool it had become, set it back down, and agreed.

"We have some time with the entire sales force on Wednesday, and I wonder if you might join me in setting some expectations with them. If we then set the same expectation in meetings with customers and prospects, perhaps we can start turning this ship in a more productive direction," I pleaded.

"Sure, Wes, what do you have in mind?"

"I've developed a simple, one-page summary of our products and how they should be sold. I'd like to make this the focus of one of our sales meetings and then reinforce it over the next few days as we meet with customers jointly with Sales. Here, take a look" (Figure 10.2).

I had put together a list of our offerings, ranked by sales priority focus, with suggestions on the sales approach for each. I had taken the liberty of including the operations offerings as well, so that Sales would have a complete guide. But I needed Connie's support to make this work.

"Let me show you how this works, Connie," I offered. "Take a look at the second line: Document Capture Services. The Sales guidance would be that this is a high priority to sell, that the product and our capabilities are mature, and that implementation is standardized and routine. Make sense?"

Connie studied the table intently; after a few moments (which seemed like an eternity), she looked up at me and said, "I like it. There are a couple of items I take some issue with, and some that are close, so I'll need to edit somewhat. Let's go over the major issues now, and then let's get back together at the end of the day to finish it up. I will need to confer with my sales engineering lead to be sure it's okay with him, as well."

"Lay it on me. What doesn't seem right?" I invited.

"Selling DocGrabber as a stand-alone technology for customer use. It's not ready for shrink-wrapped sales, and it's one of our competitive advantages for outsource document capture services. You'd be competing with some established products with their canned support services, licensing schemes, and branding. The effort would take away the focus of our development group from supporting our own operations effectively. It's a low priority anyway, so I'd say take it off the list."

Listening to Connie, I immediately knew she was right. I had put DocGrabber on list merely to be complete; I should have simply left it off. I immediately agreed.

"Next," Connie continued, "I need some more coffee. This is going to take a while. You have another half hour?"

I did. This time Connie bought for me, and I did a double-shot.

Product/Service	Sales Priority	Maturity	Implementation	Sales Approach
DocGrabber (document capture technology for use of customer operations groups)	Low	Immature. Just beginning to sell as product separate from our operations outsourcing service.	Next several sales will be custom, high-touch implementations. Pricing will also be custom; we will be moderately competitive. Best target: growing operations that use our DocKeeper storage and have new need to capture documents themselves.	Engage both Operations & Product Development Sales Engineering early for prequalification of opportunity.
Document Capture Services	High	Mature	Routine, standardized, well documented.	Use standard sales documentation, standard prices. Capacity is ready for small and large clients. Unusual needs to Operations Sales Engineering.
DockKeeper (document storage–capture methods mostly immaterial) Note: Includes MCCA Viewer as option.	High	Mature. Bread-and-butter product.	Routine, standardized, well documented.	Use standard sales documentation, standard prices. Capacity is ready for small and large clients. Unusual needs to Operations Sales Engineering.
			(Not all cells shown.)	
Info Linker	High	Immature	Next several sales will be custom, high-touch implementations. Pricing will also be custom; we will be very competitive for right opportunity.	We want two new customers beginning next quarter, for implementation in 1Q. Contact Product Development Sales Engineering with opportunities.
			(Not all cells shown.)	

FIGURE 10.2

MCCA Sales approach.

PARTNERING WITH CUSTOMERS AND PROSPECTS: DEMOS AND BACKLOGS

Friday morning of DocWorld started at 9:00 a.m., instead of Thursday's 8:00 a.m. start. This is an accommodation to the fact that Thursday night at DocWorld tends to be busy—and late. The hundreds of attendees self-select into three groups: the business dinner crowd, the vendor reception crowd, and the late-night party crowd. I had the fortune to fall into all three categories. On my own, I would have limited myself to dinner and a reception, but Mary had accompanied me and felt like partying.

Mary had been feeling frustrated at work of late; her almost entirely new group was struggling to learn new technologies, development processes, business areas, and especially their teammates. Yesterday had been an especially tough day; by evening, with a babysitter willing to stay late at home with the children, she felt like blowing off some steam. So we wound up on a yacht in the marina, drinking margaritas and dancing until well after midnight. To tell the truth, it was more Mary drinking and dancing than me; someone had to drive home!

In comparison with Mary's recent struggles, the last two days had gone well for me. Our core value proposition—extending our document management franchise, leveraging our outsourced hosting and operations capabilities, integrating documents with data, and customizing information delivery to people based on their needs and preferences—drew reactions ranging from mild interest, to intrigue, to enthusiasm.

This morning's meeting was aimed at our goal of finding two more customers for Info Link and MCCA Viewer, the new capabilities that we were building out at SDNI and preparing for via our new product-hardening scrum team. We gathered in our hospitality suite at the convention hotel. The room was on the twenty-eighth floor, with a commanding view of Seaport Village and the marina beyond, hidden behind curtains keeping the sun off our projection screen. I was hosting this meeting of a dozen of our largest customers and half that many new prospects, plus Lynn Hollander and several members of my team and Jack's. I was disappointed, though, not to see Jack or the group from Alpha Health, which had spent some time at our booth yesterday and had seemed interested. I wondered what derailed them.

As 9:30 came and went, our audience alternately strolled and staggered in, heading for the coffee and the fruit and pastries. By 9:45, the group was large and settled enough, so I began by thanking everyone for coming, explaining our purpose, and starting my pitch.

"Today, you will see the beginnings of a powerful new capability, one that can leverage what you already have and bring you a new level of information management. Info Link and the viewer are in production now at a large local insurance company, and we are devoting considerable resources to generalize it for broad deployment while we build out additional capabilities. We feel confident that the products are ready for installation and use at additional customers, so we are looking for two organizations that have strong needs and would like to partner in our next stage of development.

"This morning we have an interesting ninety minutes for you. First, we are going to show you a demonstration of what we have in production today. Next, we'll share our development agenda, explain how we approach our customer partnerships, and show you how you can insert your own needs into our plans. Then we'll do a brief demo of the code we've built in the last two months so you can see the progress we are making. Finally, we'll take questions and suggestions, and maybe even change our development plans in front of your eyes. At the end of the session, we hope you will understand what we have already, our intent to drive development directly from customer needs, and how you can join our team if you want to."

My goal in making this introduction and sharing our Agile development method was to start to shape a more productive and open relationship between MCCA and our customers. We knew how skeptical they were of our promises, based on surveys done during due diligence. Customers' dominant view was that our salespeople would promise anything to get the business, and once they had it, they would do little to keep it until the next relationship crisis or contract renewal/expiration time. The market's reaction was to ensure they had strong service-level commitments with biting penalties in their contracts, and to keep contracts short enough to ensure we had to come back and satisfy customers periodically.

Fortunately, our customers liked and respected our operations staff, seeing them struggling valiantly and mostly successfully to make good on the promises Sales made without their participation. Connie's work had begun to change perceptions of our company, and I wanted to keep momentum moving in that direction.

First on tap was the demonstration of the product we had already deployed. Janet Livingston, our new user experience manager who had come fresh from the help desk, had set herself up as an imaginary user in our test environment. She had also mocked up some documents and some data and reports. She showed the creation of her personal interest page, her preference settings, and how searches combined images, documents, structured and systemic data, and reports. Even though I knew the material and had seen the demo before, I was impressed, and I could tell the audience was also impressed.

Next came my favorite part of the meeting: SDNI had agreed to talk about its experience and its goals for further development. Pervez Milligan, the business lead at SDNI, talked for fifteen minutes about why he had chosen MCCA, the positives and some of the negatives of our engagement so far (he was polite about the negatives), and some of the things he would like to see improved about the product.

After Pervez's discussion, Hannah got up and described our development approach. She showed the backlog, which included our feature enhancement list and the hardening list that was aimed at making the product more easily deployable to additional customers. She pointed out several features that had been prioritized highly and thus worked in the early sprints of the next release. Then she reintroduced Janet, who demonstrated the new code in the development environment.

The net effect of the overall presentation was to show that we had something impressive already in production, we had a great vision of where we were taking it, and we were actually taking it there. From the questions and discussion following Janet's demonstration, I had little doubt that we had succeeded in telling the story. But we still had a way to go before our customers and prospects believed it.

One question from an existing customer summed up where we had been and where we needed to go for me. "Let's say we signed up with you," the questioner said, "and we find that we need something new in order to make the system work for us. What would happen to the new item? In the past, we've been promised that you would develop new items for us according to committed schedules, but the deadlines come and go with no communication or delivery. How would this new approach be any different?"

I had to think for a moment on how to answer this effectively. I didn't want to dismiss or insult MCCA's past, although I knew it had been uneven. We wanted to build on the strong elements of our past without dwelling on its gaps.

"That's a fair question," I started. "All I can do is to share with you what we've done already—which you've just seen—and our commitment to partner and be open with our customers. Here's how it would work. Let's say we are in progress of implementation, and we find something that is required for your success. I'm going to ignore any contractual issues here—for example, whether it's included in the base price, or who pays for the new feature—and let's just assume we have jointly agreed that it is required. At the time of the discovery, we would have already set the next release date, and a number of development periods making up the time frame to release. We would evaluate the criticality of the new feature, and we would reprioritize our backlog to accommodate the new work. I would expect much of our release plans to be shared with our customers and that you would have input to our prioritization process."

The questioner looked pacified but doubtful. "That sounds great, Wes, but we've heard promises before. There's a reason MCCA's request process is known as The Black Hole of San Diego."

"I didn't know that," I said, "but thanks for that information." The room twittered. "I hope you've seen enough today to be convinced at least of our sincerity. We'll have to prove to you our performance."

On that hopeful stage-setting thought, the meeting broke up, and the attendees headed out for their last DocWorld experiences or the golf course before heading back home.

Signposts	MCCA Transformation
	• As the DocWorld event approaches, Wes does a mostly positive self-evaluation of mid-year progress.
	• He unveils the product plan done in the context of the Lean Team, and he partners with Connie to set Sales expectations.
	• The big MCCA customer/prospect meeting goes well, beginning to change expectations by partnering more openly.
Change Guides from Wes	• **Stay focused on customers, prospects, and the channels to them as you drive Lean and Agile software improvements.** The purpose of these improvements, after all, is to strengthen value provision.

	• **The tight, cooperative vendor partnering that is a core part of Toyota's Lean system can work for you in two directions:** with your vendors, as with Mary's reconfiguration of the GRI relationship, and with your customers, as Wes is seeking to initiate at DocWorld. Your Lean transformation most likely should not end at the borders of your firm.
Coming Up Next	Mary's work at FinServia isn't going well. Mary describes how the project status becomes clear at the demonstration at the end of Sprint 1, and how the formal team retrospective begins to turn things around.

ENDNOTES

1. This is discussed at the end of Chapter 3.
2. Frank had given me this information just before my meeting with SDNI, in Chapter 4.

11

Sprint 1 Demo at FinServia—Dealing with Disappointment: July

Narrator: Mary

It's been two months since I wrote a chapter. It's a lot more fun to write about making great plans, executing on change, and beating back ignorant and unreasonable demands from Marketing than about the failures of my own development and team, and by inference, me. I'm hoping the setbacks we've been suffering are temporary growing pains and not foreshadows of terminal illness. Wes tells me I have to keep the faith; after all, he says, I chose a high-risk, high-gain transformation approach. However, given who I am and the situation I found myself in, I prefer to think that the *drive people* approach found *me.*

MARY'S SIX-MONTH RETROSPECTIVE

I know I should feel good for Wes; his work at MCCA seems to be going exceptionally well. We were out together last week at his document conference, where I had a chance to meet some of his coworkers and customers. I hate to admit that I feel competitive with my fiancé, it makes no sense, but somehow the fact that he is doing well with his soft-hearted, collaborative approach while I struggle with my more directive method makes me even more frustrated with my troubles so far.

Also last week, Wes shared with me his six-month retrospective.[1] His assessments of his top-five items were *Done, Done, Mostly Done, Promising,* and *Promising.* He wanted to compare report cards on the priorities we set months ago over a bottle of Pinot on Neville's back deck. I didn't want to play that game; it seemed like junior high school all over again. But he cajoled (nagged) me into doing the comparison, so I prepared my own report card.

- **Priority 1:** Deal with GRI contract; bring development back in-house.
  Done. Better outcome than I dared hope.
- **Priority 2:** Figure out development leadership.
  Not Yet. I can't bring myself to give myself an "F," so it's just incomplete. I put people into the roles, but they aren't playing them well.
- **Priority 3:** Become more Agile; change development process to scrum.
  Stormy. We have the form of a scrum process, but it's not working.
- **Priority 4:** Get alignment with Mervin.
  Tentative. Mervin has intellectually agreed with our Lean and Agile approach, and on the surface he shows me respect and patience. But after the last sprint demo, I think I'm losing him.
- **Priority 5:** Implement Agile management tool to help shape new culture.
  In Form Only. We bought a good tool and are requiring its use, so it looks like progress. But it's full of garbage and there is no enthusiasm or commitment to it.

Of my goals, only the GRI work has been an unalloyed "well done." The remaining items range from "tentative" (Mervin alignment) to "in form only" (Agile tool implementation). Project leadership establishment and change to scrum are both begun, but success is far from certain. I haven't received such poor grades since high school!

My assessment leaves me in a poor second place (out of two). Wes didn't gloat, just hugged me and encouraged me and listened to me complain. No wonder I like the guy so much!

The last two months have been consumed with the early stages of our new team, our new organizational structure, and our new development processes. We have entered our *forming* and *storming* stages, but we aren't close to the norming or performing. The two months began when Mervin gave us, in early May as promised, a list of the features he wants in our next two product releases. I then organized a series of meetings over a week's time with Mervin and his product management team and my leaders, including the four Chief Engineers, our experienced technical lead recently in from GRI (Max), and my one known quantity, Alex Fuegos, who was leading our Learning function. My staff brought along some of their people as well to the various meetings throughout the week, trying to prep ourselves for our planning work. We were able to get a good shared understanding of what we functionally wanted to create, and we gave Mervin some tentative timetables.

The second half of May and the first half of June were spent taking Mervin's feature goals and working to configure them into two releases. We put people on point, either singly or in groups, for each of the features, asking them to refine and elaborate on them in enough detail so we could determine how we would build them. We then had each of our four development teams (issuer, investor, provider, and management information system [MIS]) do rough estimates, and we asked the Development Support, Learning, and Infrastructure teams to determine support plans.

This entire effort was facilitated by our new Agile process management tool, Agilefocus. Each feature was entered into the system, given a rough order-of-magnitude sizing, and later broken down into tasks, each task estimated in four-hour segments. Each task was allocated to one of the four development teams or a support group. Each team or group established its own backlog. Two releases were configured, and as we estimated and prioritized the features, each team prioritized its backlog and assigned the tasks to the releases. Within each release, we set up the sprints; for planning purposes, we had chosen four month-long sprints followed by a one-month testing, fixing, and deployment period. The teams each evaluated their ability to get the work done in the release time frame, trading items and people among the teams to balance out the work.

TOOLS CAN HELP, TOOLS CAN HURT

At least this is what we *tried* to do. The reality of our practice would make any Agile/scrum theorist cry. I was counting on Alex Fuegos to be the overall driver of our planning because he had done an Agile project leadership before. However, Alex was also the owner/administrator of Agilefocus, and he became overwhelmed trying to implement the tool and drive the planning. Even though we had an Agilefocus consultant on-site to do training and help for a few days, the idiosyncrasies of the tool hurt us more than helped us, and after struggling for weeks, two of the development teams started doing their planning offline, one in Excel, one in an Agile planning freeware tool they downloaded from the Internet. Rather than telling Alex, who was committed to making Agilefocus work, they both just did it, and expected to do their planning themselves and reenter when they had the "answer." Alex didn't find out about this subterfuge for some time, by which time Agilefocus was so polluted and out of sync, we almost junked it entirely. Alex then spent most of the rest of the month-long planning period fighting to ensure we had a consistent plan data in our tool, instead of focusing on the nature of the plan itself and the teaching and alignment of the people involved.

At the end of month one, we did have a plan: we specified a first and second release, we had user stories split into tasks, and tasks allocated to sprints. We had a detailed estimate of the first sprint. Formally, we were ready to go, and we did. The results were disastrous. Rather than describe what went wrong, I'll show you, by relating our first sprint demo and the subsequent retrospective. Warning: this is not for the queasy!

RESULTS OF SPRINT 1 DISAPPOINTING: THE SPRINT DEMO

Sprint 1 ended in mid-July with the Sprint demo. My leadership team had finally solidified the following in early July:

- Alex (learning manager)
- Max (manager of development support)
- Dan O'Malley (chief engineer, issuer value stream, a recent hire from the Shareholder Services group of Mervin's old company)
- Jill Jacobsen (chief engineer, investor value stream, a recent hire from the systems group at Prosperity Investments, where she had been a fierce Agile advocate in a traditional development organization)
- Omar Hillegass (chief engineer, provider value stream, a recent transfer from our printing division)
- Luna Unigaro (chief engineer, management information, was a contractor we'd liked so much at Cremins that we'd hired her)

But by the time we started, the month of planning had thoroughly divided us.

Discord during the Sprint

We seemed to argue over everything:

- *Length of sprint.* Alex and I liked one month to begin with, but Jill (who was also an experienced Agile practitioner) passionately argued that this was too long, whereas Max and Luna thought it was too short. This also related to the next issue, the user stories.
- *Complete user stories.* Jill and Manish were adamant that we begin and end user story requirements, design, development, and testing within a single sprint. I never did figure out how Jill squared that with her insistence on two-week sprints. In my mind, she confused user stories with the tasks they comprised, but she denied that. Max and Luna both liked the idea, which drove them to advocate longer sprints. Alex and I were used to splitting user stories into more than one sprint when needed—we weren't "religious" about the details of methodology, we were committed to the principles.
- *Requirements versus test cases/scripts.* Although some of the team understood the idea of *test-driven development*, very few understood my distaste for doing user requirements. I pushed very hard for us to go from user story to design and build, with any details on requirements that were needed being documented directly in the test cases, preferably in automated test cases, for our unit test tools or custom-built test harnesses. Yet the harder I pushed on this, the harder almost everyone pushed back!
- *How to estimate tasks.* Jill and Manish were aligned again: they wanted to use *story points*, an arbitrary metric for measuring the amount of work for each story. I had done story points in a couple of different formats—arbitrary amounts (whatever number seemed to fit best); Fibonacci (where you can use only 1, 2, 3, 5, 8, 13, and 21); order of magnitude (where you can use only 1, 2, 5, 10, and 20)—and I wound up hating all of them. The points can work for a single team, but when a single leader (i.e., me) is dealing with multiple teams (in my case, four), story points must be comparable across the teams. Besides, in every case I've seen, the points are simply a layer of complication, since people naturally think in terms of "how long will this take?" Is a story point an hour, a day, or what? We wound up compromising: during early release planning, we'll do story points with Fibonacci, with each point about a half day. As we get more detailed and plan each sprint, we break down the stories into tasks and do actual hourly estimates and burndowns.
- *User stories only?* Jill and Manish, who I've started to think of as the zealots, argued that *only* user stories can be on the backlog; nothing

that is not of direct value to the system users. This resulted in what I thought were convoluted stories when the tasks would be much simpler. Although one could cook up a user story to encompass the task, such as "Build code compilation and environment migration processes," what's the use?

By the time we finished planning, I wanted to get rid of Manish, but Jill found him to be an ally, and to a lesser extent, some of the others found him useful. I tried hard to help our new team review the issues with rigor, to take ownership themselves, and to have their fingerprints on the decisions, even though I knew the "right" answers. At the end of the day, on most of these items, I made executive decisions to stop the endless debating, even though this left a bad taste in my mouth and I'm sure in the mouths of some of my team.

READY OR NOT, SPRINT AND DEMO

Meanwhile, the calendar doesn't wait for team alignment. Mid-June came at its own urgent pace, and we started the sprint. We reserved two conference rooms for the teams, scheduled the scrum meetings for the mornings, and established the scrum of scrums for the afternoon. Manish trained the scrum masters and observed and adjusted them in action (I guess he wasn't useless, just occasionally wrong-headed). Each team did burndown charts, and my management team met weekly to review progress and (try to) deal with issues. Things went wrong from the beginning, which everyone would see today.

Our demo was held in what the wags on our team had named "the cave." It was a far corner of our printing plant, long-empty of equipment, high ceilinged, and separated from the rest of the plant by movable partitions. One wall had been painted with whiteboard paint, whereas the other still had large metal shelving, now mostly empty. Some old tables and a motley collection of chairs comprised the furnishings. Light came solely from industrial lights on the ceiling and a half-dozen incongruous free-standing lamps that looked like they came from K-mart. At least the air felt cool and dry, despite a faint persistent odor of oil.

There were thirty people gathered to witness and evaluate our sputtering progress, including my boss Greg and most of my peers. We hadn't hidden our troubles from anyone this month, but most of our guests hadn't been paying close attention. They were now.

I kicked the demo off by welcoming everyone and setting the stage. I taped the agenda up on the wall, and described it. We were going for four hours, 8:00 a.m. to noon.

- We'd begin with a review of the plan for this sprint, so everyone understood what we were trying to accomplish.
- Then we'd look at the project tracking results: the burndown charts for the sprint overall and each team. This would show how much of the task list we had completed (surprisingly little).
- Next, we would see what we had actually accomplished: a demonstration of the actual software we had created this spring. Unfortunately, we didn't have much to show here.
- We would wrap up with questions. We didn't want to dive too deeply into why we hadn't done well in the sprint; that would come this afternoon during the retrospective. Nor did we want to get into planning for the next month; that was for tomorrow. This morning was about understanding what we had planned to do, and what was actually accomplished.

Reviewing the Plan for Sprint 1

"I'm going to start with a review of the plan for this sprint, with some help from Mervin and Alex. In this sprint," I began, "we selected what we hoped would be a balanced set of things to do. We chose high-priority items from the backlogs of each of our teams, most related to Mervin's highest-priority product goals. Mervin, would you please describe our primary goal?"

I try to get as many people involved in demos as practical. No reason for me to describe Mervin's goals, he can do it himself.

"Certainly, Mary," Mervin said. "There's a lot of activity in the market about shareholders' rights. Recent news about large companies suddenly failing, taking excessive risks, and paying CEOs excessive amounts has sparked actions to ensure better information is given to shareholders directly, and that they have mechanisms to influence corporate governance directly as well. Today, shareholders are largely limited to voting for a hand-picked board of directors; that doesn't seem to be working so well.

"We have several customers of our shareholder electronic document distribution system interested in treating this movement as a positive force, instead of fighting it. One of their needs is an online website for sharing information, taking polls and votes, and hosting dialogues and blogs. We are in a good position to get this business, since we already are distributing information for the companies to their shareholders, so we have the security features in place—many of the shareholders already have IDs and passwords to our site. We could just build out new pieces, make some incremental revenue, and go after new, like-minded customers hard."

"Excellent, Mervin, an exciting new business opportunity. Questions for Mervin?" I asked the group. Nothing yet.

"Alex, can you take it from our major goal to our things to do for each of our teams?" I conducted.

Alex walked over to the side of the room nearest the racks. He had set up four flip-chart stands, and he walked up to the one closest to the front of the room. He flipped over the blank cover to reveal a titled list. Rather than try to summarize Alex's whole talk, I'll just share his lists, and a few highlights:

- **Issuer Team**
  - Conduct polls
  - Conduct formal voting
  - Manage pages dynamically
  - Host blogs
  - *We planned to give security issuers the ability to conduct polls and voting, host blogs, and manage parts of the website more dynamically.*
- **Investor Team**
  - Discussion boards (hosted and not)
  - View research (free for now)
  - Alerts to polls, votes, information
  - *Investors would be able to use discussion boards to chat with each other and save the conversations so others could read them; a discussion board variant that could be hosted by the issuer (something like an Ask the Management feature) would also be created. Investors would also be able to view free research (for-sale research would come later), and be alerted to new activity on the site.*

- **Provider Team**
  - Upload research
  - Manage own page(s) dynamically
  - *The only providers we targeted were the research providers. We'd have to build pricing and payments in soon.*
- **Management Information Team**
  - Report on polls and votes
  - Report on Investor usage of new features
  - *Management information seemingly had little to do: just provide reports on the new features.*

Alex then summarized his list: "There were a few other things on the plates of each team as well, mostly production support items, since we are not big enough yet to split that completely apart from development. When we started the sprint, we had been planning for one month, so we had some directions and plans for the scope and architecture of the items, but not nearly enough. Ideally, by the time we enter this stage of development, we would have spent several additional months preparing, doing the technical design work at the same time Mervin was doing the product planning—in fact, doing both at the same time, as one effort. But that wasn't possible due to the newness of this group. Bottom line, we entered the sprint with a much higher level of risk of unknowns than we would normally prefer.

"I don't mean this as an excuse," he concluded, "although as you'll see, we could use some of those. Instead, I'm telling you this, as the demo audience, so you can understand the results you are going to see, and also understand that it will get better. So let's look at the results we accomplished. Dan, you're up."

(Lack of) Accomplishments of Sprint 1

Dan O'Malley, our new chief engineer for the Issuer Team, had volunteered to take this part of the demonstration. He began by asking the audience if they were familiar with burndown charts. Most were, but some were not, so Dan explained. He approached the white-painted wall in front and began drawing (Figure 11.1).

"The burndown chart lets us monitor, daily, the progress of the sprint," Dan explained, drawing lines and labels as he spoke. "The horizontal axis shows time remaining in the sprint—in this case, the number of days and

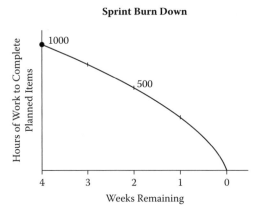

FIGURE 11.1
Burndown chart example.

weeks. The vertical axis shows how many hours of work we believe we have left to complete the items we slotted for the sprint.

"For example, on the first day of the sprint, we might have 1,000 hours of work to do." Dan placed a dot at 4 weeks, 1,000 hours. "If all goes perfectly to plan, at the end of the sprint, we're done." He placed another dot at 0 weeks, 0 work. "And in the perfect world, our estimates were just right, and we steadily complete tasks throughout the sprint." Dan drew a line between the two dots he had put on the chart. "Finally, at any point during the sprint, say at week 2, the points on the chart show hours remaining; at two weeks, in this chart, we would have 500 hours left." He finished by putting hash marks on the burndown line for each week, and writing in the 2 week, 500 point.

"Our plan was to do most of the 11 items Alex has on the charts," Dan said. "We didn't think we could finish them all. Even if we had unlimited people, some of the items require more than a month of elapsed time. We determined how many people would be working on the sprint, assumed six good hours per person per day, estimated tasks in detail, chose which we thought we could do given our staffing, and drew out our projected full-sprint burndown. Please find the charts in your handout package (Figure 11.2). Each subteam also had their own burndown projections.

"You can see that in total, we got slightly less than half the work done we had hoped. As of the last day of the sprint, we still had 2,000 hours remaining to accomplish what we thought we could do last month. The good news is that we are feeling much more confident about those 2,000 hours, and assuming that set of tasks remains our highest priority going

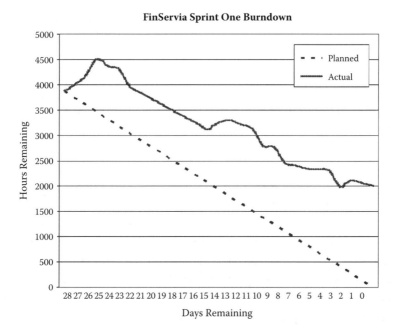

FIGURE 11.2
FinServia Sprint 1 burndown.

into the second sprint, we don't anticipate issues with getting them done in Sprint 2."

"Dan," Greg asked, "I know Mary said this isn't the time for retrospectives, but I won't be at the meeting this afternoon and am curious now. Could you give a brief narrative of what happened?"

Dan looked over at me for guidance, and I gave him a nod indicating he should go ahead and answer the question.

"I'll do my best, Greg, with the caveat that these are my own observations and I can't speak for the whole team," Dan replied cautiously. "I'll ask them to add whatever color they'd like after I finish.

"You can see that for the first few days of the month, our projected hours to finish actually went up, even though theoretically they should go down by about 140 hours per day. The overall trend line hides the underlying facts, which were that some of the teams and tasks were making good progress, while others, as they dove into the work, found significant underestimates on some tasks. Some of that was due to not fully understanding the work to be done, but probably more was because of our inefficiency in getting the work done. We have a lot of new people in new roles, and we would bump into each other, ask the wrong people the wrong questions, or assume ways to get things done, which were not right."

"Could you give me an example, Dan?" Greg followed up.

"Sure," Dan agreed. "Not to pick on Max," he said, giving Max a nervous glance, "but just by way of explanation. My team had several features to build, most of them involving links to third-party software we were integrating: polling/voting software, and a blogging system. Even though our job was mostly integration, we did need several new database fields. We assumed we could work on our features, and when we needed a field, we would ask Max's database administrators, or DBAs, and they'd simply add it to the development environment.

"However, Max already had a process in place from GRI, which required the application teams to identify *up front* all the new and changed fields for a release. The fields had to be documented in a certain format, and then data analysts—who are a separate team of people from the DBAs—would incorporate the new items into a logical model. That model would then be reviewed and approved and then handed off to the DBAs to be transformed into a physical model for additional review and approval. Finally, the DBAs would make the changes to the development environment, test them, and release to the application teams so coding on the release could begin. Changes to the database then required a formal change order, which would flow through a similar path, with physical updates to the database coming monthly."

Max now spoke up for himself. "It's not that we couldn't make faster changes," he said. "It's that we *didn't* make faster changes. Unfortunately, because we're all so new to each other, and because we had so much to plan so quickly, we never discussed the data engineering process up front; I just assumed I'd get a list of all the data needs for the release up front, while the other Chief Engineers (CEs) started trickling them over to me a few fields at a time. At first, I pushed back and demanded the application developers generate the standard documents I'm used to. Eventually we worked it out, at least for now, but we lost a lot of time trying to figure out how to do just-in-time data engineering."

Dan picked up the dialogue: "This is just one of several issues that arose. We had problems with getting developers and testers proper access to systems; we had problems building new test environments; we had problems punching holes in the GRI firewalls to access the providers of our voting and blogging software—in other words, if it could go wrong, it did."

During all of Dan's explanations, I was watching Greg. His face isn't emotive, so it's hard to tell what he's feeling. I'm sure he was disappointed and perhaps a bit scared, but to look at him was to see confidence. I appreciated that about now!

Greg thanked Dan and Max for their explanation and turned to me. "Mary, I know this is new for you—building a whole new development team, learning a new development approach for a lot of people. For those of you who don't know Mary well yet, she usually sets unreasonably high standards and then exceeds them, so this has got to be killing her. But we all need to work through this early set of issues, stay positive, surface and talk through the problems, and keep our focus on generating valuable code at a steady, reliable pace." Looking directly at me, Greg asked, "I'm assuming we coded *something* this month?"

"We certainly did, Greg," I assured him. "We have several items to show today. Can I check first to see if you would like to look more deeply at the burndowns of the individual teams, or do you want to go right to the code demos?"

I couldn't tell the sense of the group from the informal responses, so I asked for a show of hands. Most wanted to go right to the code, so it was decided. I handed the meeting off to Jill, the chief engineer for the Investor Team, to conduct the demo.

Code Demo for Sprint 1

Jill was an articulate, even insistent partisan for following defined Agile techniques within our technology team, but she had a mild fear of public speaking. I hadn't known this when we hired her (nor had I fully understood her zealous nature); the fear didn't seem to cripple her, and unless one knew of it, it wouldn't have been noticeable. She dealt with the fear by intense, elaborate preparation.

"Today, we're going to try to execute a business scenario that touches on many of the code elements we've been working on," Jill said. "The scenario is outlined in your information packet—it's the pink sheet of paper. We've created a test company, ABC Computers, which is already a customer of ours for distributing documents to shareholders and others. ABC's management is eager to try out participative shareholding, and it has selected an issue on which to base an experiment. Today ABC makes primarily large-scale server computers; should it enter the market for netbooks? Or should it stick to its knitting and avoid taking on new risks at this time?

"Our demo will begin with the shareholder services group at ABC creating a new subsite dealing with the issue. The site will be linked to our main ABC site, and also to ABC's own website. It will pose the issue and provide links to background information: documents generated by ABC, independent research on the netbook market and on ABC's strategic choices, and blogs from ABC staff members and a netbook user that ABC's marketing department recruited. Unfortunately, we were unable to complete the discussion board integration, so we won't be showing that today. There will also be a link to the poll questions, in which ABC's shareholders will be presented with a ten-point questionnaire. Finally, shareholders will be able to see the results of the poll when it is complete, and they'll be provided an e-mail to notify them that the results are ready, along with an interpretive comment from ABC's Marketing Department.

"The grand finale is the management information reports. For this demo, we built some reports that show the results of the poll, segmented in a number of different ways: large vs. small shareholders, and those who have taken advantage of the learning resources on the site vs. those who went directly to the poll."

Jill proceeded to conduct the demo for the group. She introduced several developers and testers, who began to show what we had built. Almost every step involved workarounds that were visible to the audience, awkward user interfaces, unconnected steps, crashes and restarts, and inconsistent data:

- The user interface for the Shareholder Services Department was incomplete, although its promise was evident. Just by picking from menu items, even a novice would be able to create a new subsite, set up the control information (e.g., how long would the voting be open), and add the links to research, blogs, and polls.
- The linking to the blogs worked well, because we had made an agreement with a blog provider that had a simple connection mechanism.
- The link to the polling software didn't work at all today, even though it had worked last week; we had to show the polling software separately.
- The management information reporting was mocked up because we hadn't been able to combine the polling results information with the shareholder data (large vs. small holder) or the site activity data (did user view, e.g., the research, before voting?).

It was one of the most difficult demos I had ever sat through. I could tell it was torture for Jill; thankfully, Greg and the rest of my peers were encouraging throughout, focusing on the ideas and the code that did work, asking questions carefully to distinguish what was simply not yet complete from what was intended before offering opinions on design or function. After an hour and a half of stumbling through our software, I wrapped up the meeting and we broke for lunch, before resuming in a smaller group with our retrospective.

SPRINT 1 RETROSPECTIVE[2]

Suspecting how badly the demo would go, I had decided not to provide lunch; I figured the sooner the group broke up, the less the collective dwelling and moping would be. Thankfully, the room emptied quickly, and we left Margaret free to prepare for the retrospective. Wes had insisted on coming over and taking me out to lunch, a rare event for me; he knew that I would need some cheering up. We drove over to Mission Beach and bought smoothies at a stand on the boardwalk, and drank them while walking barefoot at the intersection of the land and the water. We didn't have much time before we had to head back to where we hoped we would find our shoes (they were still there), and I had to head back to the intersection of hope and chaos.

Margaret Plans and Facilitates the Retrospective

Margaret, our GRI Agile culture consultant, had asked to lead the retrospective. I happily agreed; I wanted to participate, and I wanted Alex to participate as well. At this point in our evolution, I wasn't sure anyone else had the skills to lead such a critical event. Margaret and I had talked through how the retrospective should be done, and we had set a four-hour agenda for this afternoon.

We had two separate but related objectives: the first was to come up with concrete steps, supported by the group, to improve over the course of the next two sprints; the second was to evolve the culture one step farther along the path toward a self-sufficient, open, respectful, problem-solving culture.

The agenda was up on the wall on a large poster (the capitalized titles were on the wall; the explanation following was not, it's from me to the readers).

1. **Set the Stage.** We would get the group settled and ready for work.
2. **Gather Data.** The demo this morning had provided much of this, from a results perspective, but we needed to get the group (I hesitate to call it a *team* yet) on the same page regarding some process items.
3. **Generate Insights.** The group would work through an exercise to learn from our experiences over the past month.
4. **Decide What to Do.** Come up with a small number of things we can do to make the next demo bearable.
5. **Close.** Review how the retrospective went and determine what we want to do at the end of the next sprint.

The next sections describe how each topic was covered (though as we'll see, we only finished the first three items on the agenda).

1. Set the Stage. Right at 1:15 p.m., Margaret kicked the meeting off (we were trying to instill a cultural norm that meetings start on time). Most of the twenty invitees were here—the four chief engineers, Max and Alex, Manish, our infrastructure lead, our facilities manager, Mervin and two of his team from product management, and half-a-dozen development, analyst, and testing leads from the development teams. The attendees were seated at scattered tables, four to a table.

Margaret described our objectives and the agenda and then proceeded right into the first item, Set the Stage. She made sure we all knew each other; the group was still so new that we couldn't take that for granted. Then she asked each person to say one word describing how they were feeling right now, and she started pointing at people.

"Embarrassed."

"Anxious."

"Tired."

"Stressed."

"Hopeful" (that was Manish).

"Frustrated" (Mervin).

"Curious."

"Angry."

"Excited."

"Grateful."

"Worried."

"Pass" (which Margaret allowed).

"Interesting," Margaret summarized. "A lot of stress and worry, but also some hope. My sense is that none of us is proud of or satisfied with what we've done in the past month, but we are hanging in there together and want to try to make it better. Is that right?" she asked the group.

Mervin jumped right in. "I think that's right, Margaret. We're building a new team, using new processes, and we're trying to address a big opportunity in a new company that needs the success. We set some goals and we didn't meet them, and none of us likes that, but we see potential."

"Well said, Mervin, thank you. I'd like to try something with this group, a quick way to tell if we are all on board. Can you give me a thumbs up if you agree with what Mervin just said, a thumbs down if not, and a simple fist if you are neutral on it?"

I looked around the room along with the rest of the assemblage and saw mostly thumbs up; no thumbs down.

"Great, then we have our emotional temperature—frustrated with the past, tentatively hopeful for the future," Margaret said, and wrote, FRUSTRATED, TENTATIVELY HOPEFUL on a flip chart. "Let's go on. One more thing I'd like to do to help set the stage is develop some working agreements. Do you all know what they are? Thumbs?"

Most thumbs were up, but a few were down. Margaret took a moment to explain. "Working agreements are a small number—maybe five—that set expectations among us on how we want to behave in this meeting. For example, Mary gave me one that she would like to propose." Margaret approached the flipchart, titled a page Working Agreements, and wrote, *Generosity of Spirit*. "Mary," Margaret asked me, "could you explain?"

"It means each of us should assume that all of the rest of us are well-intentioned—we should assume the best of each other. If we do that, and we hear or see behavior that appears to be ill willed, petty, or back stabbing, we need to check it out and confirm it, because that doesn't make sense. Or if someone seems critical to us, we need to assume they mean well by it—they want to help us succeed, not tear us down." This was my favorite working agreement ever. I had tried with Margaret to make it a given, based on me being the boss, but she thought it would be more effective if I were treated as just another member of this group.

"Thank you Mary. Let's take suggestions from the floor, see what we have, then discuss and agree," Margaret said. After several minutes of discussion and some more thumbs up/thumbs down, we had our working agreements:

- Generosity of spirit.
- Cell phones and laptops off.

- Everyone contribute; OK for leader to randomly call on people; OK to pass.
- Agree on communication to others at the end; honor that (what happens in the room stays in the room, except as we agree).
- Decisions based on facts and arguments, not positional power.
- Speak up if not in agreement; silence implies support.
- Focus on improvements, not blame or criticism.

I was pleased that my "generosity of spirit" suggestion was accepted. The others combined to make up a good framework, not unusual for a meeting of this type. The positional power agreement was a tricky one, but I felt it was okay for the group to believe it, even if it wasn't really true.

2. *Gather Data.* As we moved into "Gather Data," Margaret reminded the attendees of the material we had reviewed in the morning and then suggested an exercise to refresh us on the major events of our sprint. She brought the attention of the room to a timeline she had taped up on the wall (Figure 11.3). "We're going to work together to identify and talk about the major events of the sprint," Margaret explained. "I'd like each of you to think about events that were important to you, that shaped our results, and that had practical and especially emotional impacts. Take a few minutes to jot down the most important events to you. When you're done, we'll take turns putting the events up on the timeline, and by doing this, we'll see how each of us experienced the sprint."

"Let me give you an example," Margaret said, and she went on to do a *tool demonstration*—a facilitative leadership technique that helps participants learn how to participate effectively. "As a consultant, I wasn't here for many of the important events, but one I thought important happened at one of Mary's staff meetings during the planning month. We were deciding how to do estimating, with Jill and Manish arguing for using story points, and Mary insisting that that we make the story points comparable across teams by converting them to hours. The discussion got to the point of discomfort quickly, and we seemed stuck, until Mary pulled rank and

FIGURE 11.3
Retrospective timeline.

decided how we were going to proceed. I'm not sure if this was a positive or negative event, but for me, it set some ground rules and set some precedents: that we would talk through issues, listen to each other as best we could, problem solve if possible, but that at the end of the day, Mary would make the final decisions when needed. I'm going to call this event, 'Mary makes the estimating decision.'"

Margaret wrote that title on a card in large, legible letters and placed it in the Prior Month column.

"Do we talk about this now?" Jill asked.

"Let's hold off on that until we have the cards completed," Margaret directed. "We'll talk though all the major events in context then."

"Sure," Jill said. "I can wait. Should we start writing?"

"Excuse me, Margaret," I interrupted. "I would like to say something now."

"Alright, Mary. The floor is yours."

Although I knew that retrospectives could be valuable, and I obviously thought that this one was necessary, that didn't mean I liked them. I am not, by nature, an introspective person; I don't often contemplate my own behavior. Retrospectives can easily go wrong, and they can make things worse, particularly if you're trying to deal with the true items that need to be examined and resolved and the group isn't ready for open dialogue. I wanted to take this opportunity to help keep this one on track.

"I'd like to point out a few things about the incident Margaret just noted," I addressed the room. "I didn't know Margaret was going to identify this one, and we will get a chance to talk about it in more detail if we choose. But I'd like to be sure as you all look at this event, and as you identify and note other events, you look through the lens of our agreements. If you are generous of spirit, you will acknowledge that all of us were trying to do the right things, respecting each other's views, and making decisions based on what we thought best for the project and each other. And think about what that event means for our future; in this case, for example, do you like the way I took ownership and made the decision, or do you find this overbearing? As long as the discussion is in line with our agreements, we can have a productive session here today."

Jill, who had been involved in the incident as well, couldn't resist speaking now, even though Margaret had counseled to wait. I'm glad she spoke up. "Thank you for saying that, Mary. I never for a moment imputed you with anything but good motives, and extending that assumption space to all of us is a great idea. Although," Jill smiled as she said this, "I still think you were wrong." Turning to Margaret, Jill asked, "Shall we continue?"

With the expected interaction mode successfully clarified, Margaret directed the room to take five minutes and write out their cards. It was quiet while people thought and wrote. Being the subject of the first card, I thought carefully about what cards I wanted to contribute. This idea of emotional content struck me; which events merited noting and discussion?

Margaret had brought along an attention-getting device: a duck quacking whistle she had saved from a duck-boat tour in Philadelphia. She quacked and regained the room's attention. "Let's begin," she said. "Here's how this is going to work. We start at the beginning, and we'll take cards in chronological order. If you have a card to post, volunteer it; walk up to the wall, tape it up, and describe the event and what it meant to you. Anyone else who has a similar card gets up as well, brings their card to the wall, and tapes it up with the first card. We then talk as a group about how we felt about the event, what it meant to us, and how it shaped the results, for better or worse."

"Do we also note anything about what we learned from the event, or what we want to learn about it in the future?" Omar queried.

"Well, we need to get through this in about an hour," said Margaret. "After this, we'll draw out insights and decide what to do in the future. We're going to do an exercise called Helping and Hindering, in which we'll identify things that helped us and prevented us from succeeding. How about you each take a set of cards—green for helping or do more of, and red for hindering or do less of—and jot down whatever occurs to you while we do the history. Make sense? Thumbs?"

Thumbs up, so Margaret distributed the colored cards.

We began with the planning month and worked our way through the sprint. It started out slowly and tentatively, but as we touched on sensitive issue after sensitive issue, we seemed able to talk about them with more distance and eventually even humor. It was fascinating to hear about which events were important to whom, and why; we all learned about what had happened. Some of the events that were deemed important, including some into which I had no visibility at all, included:

- **From Jill's test manager:** After the first week of development, Jill sent her an e-mail asking her when she would be done testing the code so far. This surprised her; she hadn't planned on doing any testing on such a small amount of software. Her return e-mail saying so resulted in an agitated Jill coming over to her cube and insisting she get the code to the test environment and get it tested! The skeptical test manager convinced the developers to move the code, and she tried to test it. She couldn't, because the code hadn't been written to be testable after just a week. At first, the tester thought Jill was being crazy, but now she realized that demanding testing as soon as possible after code is laid down forces developers to build for testability, and it gets the code into a stable state as quickly as possible.

- **From Mervin:** At the end of the second week, Mervin had given guidance to the Sales group not to commit to any dates on the functionality we were building. He had been hoping to be able to commit to our release date, but after seeing the burndown chart "burning up," he thought better of it. The conversation revealed appreciation from Mervin on the visibility we had provided, his disappointment with our lack of progress (no surprise there), my disappointment that he hadn't shared this with me at the time, and our need to get him a decent date as soon as we could so we'd have Sales guidance.

- **From Max:** In the middle of week three, Max had, in his words, "caved" on the data design issue. Up to that point, Max had been handing out the data design templates that GRI had required and demanding that teams follow his rules. Some of the teams complied, but therefore couldn't expect to get any database changes this sprint; Jill told her developers to store data in the file system if they couldn't get Max to move. Jill then went to Mary and asked for help, and Mary got Max and Jill together to try to work it out. Ultimately, Max agreed to make routine database changes within a day of request, and to shoot for within an hour. Unfortunately, his team was not set up to comply with those service levels, and almost no database work was done in Sprint 1.

- **From a systems analyst on the Issuer Team:** Just a few days ago, as the sprint came to an end, one of the developers came into her cube and asked her to sign on to the development environment. There, on the skeleton of the new Issue Discussion page was a button for Express Your Opinion. She clicked on the button, and a new browser instantly opened. There she saw a two-question poll on an MCCA-branded website, which said, "Is this cool? Yes, No." It was a rare light of success in what had been a dreary development sprint, and it gave her hope.

Margaret had to work hard to keep to time limits. We wound up going for an hour and a half, half an hour over. At the end, we had been able to talk through, for just a minute or two, one event from each person (*Everyone contribute* item) and a dozen more.

In announcing the break, Margaret asked attendees to walk up to the timeline and review it, and to think about the next exercise: identifying "helpers" and "hinderers," and making plans to do more of the helpers and address the hinderers as best we could.

3. **Generate Insights.** The mood seemed good during break. The group talked with each other in twosomes and small groups about the events, scanned the timeline, and some began to talk about the upcoming exercise. At the appointed time, Margaret quacked, and the group reassembled.

Margaret directed the room's attention to the front wall, where she had created a display in masking tape and signs during the break (Figure 11.4). She described the exercise, which is one of my favorites. It combines "generate insights" and most of "decide what to do" in a single pass. It also implements several principles of facilitative leadership: it has the group doing the work for itself, it helps ensure rigor in the discussion and decision making, and it is time efficient.

Margaret explained that each table should work together for 30 minutes to create Hinder/Help cards. Each table had been stocked with sticky pads, red for hinder, green for help. The first 5 minutes would be allocated for each person to think and create cards, and then 25 minutes for the tables to talk over the cards, eliminate duplicates, and prepare to share with the rest of the room. Continuing her use of the "Mary makes the estimating decision" event from earlier, she did a Helps card that said, *Senior Leadership Willing to Make Decisions*, and posted it in the Helps column on the wall.

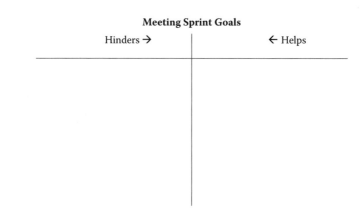

FIGURE 11.4
Helps and hinders.

"In practice," Margaret said, "I would have to vet this card with the people at my table. Together we might modify my card, or we might even decide that a better statement would be a Hinder, such as *Senior Managers Dictating Process.* The table might even submit both cards. Everyone understand?" She held out her thumbs and got thumbs up.

"Take five minutes and write out your cards. At the next quack, pick a table leader, and consolidate your cards. Go!" Margaret directed.

The room went quiet, except for the scratching of the markers on the Post-its. Margaret wandered from table to table, checking on people's work, giving hints, insisting on clarity, and being generally encouraging. After five minutes, we moved to the consolidation phase, with Margaret still doing her supervision. A half hour passed, Margaret gave us a break, and then we came back together to see what we had come up with.

Margaret called first on Omar, the chief engineer for the Provider value stream. Omar walked up to the display on the wall and began sticking his cards to the wall, as Margaret instructed. Helpers came first; Margaret always wanted hear the good stuff first.

"*Clear Product Direction,*" Omar began. "We knew what we had to do, and when we had questions, Mervin and his staff were accessible. *Scrum meetings.* We mostly kept to 15 minutes, and by the end of the first week, we had a good rhythm going." Omar listed another few items, then came to the Hinders.

"Unfortunately, we had a lot more Hinders than Helpers," Omar explained, and he started to post each one, while describing them a bit. "First we have

- "**Lack of Legal Support**: We needed to do an agreement with the polling and voting service provider, but it took two weeks to figure out who would do our legal support.
- "**Responsiveness of Computer Support**: Getting our development tools installed, and building out development and test environments consumed way too much of my time and my team's time.
- "**Flexibility of Facilities Group**: This came from someone on the MIS team, who wanted to rearrange their cubes into a circle with a meeting table in the middle, but Facilities wouldn't allow it.
- "**New Teams**: Our discussion on this was that few of us have worked together before, so we had to continually discover and negotiate what we expected. An example was a systems analyst and a developer; the developer expected very detailed coding instructions, whereas

the analyst provided just a high-level story and expected to work through the details verbally together.

- "**Data**: We'll just leave it at that."

As Omar finished up, each of the other four tables sent their spokesperson up to post their cards and explain them. All the cards were posted; the duplicates were simply pasted on top of or near their siblings. When all the cards were up, which took the better part of an hour, Margaret selected three "volunteers" to sort the cards into actionable categories. She chose Mervin, Jill, and Max—no doubt strategically chosen to have these three leaders have their fingerprints all over the outcome. Margaret joined the three at the board, and they worked through most of the break.

"Mervin," Margaret began when most of us were back in our seats, "please summarize the Helpers."

Mervin stood and walked to the board. He had taken the 20 or so cards and organized them into 5 groups.

"I had the easy task," he said. "For some reason, there are a lot fewer Helpers than Hinders." Mervin made something between a smile and a sneer. "We should continue or do more of these things. Anyway, here's what we found helpful:

- "*Scrums and burndowns.* Most of us believe this is a good fundamental approach, we know where we are, even though we might not like it, and the daily meetings force us to talk with each other more than we might otherwise.
- "*Small, tight teams.* Our CE structure worked well: it helped us to have development, analysis, project management, and testing all reporting to one leader who is focused on customer value.
- "*Product vision.* We have a clear idea of what we need to do for the next several months, and the product managers and development teams are working well together, formally and informally, every day.
- "*Focus on delivery.* All of us are trying to find the best way to deliver the product, without taking shortcuts that would compromise quality or longer-term success.
- "*Team members, not contractors.* We're relying on our people, we're growing their knowledge and capabilities, and we're using consultants and contractors only for teaching and temporary needs.
- "*Openness.* There has been a lot of conflict as we've begun to learn to work together, but we haven't tried to hide it.

- *"Team member expertise.* We have hired a strong group of people with what seem to be the right set of skills, once we figure out how to deploy them!"

Margaret thanked Mervin and asked the room if anyone had something to add to the list. The group seemed satisfied, so Margaret moved on the Hinders. Jill took Mervin's place at the board.

"As you all know, we had a lot of things to overcome this month. We did our best to put our Hinders into actionable categories. Why don't I just begin," Jill said, as she pointed to the categories one by one of where we had difficulties:

- *"Inaccurate estimating.* The initial estimates were done mostly by people other than those doing the work, and they've proven to be overoptimistic. Even though some of us think we've done a lot of great work this month, we wind up looking like we've failed.
- *"Confusion of total time with elapsed time.* Some of the stories in the sprint were just not possible to do in one sprint. We either need to break the stories down more, or we need to spread some over more than one iteration. The reporting integration is a good example: there was just no way to set up integration across our environment and the vendor's in a single month.
- *"Arguing over methods.* We included use of Agilefocus in this category. We each come to this job with experience and preferences, and for better or worse, they vary. We've already talked about the data and requirements issues, and those are just the most prominent of a lot of this. We're going to need to settle down into some accepted patterns, or we'll never get anything done.
- *"Poor support from systems infrastructure and facilities.* It took way too long to get changes from these two areas. We entered the sprint without support lined up, and we surprised them with the amount and urgency of our demands. From now on, we need to include these groups in our planning.
- *"Inadequate code and build control.* The existing infrastructure from GRI never contemplated Agile development. We need to continually build, regularly move code from development to test environments, and work on code in several areas at once as we do end-to-end stories instead of working serially on code modules.

"That's what we came up. It's a lot of issues, but we think it's a manageable list, although some of the items are going to be difficult to address," Jill concluded.

As she had done with Mervin, Margaret thanked Jill and asked if there were any disagreements or missing items. Luna, our chief engineer for Management Information, who had been quiet most of the day, volunteered an item.

"Our table had a card labeled *Inadequate Meeting Schedule*," she said. "We thought it was an important issue, but I don't see it reflected on your list, Jill."

"We did see that card," agreed Jill. "But we didn't include it on our list. Is it important enough to be added?" she asked.

"We thought so," Luna answered. "We have the daily scrums for each team, throughout the morning, and then the scrum of scrums in the afternoon. Most departments have their own staff meetings weekly, and we have Mary's staff meeting on Friday morning. But we don't have a regular forum in which we can deal with issues like the ones we are talking about. The scrum of scrums typically doesn't have Mary and enough of the CEs present, whereas Mary's staff meeting is missing the scrum masters and other key leaders."

There were murmurs of agreement around the tables, and then Manish, our Agile consultant from GRI, spoke up. "Luna, perhaps the issue is broader than not having the right meetings. Perhaps we are hindered by *not being good enough problem solvers*. We are trying to implement many Lean and Agile concepts, but we perhaps we haven't focused enough on one of Lean's central tenets: to arrange operations so that variance from the expected is immediately evident, and to solve the problem that caused the variance quickly. We are in the process of creating what is *the expected*, but perhaps we should work to be able to better solve problems created by incomplete *expected* and variances from what we *do* expect."

"Manish," I asked, "what exactly are you proposing?" I continued to find Manish's methods orientation annoying. I wish he would just say what he wanted us to do!

"Perhaps," Manish elaborated, "we have missed some key training and process elements—in particular, PDCA,[3] A3 problem solving, and *obeya*.[4]"

Dan O'Malley, the Issuer Team CE, said, "Excuse me, before you answer that, what the heck are you talking about? I hate it when you use those abbreviations and Japanese words!"

"Oh, sorry," said Manish. "I can get wrapped up in the lingo. *PDCA* is plan, do, check, act—a simple but effective problem-solving technique. It basically means study a problem, fix it, monitor it, and adjust to what you see in monitoring. An *A3* is a one-page format for summarizing a problem and its solution, and it typically includes an informal process of socializing the problem and proposed solutions, which helps get decisions made well. A3 is actually a size of paper used in Japan, a bit larger than our standard 8½ × 11. Both PDCA and A3 are central to Lean manufacturing."

"Thank you, Manish, now that we've taken out the jargon, you can answer Mary's question," said Margaret. "What are you proposing we do?"

Manish was more specific now. "We have a new group, with lots of problems, which we've done an excellent job of surfacing. It may well be that our critical path to success is getting better at solving the problems we find, which could include some training on PDCA, a better problem solving tool, like the A3, and as Luna asks, a new or different forum, in particular, an *obeya*."

"Enough with the jargon!" Dan exclaimed. "Obeya?"

"Sorry, Dan," Manish apologized again. "I'll try to be more careful to explain. *Obeya* is simply a room in which each scrum team keeps its charts and plans, making visual the team's progress and problems. Instead of having each team with its own room as we do now, we could combine the rooms into a single large space, and then have a periodic senior meeting in the room as well. Mary and her team, plus selected leaders of each of the component teams, could walk from team area to team area, getting current on plan and problems, and using PDCA and A3 to help crystallize and solve issues."

Any doubts I had about Manish's value evaporated. It was so obvious! I had gotten so tangled up in our Agile software processes and debates over it that I had put the critical larger cultural lessons of Lean on the back burner. I had fallen right into the trap of using the processes and tools and not building the supporting cultural foundation of standardized work (wherever possible) and problem solving.

"How about we put up one more Hinder?" I asked. "*Inadequate Problem Solving.* Does that do it for everyone?" By this time, everyone knew I was looking for a thumbs up or thumbs down, and they were up.

I could see that Margaret was pleased. "Great job, team. All we have left now is to put some details to exactly what we plan to do about these Helpers and Hinders, who is going to do it, and when. Unfortunately," she said, as she looked at her watch, "it's 5:00, and it's going to take us at least another hour to finish. Do we want to keep going, or reconvene tomorrow? What do your schedules look like?"

I couldn't stay tonight. I had to pick up my kids up in a half hour. "How about we finish over lunch tomorrow?" I asked. "I'll buy pizza, and we'll wrap this up. How many could make it tomorrow? Thumbs?"

There was a rush to look at Blackberries and iPhones, and then most of the thumbs came up. Mervin apologized for not being able to attend, but he said to go ahead without him, he was comfortable with the direction.

"OK," Margaret said. "Tomorrow at 11:30, right here. Plan on an hour and a half. We need to decide what to do, and then do an after-action review on this retrospective itself. Have a good evening."

It had been a long day, but a productive one, I thought. It had started badly with the project review and the demo, but then it got better as we worked our way through the retrospective. Manish's insight had turned the corner for me, from something approaching despair to hope. Of course, we were going to have problems, I had blown up the organization completely and we were starting over. I knew that intellectually, but the perfectionist in me hadn't let me emotionally reflect that. Now that I had a way forward, I was more accepting of the mish-mash of problems and issues facing us. How simple that we should value our problems and become better at solving them! And how embarrassing that I had not recognized the reality of our situation and the way out! I guess that's what teams are for—did I call us a team?

Signposts	FinServia Transformation
	• FinServia development holds its first demo. Less than half the planned work was completed, and what did work was rough but not a total failure.
	• The group holds a retrospective and identifies factors that help and hinder their success, and they make some plans to improve.
	• Mary is hopeful that the discussion in the retrospective and the action items identified will help the group forge into a more effective team.
Change Guides from Mary	• **The sprint demo, as an integrating event and a visual status report, is an irreplaceable element of Lean and Agile development.** Sometimes teams complain that the preparation for the demonstration takes them away from development itself; normally, however, the truth is exactly the opposite, and the demo drives focused effort to finish and integrate.

- **Learning retrospectives can be critically important and are a core part of both Lean and Agile methods** (the "check" in PDCA). Don't skimp on taking enough time and diving deep enough, especially when a project hasn't quite found its way yet.
- **Lean thinking has problem solving at it center.** Strengthening organizational capacity to identify and solve problems is a key tenet of any Lean and Agile transformation.

Coming Up Next   Wes resumes narration with "Jackass" Langley's attempt to reassert Sales' control of MCCA. Will MCCA's Lean transformation fizzle before it fully takes hold?

ENDNOTES

1. See Wes' list at beginning of Chapter 10.
2. I'm using the basic framework for agile retrospectives from Esther Derby, *Agile Retrospectives: Making Good Teams Great*, Esther Derby (Raleigh, NC: Pragmatic Bookshelf, 2006).
3. PDCA, plan, do, check, act, is Dr. Edward Deming's classic approach to quality improvement. A useful explanation can be found in Dave Nelson, Rick Mayo, and Patricia E. Moody, *Powered by Honda* (New York: John Wiley & Sons, 1998).
4. *Obeya* means "big room" in Japanese, and is simply a physical location where the project leaders can assemble and regularly collaborate. See Morgan and Liker, *Toyota Product Development System*, pages 152–153.

12

Jack's Gambit at MCCA

Narrator: Wes

When I got to my office this morning, I immediately knew something was wrong. Waiting for me in a stuffed chair in the executive reception area was Phillip. For Phillip to be here this early, I thought, there had to be trouble. I wondered what it could be; our management scrum was going well, and our sprints for SDNI and product hardening were productive and satisfying, if a bit rocky. I soon learned that the drama was in another area altogether.

PHILLIP SPILLS THE BEANS

I invited Phillip into my office and gestured him toward my desk side chair. I asked him to wait a moment while I got a cup of coffee; he was already well-provisioned with his usual cup. I came back in a moment to an agitated Phillip, something I had not often seen.

"Wes," he began, "we've got a situation developing. I'm not sure if you knew, but Rico has been out the past few days. He took personal days, even though he had a lot on his plate and hadn't planned a vacation. Yesterday, he came back to work, and I found out what he's been doing. You remember Alpha Health at DocWorld? According to Rico, they were interested in our products, but we're missing the kind of versioning they need in order to maintain regulatory compliance. Jack didn't see that as a barrier, however, even though Lynn and you gave clear direction to Sales to sell what we've got and what we are building, and not to chase other opportunities. So Jack hired Rico to build out a demo for him on his own time—he's done this before, it's worth it to Sales given the commissions to be made on a successful sale like this. Rico finished the demo on Tuesday, two days ago, and now he's back at work."

Wow! I was stunned. It took me a few moments to process what Phillip had just told me—that Jack had completely defied the higher degree of alignment and planning Lynn and I were working so hard to install. He had reverted to historical pattern, going for the big win (and commission check) with little regard for our ability to deliver or our preexisting strategy, taking a completely sales-driven approach instead of working within the leadership team. Jack must see our team as a competition, I conjectured, with Connie and me conspiring to "rob" him and his sales team of their traditional highest place of honor, constraining him from his (personally) rewarding deal making.

I am not the battling kind. I don't enjoy conflict, and I don't do well in organizations that depend on conflict to get things done. I've consulted to such companies, where the senior executives thrive on macho brinksmanship and where competing and winning internally is as important as winning against external competition—where results, however achieved, are all that matters. Was MCCA going to be that kind of company?

I wasn't sure what to do with the information Phillip had just given me. I thanked Phillip and told him I needed to think about what to do, and I sent him back down a floor to return to work. Then I sat at my desk thinking for a few minutes until I settled on a course of action.

GETTING ADVICE FROM CONNIE

I checked out the instant messaging panel on my computer and was relieved to see that Connie was already in her office. I asked if I could drop by, and when she said OK, I stopped at the coffee station in the executive suite and poured a cup for Connie and another one for me, and hurried to her office. I was relieved to have someone with whom to share my dilemma.

"Morning, Wes," Connie greeted me. "What can I do for you today?"

"I'm afraid Jack has thrown down the gauntlet," I said. "I can hardly believe what he seems to be up to. I need to get some advice."

"Sit down, take a load off. Tell me about it," Connie said.

"I was suspicious about how he's been behaving lately," I explained. "His acceptance of your new structure and the cooperation he displayed at DocWorld seemed too good to be true. I also wondered why he had skipped our big finale at DocWorld. I've just been given some information, and I fear he has been going behind our backs looking for a home run, which would put him back in the driver's seat in this company again. I'm not sure what to do about it."

I explained what Phillip had told me—that Jack had paid Rico to work on his own time to write a demo of our software, enhanced with the specialized feature needed to support Alpha Health's special needs. Jack knew full well that if he brought that idea to me, it would face scrutiny and almost certain rejection based on our existing product plans, because supporting pharmacological research was not one of the opportunities we were pursuing. What, I wondered, was he up to? What should I do about it?

Connie listened intently to my story, quiet but focused. As I wrapped it up, she laughed ironically, smiled, and shook her head.

"I wondered when we would have the 'Come to Jesus' event," she said. "It looks like it's coming soon. I've been getting a lot of passive-aggressive behavior, but no out-and-out, 'screw-you' resistance like this. How about you and I walk over to Jack's office and ask him directly what he thinks he is doing?"

A logical thought. Why hadn't I just done that? I suppose because, on some level, I'm afraid of Jack. He knows more than I do about our products and customers, even though I'm the marketing and product guy. And from my first day on the job, I had seen him willing to stand his ground and fight for what he wanted, in both fair and unfair ways. I am conflict averse, no doubt, but I don't think I feared an argument about what the right policy might be; instead, I was bothered that Jack always seemed to be motivated by what was good for Jack. After all, when two participants to a dispute are motivated by a common goal—i.e., what is good for the company—there is the possibility of dialogue and learning and agreement. But when one is motivated only by what's good for him and the other is motivated by what's good for the company, that possibility fades quickly.

I must have appeared to be in shock as these thoughts raced through my brain, because Connie asked again. "Wes, do you want me to come with you to see Jack? You don't have much of a choice if you are to demonstrate the respect for each other that we need to model. You have to talk with him directly about this. But I'll come with you, as support and a witness. Plus," she chuckled, "I wouldn't want to miss this."

I snapped out of my internal dialogue and joined Connie as she marched out of her office toward Jack's, on the other side of the executive area. We approached Jack's assistant sitting in her guard-dog position outside his office and asked if Jack was around this morning, and if so, if we might see him.

"Sorry," she said, "he's out of town today."

"Do you know where he is, and when he'll be back?" I asked.

"Sure, Wes. He's at a customer in Dallas. Alpha Health. He'll be back tomorrow. Hey, while you two are here, can I check a meeting with you? Jack needs to set up a special meeting of the senior team to talk about a new opportunity he is working on. You two here tomorrow afternoon?"

So that's how he planned to play it, I thought. Connie and I directed Jack's assistant to deal with our assistants to plan the meeting, and we walked, somewhat humbled, back to Connie's office. Connie returned to her desk, me to the chair beside it.

"Suggestions?" I started the conversation.

"All we can do it wait and then listen," Connie said. "We've tried to treat him with respect; when we heard the information of concern, we attempted to talk directly with him. At the foundation of a team, Wes, is respect for the individuals on it, but in return, each individual must respect the team. So we'll listen tomorrow, we'll measure Jack's respect for the rest of us, and we'll decide what to do then."

As usual, I appreciated Connie's simplicity and clarity.

"You don't think we should try to phone him today?" I asked.

"To what end? He's clearly got this orchestrated in his own way. No, we let him do it. Right?"

"I like that answer because it's easy, Connie, and because I'm not sure what I would say that wouldn't sound accusatory or whiney," I said.

"We wait," Connie concluded. "Anything else I can help you with? No? Then thanks for the coffee, and see you tomorrow."

JACK'S PROPOSAL

It seemed like hours between the time I arrived at work at 8:00 a.m. and the beginning of Jack's special meeting at 10:00. Fortunately, I had a diversion on my schedule: a meeting with Hannah and Melissa to talk over some issues the SDNI team was facing regarding what the customer wanted from us for free (of course) versus what the contract called for. We probably needed to talk with Jack to fully resolve it, but that wasn't going to happen this morning.

At 10:00 on the button, I walked into Lynn's outer office, where many of the senior team members were waiting for the meeting to begin. Jack was flirting with Janice, Lynn's assistant, while Sasha (VP Finance), Cynthia (VP HR), and Connie chatted quietly together just inside the door. Respect … respect, I thought, glancing from Connie to Jack, and gathering up courage to greet him. Just as I began to approach Jack, Lynn's door opened, and she poked her head out.

"Come on in, we're ready to begin," she invited us.

We filed into Lynn's extravagant office—me last. I had a surprise when I crossed the threshold. There, next to Lynn's enormous desk was Jack Langley, shaking hands with Franklin McDonald himself. Frank, as he likes to be called, was the closest thing we had to an owner, being the responsible partner at Fletcher, Wilkens, and Johnson (FWJ), the private equity firm that bought MCCA from its founder and was investing in our growth. We took turns greeting Frank, and then took our seats at the polished wooden table that grew like a mahogany tumor from Lynn's desk.

Lynn greeted us and then got right down to business.

"We're here today at Jack's request, to consider an opportunity he has been cultivating on our behalf." Was Lynn being polite and respectful, or had she been working with Jack on Alpha Health all along? I found that hard to believe; if it were true, I would find it hard to stomach. "Because of its implications for our strategy, Jack has invited Frank to join us. Frank was on the West Coast already, so he was able to drive down from LA to be here in person. Jack, the floor is yours."

Jack was looking particularly powerful today. His hair was trimmed, his face shaved close, with a slight fragrance of after shave or cologne wafting from his direction. His suit, which cost a thousand dollars if a nickel, fit perfectly; his shirt, tailored and monogrammed, with MCCA cuff links resting on his Rolex; and his tie, a red silk rep. The contrast with the rest of the group was sharp. Jack, Lynn, and Frank looked as if they were one team, the rest of us, in low-key business casual, another. I hoped that would not be the case today.

"As many of you know, I have been working to sell Alpha Health our new product suite," Jack started. "I believe some of you met them at DocWorld. Alpha is a diversified pharmaceuticals company, interested in branching out into new fields. One of those fields is information technology.

"Their interest in technology was sparked in part by difficulties they have been experiencing managing their research. They are required, by regulation and risk control procedures, to maintain very extensive records of their research and clinical trials. For many years, Alpha has used in-house technology to manage its document trails, until two years ago, when

Alpha did an extensive search for alternatives, picked what it thought was the best product, and entered into an agreement to purchase and implement it."

"Jack, may we ask questions?" Frank queried.

"Of course, Frank. What would you like to know?'

"The product they chose, please," Frank asked.

"Pharmatrail. It's a specialized records management product aimed at helping pharmaceutical companies manage their research and clinical trial records and manage submissions to the Food and Drug Administration (FDA) and regulatory bodies in other countries. You know them, Frank?" asked Jack.

"No, never heard of them," said Frank. "There are a lot of players in various niches of the document/knowledge management space; our goal with MCCA is to play in the large middle of the market, so we didn't do much investigation of companies like them."

"Not important anyhow—let's continue," Jack said. "Unfortunately for Alpha and Pharmatrail, the implementation imploded on itself a year into the project. Alpha has some requirements that Pharmatrail could not, or would not meet, and Alpha chose to declare Pharmatrail in default and cancel the project. Alpha still needs the solution, but its senior managers are wary: they aren't sure a good solution for them exists in the market. And if no good solution exists for them, a mid-tier pharma player, no good solution exists for other pharmaceutical companies either. Here's where we come in."

I wanted to reach out and shake Jack, but I restrained myself. *Be calm, show respect,* I told myself, *listen to the story.* Jack was on a roll now.

"I have an old college friend who sells for Alpha," Jack continued, "and I saw him at a reunion several months ago. We got to talking over beer late one evening, and this opportunity grabbed me. I got an introduction to the right people at Alpha, sold them on our company, and began talking about what kind of business relationship might work for us both. They sent several people to DocWorld, met some of our leaders—Wes and Phillip, I believe—and talked with several of our customers for references. We passed the DocWorld test, and I was invited back to demo our solution for them. I had our tech group whip up a demo with some of the special features they need, and I was out yesterday to do the show. It went over well, I'm happy to say, and we are now ready to move forward with a joint venture."

"A joint venture, you say," interjected Frank. "Interesting." I wish I knew what that meant: were they hearing this for the first time as well? Or were Lynn and Frank already on board? That was hard to imagine.

"Yes, Frank. As I mentioned," Jack explained, "Alpha would like to enter the software market. I have a draft term sheet here." Jack took a stack of paper out of his leather folio and handed out copies to the group.

"The basic terms are as follows. We form a new legal entity, which Alpha proposes to call Alpha Technologies. The idea is that Alpha's success in pharma would provide a good brand name, and that the other pharma companies would mostly not see Alpha as a competitor if we create a separate entity. The pharmas tend to have a few blockbuster drugs each and none seem to be directly competing with Alpha Tech in a way that would interfere with a decision to buy software from Alpha if it fit. We contribute the software base, and Alpha contributes the intellectual capital to bring the product to market. When the product is ready, Alpha Pharma buys the software from Alpha Technologies, proves it ready for prime time, and then Alpha Tech markets the product to pharmas around the world. MCCA supplies software development and support services to Alpha at cost plus 10%, and we make a profit on each sale and support agreement."

Jack had gone much farther than I had guessed. He had worked out the whole business arrangement without ever consulting me, the head of product development and marketing. To cap it off, he went on to present the financial analysis. He handed out another set of documents, and went through the pro formas. If everything worked out as he laid it out, Alpha would be a very significant business, perhaps 25% of our company in three years.

Lynn contemplated the numbers and asked Jack what the next steps should be.

"Assuming we're interested," Jack said, "Alpha would like to start drafting the joint venture agreement and then get its leaders together with you, Lynn, as soon as possible. And Wes, we would need to put a team together to start building out the new features; we won't have much time to get it done." No surprise there.

I wondered what I was missing. Had Jack planned a role for himself at Alpha, perhaps as president of Alpha Technologies? With some equity kickers? There had to be an angle, in addition to his need to show us all who was really in charge at MCCA. I may never know.

Lynn ended Jack's presentation and asked the rest of us what we thought. I had many thoughts: anger at Jack doing this behind my back, frustration that he had introduced an entirely new strategy outside of our current path, and doubt that we could profitably build and sell the products when others specialized in the industry had failed. But I was frozen in this forum; I didn't know where Lynn and Frank stood, and lacking that intelligence, I didn't know how to proceed. If they were already on board, anything I said would seem like sour grapes or unsupportive. I chose to keep my mouth shut here and speak with Lynn in private afterward. Connie was not so circumspect.

"Lynn, I'll start," Connie said. "Building a great company requires a long view," she started. "I admit my experience is limited: I'm an operations gal, and the only two places I've ever worked are Toyota and here. But what Jack is proposing violates everything I know about building a great company. We need to *build our capabilities first,* and *then* sell them, instead of the other way around. We need to have a strategic plan and stick with it, instead of chasing every opportunity that shows up over a beer at a party. And most of all, we need to respect each other—and Jack, that's what really bugs me about your proposal. We're supposed to be a team, and here you go this far down your own path without talking to the rest of us. You should be ashamed of yourself!"

My admiration for Connie knew few bounds at the moment. I couldn't have said it any better, I really couldn't! Connie may not be the most polished member of our team, but in my mind, she was certainly a contender for most valuable.

The room was awkwardly silent for a moment after Connie spoke. Jack's face was starting to show some color as he struggled to formulate a response. Lynn nodded at Connie, thanked her for speaking up, and asked Jack to respond. Be reasonable or attack? With Frank here, he tried to be reasonable.

"Connie, you make some good points," he said patronizingly. "I can't agree with your first two points, however. Great companies must be driven by customer needs, and here we have a customer with a crying need asking us for help. We grow by listening and meeting needs and that means sometimes selling business that we don't quite yet know how to fulfill. Look at the SDNI business. When I sold that, it was nothing more than a bunch of screen simulations strung together. Now it's become the growth engine for the whole company. This is another SDNI, ripe for the taking. And as for respect, I had to keep this quiet while I worked out the details. If I had involved all of you, we'd have spun around and around on these issues while Alpha got away. Talk about respect—I'd appreciate some respect from you for building this company and bringing in the business that supports you all!"

The tension in the room by now was thick. The only one who seemed calm was Lynn; she seemed perfectly at ease conducting this meeting while her team argued. She next turned to Sasha and asked for her financial assessment. What did she think of the opportunity? Sasha begged off giving any assessment until she had a chance to study the numbers, although she was concerned about how much investment might be required on our behalf until the joint venture started to cash flow.

Finally, Lynn turned to me. What did I think? No escaping now.

"Starting on a personal note, Jack," I addressed the dapper salesman, "I agree with Connie on the respect issue. I am disappointed that you chose not to confide in me on this, and that you went behind my back to pay Rico directly to develop the demonstration software. I had hoped that our team was developing into something more substantial." I stared right at Jack, until he looked away. I saw Connie out of the corner of my eye, sending me beams of encouragement through hers (at least it seemed that way).

"As for the opportunity," I turned to the business issues, "I can't comment on the development cost estimates you have laid out in the pro forma until I study the software requirements. I'm concerned that you have a fixed dollar amount and time on which the success depends prior to us doing any study. I can say that our team is flat-out on the SDNI project and the work to harden the software to make it profitably salable to others. We do not have the capability right now to take on another major effort without hurting those two. Even with unlimited money, something would have to give."

"Wes," Jack responded, "that kind of defeatism is exactly why I kept this confidential until we had a deal. I've done this many times before, while you were with that highfalutin consulting outfit, and I'm willing to bet that with enough money in front of them, Phillip and Rico and the boys could get this done."

"Perhaps," I said. "Perhaps. But I wouldn't want to bet on it, and even if they succeeded, that kind of money-driven heroics isn't going to get us the foundational capabilities we need to sustain success."

"We're talking millions here, Wes. We do what it takes to win," Jack concluded.

Lynn reestablished her control of the meeting by summarizing and closing. "I think we've heard enough. I'd like Sasha and Wes to spend the next few days analyzing the details of the proposal, and then get on my calendar for Monday to tell me what you find. Jack, thank you for your hard work on this; we'll try to get you an answer by the middle of next week. That's it for now; you may all leave."

We uneasily got up to leave, all of us, that is, except for Frank, who stayed back with Lynn. Sasha and I retired to her office to plan our work over the next few days, but we had only just begun when Sasha's phone rang. She looked at the display, saw it was Lynn, and picked up.

"Hi Lynn," she answered. "I'm here with Wes, beginning our analysis. Can I help you?"

A short pause, and then Sasha put Lynn on speaker.

"Wes, Sasha," Lynn's disembodied voice floated out of the speaker, "don't worry about doing more analysis of Jack's proposal. Frank and I have finished our review, and we're going to pass on it. It might be a good opportunity, but it's not where FWJ wants our focus. Please keep this confidential, as we haven't talked to Jack about this decision yet. Thank you both for your thoughtful consideration."

Click. Lynn abruptly ended her instructions and Sasha and I were left to speculate about what it all meant. What would be Jack's reaction? How would Lynn handle Jack's Lone Ranger act? The answer would have to wait the passage of the weekend.

MARY AND WES CONSIDER LYNN'S OPTIONS

"I'd fire his ass so fast it'd catch on fire!"

Mary didn't have to carefully weigh the competing factors surrounding the Alpha proposal. As I explained the situation to her Friday evening, sitting on our lawn chairs on the Del Mar beach watching the kids play paddle-ball, I could see her getting angrier and angrier.

"I'd have fired him right there, in front of the rest of you, as soon it became clear that he'd prepared that whole proposal behind your back, behind Sasha's back, and in flagrant violation of the sales engineering structure Connie and you had put in place. Boom! Gone! History!"

I sometimes wished I had Mary's clarity of belief, her certainty in her own conclusions. I was certainly angry about Jack's antics as well, but although firing him held some attraction, it seemed extreme.

"That sure would have felt great, Mary," I agreed. "But don't you have to give Jack some slack here? After all, he's doing what he's supposed to be doing: finding new sales opportunities. Sure, he didn't follow all the rules, but the rules are new, and salespeople aren't usually the best rule followers, are they? Besides, this kind of activity is exactly what helped MCCA find our new opportunities, growing out of the SDNI work. Jack sold a lot of things we didn't have then, he committed to fixed-price delivery, and it seems to be turning out well. Isn't he just doing what he's always been rewarded for in the past?"

"Wes, I'm surprised to hear you defending him," Mary retorted. "Are you just arguing because you like to, or do you really believe he should get away with this?"

"I think I'm just arguing for fun," I grinned. "Jack's made his choice, and it's not to be on the leadership team we are trying to build. But that's easy to say for me; it seems a lot harder for Lynn, who has to deal with the fallout Jack's departure would bring from customers and the sales force."

Mary was distracted for a moment while she called out to her children to start getting ready to go home. As she turned her attention back to me, she said, "No, Wes, I'd say it's a straightforward and compelling choice for her. If she doesn't fire him, she sends you all a message that it's okay not to play well together. If she does fire him, she shows you all that teamwork is not optional, and that challenging the basic tenets of her leadership is not allowed. Lynn has no choice. Five to one, come Monday morning, Jackass Langley is gone."

"I'll take that bet," I said. "You might be right, but I doubt it'll happen that fast. Stakes?"

"Shoulder rubs," Mary said, without hesitation. "How about I win, I get five, if you win, you get one?" I had thought the five to one was the other way around, I get five, Mary got one, but whatever.

In response to my nod, Mary said, "I can already feel the tension relief beginning. Let's see if we can tear the kids away from their friends and get going home."

LYNN HOLLANDER MAKES HER CHOICE

I made a point of coming into work early Monday morning, anxious to see what the fallout from the Alpha Health debacle would be. All was quiet in the executive suite when I arrived. Lynn wasn't yet in her office, and my gentle probing of her assistant, Janice ("anything unusual happening this week?"), revealed nothing. That wasn't definitive, however; Janice had a PhD in keeping confidential items confidential.

I walked past Jack's office and noticed nothing unusual there, either. His door was closed, again not unusual; we all closed and locked our doors when we were out. Neither was his absence at this early hour unusual. I had no choice but to contain my curiosity, unlock my own office, and start my day.

I had been absorbed in my e-mail and preparation for the week for an hour or so when Janice poked her head into my office. "Lynn's office, five minutes, Wes." *Here it comes,* I thought. Would I owe Mary five neck rubs? I guess there were worse things to lose.

The senior management team, including Sasha, Connie, and me, entered Lynn's office. Cynthia was already there, conferring quietly with Lynn at her desk. Once we were all gathered around Lynn's odd table-desk, Lynn began.

"I'm sure you all have noticed that Jack Langley is not here this morning," she said. "Last week, Jack called this group together, along with Frank, to present a proposal he had been working on. It was an interesting opportunity, and perhaps, if it had been generated in a different way, at a different time, MCCA might have been interested in pursuing it. However, as you know, I decided it was not the right thing for us, and I communicated that decision to all of you and to Jack soon after the meeting."

"I also communicated something else to Jack—that the way he went about preparing the proposal was totally unacceptable to me and to this team. Jack had his reasons, of course; he shared some of those with us at last week's meeting. Taking Jack at his word, he believed that it was in the best interests of the company for him to bring the proposal closer to finish line before involving the rest of us. Be that as it may, that was not his choice to make, and I, with Cynthia's assistance, made it clear that this type of behavior could not be tolerated."

Lynn paused for a moment to take a sip of water and catch her breath. The room was silent, tense with anticipation.

"Skipping over the details of the remainder of our conversation, the final result is this: Jack Langley no longer is employed by MCCA. You don't need to know the details of how this came about or what the terms of separation are; it's better that you don't know. You do need to know that the separation was amicable, and that Jack is constrained by agreement from saying negative things about our company or engaging in competitive activity for one year from today. Ultimately, Jack and MCCA, as we are remaking it, are not a good fit for each other, and we recognized that and are moving on."

Cynthia took over the narration. "We were informed just this morning that Jack has taken a position at Alpha Health, as the president of its new technology subsidiary. He is moving immediately to Houston, so we won't be seeing much if any of him here."

"We will put out a companywide memo at noon, with standard departure language," Cynthia told us. "For now, all of Jack's former direct reports will report to Lynn, while we search for a new VP of Sales. We would appreciate it if you would all keep gossip and speculation at a minimum. It is okay to explain that Jack had pitched the Alpha deal and we chose to decline it, and that he has subsequently taken a position at Alpha. It's also okay to explain why we declined the Alpha deal—not a good fit for our strategy and focus, with which we are very comfortable and committed."

"We expect there will be speculation about whether the way Jack prepared the Alpha proposal resulted in his departure," Cynthia said carefully. "There is no way to avoid this kind of speculation. Too many people will know about the Alpha proposal, and all of those who should have been involved but were not will understand Jack's method. Your message should be that we don't know if there was any linkage, but that Lynn and the rest of the senior team reiterate that teamwork, trust, and respect are fundamental to our company's success, and behavior inconsistent with this principle will not be tolerated."

"One more thing," Cynthia concluded. "Wes, a team member of yours participated with Jack to prepare software for the sales pitch. Could you come to my office now and talk with me on what we need to do about that?"

Rico.

Cynthia and Lynn opened the meeting to questions. The tight scripting of Lynn and Cynthia's communication sent a message that this was not the right time for dialogue, and the attendees were sensitive to it. After just ten minutes, the meeting ended. I waited in the anteroom for Cynthia, to have my conversation about what to do with Rico. While I waited, I worried about him: I had become fond of him, despite his mercurial nature, and our product development had become more, not less, dependent on him as we had grown the team and leveraged his brilliance helping others as well as coding himself.

Fortunately, Cynthia did not have strong demands of me with respect to Rico. She knew that back-door, off-hours, informal cash-driven arrangements had been standard procedure at MCCA for years, and she was sympathetic to Rico; faced with Jack Langley wanting help and offering cash, it would have been difficult for Rico to do anything other than participate. Cynthia asked me to talk with Rico, explain what had happened, and ask that he not participate in any future off-the-official-books transactions of this nature in the future. She also asked that Phillip and I reinforce the ethics policy, which already prohibited this type of arrangement.

Relieved, I retreated to my office to absorb the momentous events of the morning. I was proud of the courage and leadership that Lynn had demonstrated. I was also worried: I knew that Jack's departure would put a larger burden on me and my team. We had just lost the person who knew the most about our customers and market. I hoped that other members of the sales team would step up and that our product development was starting to reveal some compelling solutions.

That afternoon, after the announcement, I met with Phillip first, and then Rico. It was hard for Philip to contain his joy. He had hated Jack for years, thought him a self-serving bully. He interpreted the events as someone—Lynn—finally standing up to Jack and firing him for his arrogance. I couldn't comment one way or the other. I explained what Cynthia wanted from us, with which Phillip was happy to comply. At that moment, I thought, Phillip would have agreed to almost anything.

I approached my conversation with Rico with some trepidation. When I first met Rico, his status at MCCA was in turmoil. He was the brilliant center of our software, and in that way indispensible. On the other hand, he was independent, sensitive, gruff, temperamental, and unpredictable, often at the center of blowups and interpersonal turmoil. Things of late had seemed to be going well, and I was afraid to upset the apple cart by rebuking him about the side-work for Jack, and gaining his explicit assurances that he'd rigorously adhere to the ethics code going forward. I wasn't worried that he'd want to be unethical, of course; my concern was just about his sensitivity to criticism. But having no choice, I phone Rico and asked him to come up to my office.

I was astonished at Rico's demeanor as he entered my space. His confident, aggressive, even arrogant air had been deflated. If he'd had a tail, it would have been between his legs! Rico walked over to my desk, took a chair across from me, and began talking.

"How much trouble am I in?" Rico asked.

"Why do you think you're in trouble, Rico?" I asked right back.

"I heard about Jack getting fired for insubordination on the Alpha deal," Rico said. "I figure that since I helped him, my ass is grass as well."

I was going to enjoy this, at least for little while. Rico had always acted as if he were in the driver's seat at MCCA, as if we needed him a lot more than he needed us. Perhaps the shoe was on the other foot now? I was also guiltily ecstatic on how Rico described Jack's fate—amazing how quickly the word got out and how dramatically the events had been interpreted.

I responded, "How do you feel about that?"

"I'm sorry, man," Rico said. "Jack came to me, like he's done before, and asked me to whip him up a demo. I guess I know now what I was supposed to do, but at the time, it just seemed like business as usual."

"What should you have done, Rico?" I queried.

"I should have put Jack off and gone to Phillip for guidance. I know we're working hard to manage priorities and sequencing within our Agile process, and this was a big roundabout. I won't do it again, I promise."

"That's all we need from you, Rico. We understand there was an established way Jack had of working with you and others, and that it was probably confusing. HR has asked that I have you review our ethics policy, and then sign this document reaffirming your understanding of it and your pledge to comply." I handed Rico the document Cynthia had provided.

Rico reached across the desk and took the document. "I'll do it tonight, Wes. Thank you, and give my thanks and apologies to Cynthia and Lynn as well. I was afraid that just as this company is getting to be a great place to work, I would be drummed out! We finally have support for the developers, productive relationships with our customers, and management that wants to know the truth. Wouldn't it be just my luck to have to leave?"

"I'm glad you're enjoying our company more now, Rico, and I'm grateful for your contributions and leadership. Let's keep it up. Now get out of here, sign the document, and bring it back to me tomorrow."

All that remained to wrap up the Alpha Health episode was to call Mary and tell her she was entirely right, for a change. I returned to my desk, swallowed some Diet Coke, and dialed Mary's cell.

Signposts	MCCA Transformation
	• Jack Langley, who had been quietly compliant with the changes at MCCA, reveals the full extent to which he is not on board. He brings a take-it-or-leave-it business proposition to MCCA's leadership team, developed on his own and outside the company's agreed direction.
	• MCCA President Lynn Hollander rejects Jack's proposal, and Jack leaves the company.
	• MCCA remains on the path Lynn, Wes, Connie, Sasha, and Connie have drawn.
Change Guides from Wes	• **In many transformations, there comes a moment of choice. Will the leaders stick to their guns and support the direction, or will they revert to old ways?** Unfortunately, these moments don't always come with a label; that is, a caption that says "crucible moment!" Watch out for them, and be courageous.

Coming Up Next	As Mary and Wes's tumultuous year comes to a close, they meet with Neville to reflect on their progress and explore how to sustain the Lean and Agile improvements in the coming years.

Section V

Looking Back and Looking Ahead
December

13

Sustaining Lean and Agile: December

Narrator: Wes

Christmas in San Diego! After spending almost my entire life living in the north (in Chicago and St. Paul), a holiday season in California just didn't feel right. Of course, I had seen the holiday season in sunny climes. I had even spent one December cloistered in a foreigners' enclave in Saudi Arabia. Somehow this felt stranger. It was supposed to be Christmastime here, unlike in Saudi, and the external trappings were here, like mall Santas, colored lights on the trees, and of course, the incessant advertising. But I couldn't completely come to grips with Santas in shorts and colored lights on palm trees.

Also, as we crept into December, the pace of our businesses began to slow down. Right at that inflection point where business slows and Christmas activity becomes intense, Mary and I received an invitation from Neville and Cornelia for a repeat performance of our dinner earlier in the year. They were eager to hear how our voyages were progressing, whereas Mary and I were equally anxious to do some brainstorming about what should come next.

COMPARING THE MCCA AND FINSERVIA EXPERIENCES

Our first dinner with Neville and Cornelia had come early in Mary's and my efforts in trying to make our software development more effective. With Neville's help, Mary and I had chosen two different ways to make change, based on the situations we faced and our own proclivities. Mary had chosen a directive approach that I had labeled *drive people*, leading with process and tools, whereas I had chosen a more participative approach I cleverly called *people driven*. Here at year-end, both approaches seem to have worked fairly well, although the trajectories of the companies had been quite different. As we drove the twenty minutes to Neville's home, I thought about our experiences while Mary rocked out to Santa Baby (her new iPhone plugged into the car and she couldn't resist it).

At MCCA, we had quite a year. It began with Lynn Hollander settling in as President and building her new management team, including me, and ended with Jack Langley exiting and our search for a new Sales VP. Along the way, though, we had lots of successes, which I mentally ticked off as I drove:

- We had grown the product development team.
- We added new roles and new processes.
- We had shown results by completing new releases of most of our strategic product suite.
- Our flagship customer and riskiest engagement to date (San Diego National Insurance) was tickled pink with our performance, and we were in the middle of contract revision negotiations that could relieve us of the unlimited risks to which Jack had initially committed us.
- Best of all, two major agreements to implement our new product suite had been inked. One was with an existing customer that had been so impressed with Connie's operational improvements that it had been willing to try our other services. The other was with a company completely new to MCCA.
- We were now building out our installation services, which we had put under Connie's capable direction, in the belief that installation would be more akin to standardizable processes in which her group excelled (i.e., Lean manufacturing) than the learn and adjust processes (i.e., Lean product development and Agile software development) in mine.

Of course, not all was rosy at MCCA, and I also considered where we needed to do more work:

- Our new processes didn't always fit.
- Our new roles were performed more or less effectively.
- Team members periodically fell back into old ways.
- Integration of testing into the development process was incomplete.
- Disputes between product management, program management, and development management at times simmered and at times boiled

over. Sometimes, I felt as if my primary function was to get people to talk with each more effectively.

But by and large, I was proud of what we had accomplished, and perhaps more important, so was my boss Lynn Hollander.

Mary's year had been even more tumultuous than mine:

- She started the year having to reboot her whole group, as opposed to my more incremental and participative approach.
- And she got lucky with her outsourcer, GRI, and was able to reposition it from an unresponsive obstacle to a helpful change partner.

However, it took more time for her team to begin to gel than she had hoped, and Mary had to suffer through several months of feeling that ultimate success was touch and go:

- The differing backgrounds of her leadership team (from Jill's dogmatic Agile process dedication to Max's slow emergence from the GRI straitjackets) caused the *forming* and *storming* phases of their team's building to extend for several tense, frustrating months.
- The leadership variability was multiplied throughout the group's ranks: with so many new people (and some trying to learn quite new ways of working together), the "teamwork" was rife with missteps, communication gaps, and simple mechanical gaps ("*install a new PC?*" "*location of configuration files?*" "*set-up of security profiles?*").
- The low point of Mary's year came at her first Sprint demo. Fortunately, the climb out of the hole began that same day, with an intense and emotional retrospective. Looking back, it was clear that on that day, Mary saw her group begin its transformation into a team, and she saw herself transform from the change driver to the change facilitator.

She had recently had a big win when a new customer demanded a software function be built quickly, in order to come onto the FinServia system, and because development was being done in short, mostly complete synchronized iterations, the development teams were able to adjust their schedules and deliver the new features from start to finish in less than two months. The old Cremins Financial Services Division, with its ponderous processes and outsourced development, would never have been able to come close to that performance! FinServia still had a long way to go to become the self-sustaining, culturally mature organization she and Greg had come from at Cremins Corporation's real estate division—but it was arguably on the way.

We arrived at Neville's, where he invited us to sit outside on the back deck. It was warm enough, but just barely, mostly because we were protected from the wind by the house and had the last of the waning sun. Once the sun finished its descent, we'd have to go back in, but for now, it was a lovely way to begin our conversation.

Cornelia had made her "world-famous" guacamole, and Neville had mixed up the traditional English yuletide treat—margaritas! "To celebrate your upcoming wedding," Cornelia toasted. "We just made our reservations for Maui. How wonderful of you to force us to Hawaii! I've wanted to go for ages but could never convince Neville. He has to visit his family in Europe every year, and we never seem to find the time or money to go anywhere else."

Mary was delighted. "I'm so glad you are coming," she said. "I was worried that by getting married in Maui, we would either have no one come, or we would alienate our closest friends by forcing them on a long, expensive trip. So far, it seems to be working out well."

"We wouldn't miss it, Mary," said Neville. "I've always wondered what kind of man it would take to put up with you, and now that I've come to know Wes, I need to see the knot tied!"

I wasn't exactly sure what Neville meant, but I thought it better to let it go than to examine the sentiment.

As we sat and tried not to shiver while the sun sank to its nighttime home, Neville changed the topic and led off our business catch-up session.

"Enough mush-mush," he said. "Let's talk about something really interesting, like Lean and Agile software development," he began. "When was it that we sat together at your house and explored alternative ways of helping organizations become more Lean and Agile? Seems like it was this kind of weather, more or less, wasn't it? I remember having to eat indoors even though you grilled, Wes."

"It was about ten months ago, Neville," Mary answered, "in February. I remember because it was a few weeks before my trip to GRI, which was in March."

Neville nodded and said, "I'm proud of how well both of you have done." Neville had been in touch with our progress, mostly through Mary, throughout the year. "How would you feel about taking out the model we

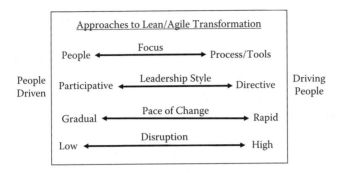

FIGURE 13.1
Approaches to Lean/Agile transformation.

built back in February, and see how your actual results fit or didn't? I kept my copy, let's see, here it is" (Figure 13.1).

"Let's start with people," said Neville. "Wes, you were doing the *people-driven* thing, so what did you find?"

"I tried to work all my change through my people," I answered. "Remember talking through roles with me, Neville? I did my best to find existing team members to fill the key roles of development manager, product manager, and program manager, and each of them has done well. We did a lot of training, support, and mentoring, mostly from the GRI consultants we found through Mary. Then we also followed your suggestion of using scrum to manage our change process, and that also worked well. I believe we now have an engaged team that is managing its own pace of change, moving in a good direction."

"And Lynn's support has been strong throughout, with the added exclamation point of moving Jack out of the way," Neville concluded. "Did you lose anything by not focusing more strongly on processes and tools, Wes?"

"Probably," I agreed. "My guess is we are doing a lot of processes more poorly than we should be, and our tools—well, let's just say that we need to put some focus in that direction soon. We also have some organizational imbalances and gaps that need some attention. I know that Mary's organization is way ahead of us in those areas now."

"We are, Wes, because that's where we focused from the beginning," Mary chimed in. "Neville, we are just starting to stabilize now, after months and months of struggle. We are pretty far down the path toward a fairly sophisticated implementation of Agile software development, even though our broader Lean culture is still immature."

"Mary," prodded Neville, "we both know that a Lean culture requires a high degree of team member involvement. Staff has to understand the value stream, drive to eliminate waste, and find and eliminate problems. You took a directive approach to making your change. From the top, you configured the organization, populated it with people, handed out missions and roles, designed processes and required their use, and bought tools to support the processes. Has it been possible to build the culture you need even while cutting your staff out of the basic design of their group?"

"You put your finger right on it, Neville," Mary said. "Even though I defined what I thought was the 'right' organizational structure, the 'right' processes, and the 'right' tools, I couldn't define *everything* that had to be done. As people stepped into roles that had been defined for them by me, it took time to find the gaps, and even more time to find the misfits between job and person. And because I tried to hire strong people, I either got a lot of push-back on the designs I had made, or even worse, narrow focuses on just what I had defined for them. We're starting to get better now as people get more comfortable with their jobs and with each other, and as I've tried to make clear that I expect a lot more from them than simply doing their jobs as I defined them."

Neville rejoined, "You've touched on a central issue in management in general, Mary. If you *overspecify* a position, or a process, you get compliance but not creativity and growth. On the other hand, if you *underspecify*, you take your chances on whether you will get what you want and need. You and Wes chose different paths, and your results are accordingly different: Mary is probably closer to the environment she wants, with the absence of it being self-sustaining, whereas Wes seems to have created a self-sustaining and adapting environment but isn't as far along on the specific mechanisms desired. Does that sound right?"

It did to me, and I said so. I also commented on the other dimensions of the chart we'd built months ago. "I think our chart held true on the dimensions of disruption and pace as well, Neville. MCCA didn't have a lot of disruption, whereas FinServia certainly did. And we didn't change as much as FinServia. Even the things that our Lean Team scrum put into our backlog got done much more slowly than I hoped, whereas Mary has her Chief Engineers (CEs) and synchronized sprints well along."

"Okay," agreed Neville, "looks like our model held, and it helped you two think through and execute on your transformation programs. What's next?"

I looked over at Mary to see if she wanted to direct this, and she gave me an eyebrow-lift that indicated I should go ahead.

"We've made it this far," I said. "We've both made fundamental directional changes. I've made major improvements in our delivery, and Mary looks set to do so. My question for you, Neville, is what comes next? How do we sustain the momentum?"

SUSTAINING A LEAN AND AGILE SOFTWARE CULTURE

"Ah, great topic, Wes. You are about to marry one of the great experts in this topic, although I doubt she'd admit to that," Neville said.

"I don't feel like such an expert right now, Neville," said Mary. "I guess I did work with a great team for many years, but I wasn't the leader—that was more Greg and you. I just built software."

"Don't underestimate what you know, Mary," Neville retorted. "Let's do a test. Once you get your Lean and Agile development working fairly well, what do you need to do to sustain it? List me your top five items."

"Where am I, Neville, back in school?" Mary asked. "Okay, I'll play along. I'd say the most important areas are about people: *building and maintaining towering technical competence,* and *reinforcing cultural values.* The values would be *elimination of waste, continuous improvement, problem solving,* and *respect for people.*"

"Good," said Neville. "Passing so far. Wes, how about you? Can you add an item or two?"

"I think so," I said, "although Mary has covered quite a landscape with her point on reinforcing cultural values. Coming from a strategy consulting background, I'd have to say that we'd need to have a *strategy-setting and management mechanism,* which would give us time to do the up-front study of new developments needed to make them successful."

"Excellent, Wes," said Neville. "At Toyota they call their strategy process *Hoshin Kanri,* which loosely translates as *policy deployment,*[1] and I know you are familiar with the Lean product development (LPD) practices of *Kentou,* or *study.*"

"I am," I said. "I've seen firsthand how taking the time to understand customer needs, consider multiple options, and set a well-examined path forward can clear the way to success. I've also seen that this requires foresight and a long view, which many businesses fail to develop sufficiently."

FOCUS AREAS TO SUSTAIN LEAN & AGILE DEVELOPMENT

1. Towering technical competence
2. Cultural values: value focus/elimination of waste, continuous improvement, problem solving, and respect for people
3. Strategic Planning and Study
4. Customer-focused, hands-on leaders
5. Lightweight processes

FIGURE 13.2
Focus areas to sustain Lean and Agile.

"Well said, Wes. Mary, would you like to add the next items?" Neville asked.

"No, not really, Neville. I'd rather you finish, and then we talk about each of them."

"All right, Mary, if you insist. I'd pick two more: *building and maintaining top-quality customer-focused, hands-on leadership*, and *ensuring that processes don't become heavy with waste over time*. Good?" Neville checked with us. We liked the list, so we jotted it down (Figure 13.2). Then we discussed each item in a bit more detail.

Building Towering Technical Competence

"Start with the technical competence, Mary. How did we do this when we were in the Real Estate Division?" asked Neville.

"We used our learning roadmap, and we insisted that a primary responsibility for every manager was the development of their team members. This involved not only planning and encouraging development, but actually teaching themselves, whether one on one with their employees or in other settings, and in setting the stage for ongoing knowledge creation and sharing. We built that expectation into all of our management tools, including annual performance management, bonus plans, individual development plans, and even succession planning."

"I don't think I ever saw your learning roadmap," I said to Mary. "I do recall the high degree of skill of your teams, though, and I wondered how you built and maintained it."

"It's nothing magical, Wes. We just worked together among our leaders to identify the key roles in our group and specify the skills and knowledge we expected each role to have mastered. Then we listed ways our team members could gain and demonstrate those skills. We did this over several years, starting with the most critical skills and gradually building the matrix out over time. You want me to draw you a quick sample?"

"Please," I said. I was having a hard time visualizing what Mary was talking about.

Mary grabbed the clipboard Neville had the foresight to bring out for our talk, and she drew the conceptual diagram of the learning map (Figure 13.3; I've taken the liberty of expanding on Mary's diagram for clarity).

Referring to her diagram, Mary explained, "See, across the top we have our major roles—in this example, *developer, tester, analyst,* and *leader*. Down the left, we have the skills and knowledge needed: *test-driven development, sprint planning, user story writing,* and *systems architecture*. For each skill, we describe how to gain it. In our actual map in the Real Estate Division, we had specific books and training listed. Finally, at the intersection of each role and each skill, we elaborate on the relevance and extent of mastery required of the skill to that role. For instance, in the *test-driven development* line, you see that developers, testers, and analysts must be fully proficient, with somewhat different focuses: the developers have to know how to use automated unit test tools in their day-to-day work, whereas scrum masters and other leaders need to understand the importance of the techniques and insist it be used appropriately in the development process."

"This would be a great thing for my Lean Team to own," I said. "I could probably get someone in HR to actually manage the matrix itself and help us maintain and communicate it, and build it into our annual performance and bonus planning.

"You can also use it in the hiring process," Mary said. "Although it's certainly not complete for the purpose; often, we hire for characteristics other than just the skills and knowledge, such as character, brains, and guts."

"Mary," said Neville, "that is a great lead-in to our next item, cultural values. How do we create and sustain the right ones?"

Skill / Role	How to Gain Skill	Developer	Tester	Systems Analyst	Leader / Scrum Master
Test-Driven Development	Read book, go to training, mentor with internal expert, experiment with unit testing tools	Critical, esp. unit testing tools	Critical, details and model	Critical, esp. test condition writing	Familiarity to facilitate and insist upon process
Sprint Planning	Certification programs, training, reading, participation, mentorship	Familiar	Familiar	Familiar	Highly expert
User Story Writing	Read books, training, participation, mentorship, practice	Critical, ensure they get good stories	Critical, ensure testability	Critical, will be a central tool	Familiarity to facilitate and insist upon process
Systems Architecture	Education (college, graduate school), lengthy experience, reading, and professional development	Critical, especially in senior engineers	Familiar	Important, in senior leaders	Critical, must know enough to ensure team does well

FIGURE 13.3
Towering technical competence learning map.

Building and Sustaining Cultural Values

"That's a tough one, Neville," said Mary. "It sounds so 'soft,' but it's so hard! If we can build into all of our leaders and team members, as a routine way of life, maintaining a laser focus on customer value and a strong distaste for waste, plus a passion for continuous improvement, problem solving, and respect for others, then all the other items would take care of themselves. I know I've tried to install the right tools and processes, but wow, it's been an uphill struggle getting the people to use them effectively together. As I think back to the Real Estate Division, all I can think of is Greg's leadership. He talked about these values over and over again, he expected us to behave in alignment with them, and he acted to reinforce them. Is that all it takes—a leader who talks the talk and walks the walk?"

"Certainly without a leader like Greg, it would be impossible," said Neville. "But Greg is unique—brilliant, completely committed to Lean and Agile at the principles level, great at building and maintaining relationships, and able to size up and lead people to perform at high levels while creating teams. No offense, but neither of you are yet a leader of Greg's caliber, although it might not be too long until you get there. Does that mean you don't have a chance of building and sustaining cultural values?"

"I don't think so, Neville," I said. "I'm a very different leader than Greg, from the little I saw of him; I'm just feeling my way forward and learning as I go, whereas Greg seems to know just what to do based on his experience, knowledge, and intuition. But I think I can do it. I believe I can instill the values through just what you said, talking about them, and continually acting in alignment, in addition to making good hiring and performance management decisions. And although Lynn doesn't have either Greg's or even my commitment to Lean and Agile principles (because she's just learning about them now), she has good instincts and courage. Doesn't her getting rid of Jack, however that transpired, show that?"

"I think it does show her leadership and wisdom," agreed Neville. "Acts of courage like the Jack incident shape culture for a long time. I've always said that there is no more powerful act of management than getting rid of a bad egg. It shows the remaining team that the leader understands the nature of the bad egg and is willing to take action to excise it on behalf of the team. *Addition by subtraction*, you could say. Fundamentally, building culture is about people—leadership from the top down, hiring the right people from outside, promoting people who fit the values you seek, training and rewarding team members who demonstrate and encourage the right things. And at crucial moments, like Jack's rebellion, we have 'cultural crucibles' where expediency can argue for an easy solution, but value creation demands the hard, aligned choices."

"As I've thought about it and tried to live it, Neville," I said, "my leadership focus has been on several things:

- "Showing respect for our team members
- "Having generosity of spirit—assuming everyone wants to do the right thing and contribute, until they show definitively otherwise

- "Trying to establish 'normal' so we can tell when we are varying, and then try to address the reasons why
- "Encouraging identification of problems and providing established mechanisms to seek resolution
- "Relentless focusing on customer value and elimination of waste—anything that isn't on the path to creating that value

"I've tried to keep it simple, to stick with this list of focus items, to repeat over and over, to expect from my team, and reward those of my team who help me reinforce and execute. I think it's making a big difference, setting these explicit values."

"I'm doing something very similar, Neville," added Mary. "My list isn't quite so explicit—I'm not as cerebral or strategic as Wes. Instead, I'm more about getting the work done. But I hope I demonstrate and reinforce Lean and Agile values as well, and that the organizational structure, tools, and processes we've struggled to install help as well. We're training on plan, do, check, act (PDCA) and A3 problem solving, and I can see that beginning to make a difference."

"I'm sure they do, Mary," agreed Neville, "and both your approaches can and will work. Wes, I would add an item to your list of cultural items you rattled off, and that is creating, storing, and disseminating knowledge. That's a broad idea that can cover the creation of towering technical expertise, the teaching of that knowledge to others, and the insistence of adding rigor in our decision making."

"In any case," I summarized, "we seem to agree that building and maintaining cultural values stems from the leadership. Mary, it's up to you and me!"

STRATEGIC PLANNING AND STUDY

"It's always up to the top leaders," agreed Neville. "But even great leaders can use proven techniques. In my own job this year, after taking over for Greg at the Real Estate Division, I've been applying a Toyota-derived strategic planning method the Japanese call *Hoshin Kanri*, which (as mentioned) translates roughly as *policy deployment* or *strategy deployment*. Greg didn't use any formal strategic planning approach at all, other than budgets; he seemed to know where he wanted to go and involve the rest of us informally, or through our annual performance management/

objective-setting exercise. As I took over the job, however, I felt I needed something a bit more formal."

I was intrigued. I had done a lot of strategy work in my consulting days, and I had heard of strategy deployment; its claim to fame was focusing more strongly on the *deployment* element than the *strategy* element. At MCCA, we didn't have a formal strategic planning cycle, and I was pretty sure that neither did FinServia.

Mary confirmed my assumption. She said, "Greg isn't doing anything different at FinServia. I doubt he'll change his ways, and I'm not sure he needs to. But is this something I might find useful in managing my own group?"

"Absolutely," Neville said. "It's pretty simple, and you can start at whatever level makes sense. Should I go over the elements now? You'd need to get some help, or at least read a book or two before trying it out, but if I describe it, you could perhaps judge whether it's worth pursuing. So far, I'm finding it very helpful."

I asked that Neville proceed, and Mary agreed.

"The basic idea," Neville explained, "is simple. At the highest relevant organizational level, the leaders set an overall strategy, which is called *True North*. It's called that by analogy with the magnetic north pole, which 'pulls' other strategy and plans to it. The strategy is boiled down into a simple, one-page summary, called an *A3*, with which I believe you are both familiar?"

We were, but mostly with A3s used to address problems. Neville had a blank sample in the house, which he fetched for us (Figure 13.4).

"I did one of these charts with my team, which set the True North for the company," Neville explained. "It was surprisingly difficult. We found we didn't have measures for some of our key results and goals, and we had an awful time sifting through the details to get to just one page. Once we had True North, we had to construct subsidiary strategies, and there are many ways to split up the second level, whether by division, function, department, or whatever. We did it by major function: product development, implementation support, customer service, people, and profitability. Each area did its own A3, which aligned with the master A3. The process of constructing these subsidiary A3s is called *catchball*—the metaphor is throwing a ball to a partner, and having it go back and forth until alignment is reached."

"Interesting," I said. "But not so unusual; it sounds like a straightforward cascading of objectives."

Strategy Deployment Chart	Focus
Performance Summary Charts or graphs that show how the company or unit has done over the most recent historical period, and what the goals are for the coming period. Show the most critical relevant measures.	**Action Plan** Show the major goals for the upcoming period, preferably with quantifiable targets, and list the activities to be undertaken to reach the goals. Activities should have dates and responsible persons.
Commentary on Last Period's Results Summarize, ideally in a table or chart, the major initiatives (plans) from the last period and evaluate their effectiveness. This sets the stage for the upcoming plan.	
Rationale for Coming Period Activities Given the goals shown in the top box, and last period's results, explain why the activities in the Action Plan box are appropriate.	**Follow-Up / Unresolved Issues** Immediate action items to enable the Action Plan, or open issues that need to be addressed quickly.

FIGURE 13.4
Strategy deployment A3 template.

"It is," Neville agreed. "The difference is the back and forth. Many planning processes are one-way trips, top-down. This is up, down, and all around. We had some very heated and revelatory conversations! At the end, each department had an A3 with its strategy, goals, and planned activities that aligned with the master A3 and peer groups. I found it much more powerful than Greg's informal approach."

"Which you'd expect in a Lean planning process, lots of involvement and frank, fact-based, problem-centered discussion," I said.

"So what happens once the A3s are created?" Mary asked.

"PDCA, of course," laughed Neville. "*Plan, do, check, act*. The strategy A3s are the *Plan*, and the Activities are the *Do*. Management then focuses throughout the year on checking on the results and adjusting as needed. It's been a welcome change to our management regime. We used to have staff meetings to report status, deal with issues, and so on, but the Hoshin structure, along with PDCA, makes the management regime more effective."

I liked the idea and said so. "This type of planning and aligning action could really help sustain Lean and Agile development," I agreed. "It could put activities into a stronger context, and it could structure management action effectively. In some ways, it's not that different from the Lean Team management scrum we already have. We have our goal—driving toward Lean and Agile, plus our specific product development needs. We have our activities—our backlog. And we check and adjust at the end of each management sprint, including our regular retrospectives."

"Agreed," said Neville. "Amazing how similar the Lean techniques and the Agile techniques are. Great thinkers think alike, no?"

Customer-Focused, Hands-On Leaders

By the time we finished talking about *Hoshin Kanri*, the sun had set, it was getting chilly, and we were getting hungry. Walking inside to dinner, I thought how lucky I was to have Mary and Neville as guides. (Of course, I was lucky to have Mary in many other ways as well.)

Over dinner, though, we put the work discussion aside, much to Cornelia's relief. We heard about Neville and Cornelia's recent trip to Europe, and we told them about our upcoming wedding trip. The wedding was coming so soon! Tonight, we were looking ahead in both our personal and professional lives.

After dinner, we got coffee and headed into the casual, comfortable living room. We had finished our discussion of strategy and planning and returned to tackle the topic of leadership. Sustaining Lean and Agile software development requires good leadership—leaders who focus on providing customer value efficiently, who know the business and the operations. How can we ensure we have the right kind of leader?

The three of us didn't have many disagreements on this topic. Mary and Neville had worked together, with Greg Allenby, for many years, so they shared formative experience here. I had formed my opinions through my strategy consulting practice, and what I thought I knew lined up well with their views. We touched on many factors and a few anecdotes, and finished up agreeing on these four:

- *Leaders should see for themselves.* Ensure that leaders spend time with customers and in operations. The stories of this at Toyota are legion—like the Sienna minivan chief engineer who, in preparation for his task, spent months driving minivans through every U.S. state and Canadian province to understand firsthand what North American customers need (like a place on which to set takeout food),[2] or the new Toyota engineers who are directed to stand in a circle on the manufacturing floor for hours and told to observe.[3] Toyota even has a special word for direct visual learning of this type: *gemba*.[4]

- **Leaders should focus on learning and become experts.** The Lean principle of *towering technical competence* refers just as much to managers and leaders as to engineers. Management is not a skill in and of itself, it must have context; managers and leaders must be highly expert in their areas. This principle is demonstrated by the idea of the chief engineer; for example, the leader of an automobile development project must be an engineer—not a marketer, not a financial professional, not a salesman. Similarly, don't put someone who is not a software engineer, or at least someone who has deep experience and expertise in software development, in charge of a software project! Of all the errors Mary, Neville, and I have seen, this seems to be the most frequent: business managers who don't trust any *technology* people put a *business* person in charge of a project expecting to get business leadership, and they wind up getting simply incompetent leadership.

- **Leaders should do performance management and development planning.** The formal, traditional tools of performance management should be leveraged to help leaders grow by specifying expected results and behaviors. For example, a simple requirement in a performance plan to spend two days a year with customers and writing up a report on each day to share with colleagues can begin to create change, so long as managers inspect what they expect. Managers of people must have special expectations to grow their own people.

- **Leaders should be facilitative.**[5] Software development is an endeavor that seems different than most anything that came before it. It's an endeavor that requires many people to learn and think together, putting their thoughts and ideas into code that actually does things. There is no physical embodiment of the work whatsoever. It's as if a university president had to get all the professors to collaborate on writing a complex book that not only made sense, but would withstand rigorous testing of every single line!

    In order to succeed at this new kind of work, leaders need to get every team member intellectually engaged, and ensure that team members have the skills and framework to succeed. The four facilitative leadership principles, which drive skill building and expectation setting, are:

- *Show respect for people by minimizing process waste (i.e., don't waste people's time).* Setting clear objectives for meetings, detailed agendas, meticulous preparation, and structured interaction models will multiply the effectiveness of leaders.
- *Get all the participants' "fingerprints" on decisions.* Because each team member contributes ideas, decisions, or code, the more they are committed to a course of action, the better the execution will be. Voluntary, enthusiastic participation results in great software; forced, reluctant, just-doing-my-job engagement does not.
- *Do nothing for the team that they cannot do for themselves.* Leaders must encourage initiative and self-reliance for each team member and for each intact team.
- *Demand rigor.* Decision making must be fact based; great leaders cannot let emotional, hierarchical, or personal factors suppress the consideration of a variety of options and decisions made based on facts and logical arguments.

Lightweight Processes

By the time we got to *lightweight processes*, we were all getting tired, and Cornelia had excused herself to finish up the dishes, bored with our conversation. So Neville summed this up quickly.

"First and foremost, leaders must understand the difference between *standardizable tasks* and *knowledge-building tasks*," Neville began. "Rigorously standardize and continuously improve the former, and leave teams a lot of freedom on the latter. Methods for knowledge building should come from the teams themselves, through their own knowledge and experience, and be enforced by the culture, not via detailed methodology audits or the like. Software methods are something for teams to learn and apply, not to follow.

"Secondly, apply our abhorrence for waste to our development process itself. Doing a document because *it's required* must be rejected culturally. Process must be examined in retrospectives and in other ways, and continuously improved. Avoid handoffs, use one-piece flow, be Lean and Agile.

"Third, respect the people and the teams. Use responsibility-based planning[6] and integrating events, not enormous centralized project task plans. Address failures at their root cause, which is usually wasteful or overspecified processes, or people in jobs for which they are not qualified or adequately supported. Very rarely, in commercial software development, is a technical problem technical at its root.

"How's that?" Neville concluded, feeling proud of himself.

"Awesome," I said. "Nice and simple. If only it were as easy to implement!"

"If it were," said Neville, "everyone would do it, and you'd get no advantage from excelling. As it is," he wrapped it up, "you have a fertile field."

As Mary and I began to pack up to go home, grateful to Neville for his counsel and mildly sorry for boring Cornelia right out of the room, Cornelia rejoined us.

"Thanks for coming over and keeping Neville entertained," she said. "He likes nothing more than to share his wisdom," Cornelia said with a hint of sarcasm.

"His advice is worth every penny we paid for it," laughed Mary.

"That's the appreciation I get," said Neville. "Drive carefully, and if we don't see you before then, see you in Maui."

"Yes, see you in Maui," I said, "Aloha!" I took Mary's hand and we headed for the door. It had been a good year for Mary and me, and we were both excited about the personal and professional years ahead.

ENDNOTES

1. Policy Deployment, or Hoshin Kanri, is described in Pascal Dennis, *Getting the Right Things Done: A Leader's Guide to Planning and Execution* (Cambridge, MA: Lean Enterprise Institute, 2006).
2. Liker, *Toyota Way*, pages 228–229, tells the story of the Sienna minivan Chief Engineer's drive through North America.
3. The famous *Ohno circle*, named for Taiichi Ohno, one of the founders of Lean at Toyota, refers to a process of putting engineers into a small circle drawn on the product floor and having them watch and think for up to eight hours.
4. Liker, *Toyota Way*, page 224.
5. I learned the term and the principles of Facilitative Leadership from Lucy Buckley.
6. Responsibility-based planning is a project management approach used in Lean product development in which component teams are given a mission and a time frame for delivery, but are not micromanaged at the task level. Kennedy, *Product Development for the Lean Enterprise*, pages 137–138.

Section VI

Summary and Conclusions

14

Transforming to Become Lean and Agile

Finally, after spending a fictional year in the capable hands of my fictional narrators, Wes and Mary, I (Michael Levine, the author) am writing this final chapter, to summarize the ideas illustrated in our two tales. We've seen two different leaders take on two different organizations. Mary is highly expert in Lean and Agile software development, whereas Wes is less so. MCCA was a chaotic culture, driven by the latest sales commitment, with little process of any sort, whereas FinServia was a rigid, nonresponsive bureaucracy frozen in excessive process specification and compliance. The two leaders reacted to differences in the situations of the two companies (as well as their own preferences), and they chose two different approaches to making transformations toward a similar goal: implement Lean and Agile software development.

Figure 14.1 sums up the differing characteristics of MCCA and FinServia that led our fictional narrators to choose different change approaches.

SUMMARY OF THE *PEOPLE DRIVEN* APPROACH

Wes chose the *people driven* approach. The basic idea of this approach is:

- to engage the existing team members in the change,
- to gain their commitment and participation, and
- to drive the transformation as a team.

Further, it relies on:

- setting a compelling vision for change,
- having the necessary skill to communicate and gain commitment, and

Characteristic	Lean to *People Driven*	Lean to *Drive People*
Current Performance	Uneven	Poor
Urgency of Change	Moderate; possible to stumble along	High; failure assured if not successful
Technical Expertise of Leader	Low to moderate	High
Style of Leader	Participative	Directive
Staff Trajectory	Growing	Shrinking
Individuals Critical to Mission	Some key leaders and technicians	Few if any
Ability of Organization to Reform Itself, Given Support and Chance	Possible; not set in any particular way; see need to change	Unlikely
Support from Senior Executives	Supportive, but wary	Supportive and trusting

FIGURE 14.1
Drive people or people driven.

- training and mentoring team members to help them make good directional decisions.

Disruption of existing work can be minimized, as is risk of alienating and losing team members along the way. It offers the best chance that Lean and Agile methods will be effectively tailored for the situation and people at hand. It is a best fit for any organization that is working well in at least some aspects and for which downside risk exceeds any probable gain from moving quickly.

The downside is that the team members don't "get it," and needed change happens too slowly or not at all.

SUMMARY OF THE *DRIVE PEOPLE* APPROACH

Mary chose the *drive people* approach. This approach:

- puts less initial value on team member engagement and commitment, and
- puts more initial value more on directive change imposed by the leader.

It requires a leader who knows what she wants, at least in the initial stages of change, and a stomach for at least temporary disruption. Initially, the focus is more on:

- implementing new processes and tools,
- changing the organization, and
- getting new people on board and existing people in new or changed roles.

Building the Lean respect-based culture and securing a self-sufficient, continually improving team lags the initial enforced process changes. *Drive people* offers the best chance for making rapid change and laying the groundwork for sustained long-term excellence in the direction set by the leader, so long as the people focus comes strongly on the heels of the process/tools shock (Figure 14.1).

The downside is the disruption, the dependence on the quality of the vision of the leader, and the risk of not making the transformation to a less-directive environment.

In practice, of course, setting the path for Lean and Agile change will occur in many ways. In some cases, the choices will be made specifically and consciously as Mary and Wes did in these tales, with Neville's help; in others, the path will evolve as the sum of the decisions of many leaders and team members. The path may well contain elements of both *drive people* and *people driven*. For example, in my own experience, I much prefer the *people driven* approach, but there have been times when I, as the executive leader, have been highly directive on certain tools and processes.

Every organization must find its own way forward. Success depends on understanding and committing to the principles of Lean and Agile, not on the details of any particular detailed set of processes or tools. Focus on the underlying ideas, and *implement them in the way that makes the most sense for your own organization.*

Some of the principles to help you on your own journey of organizational transformation are summarized in the following sections.

VISION AND LEADERSHIP

Set a Simple and Compelling Vision

The vision must be business focused above all else, and it should be measured by success in meeting the needs of customers, shareholders, team members, and the community.

For example, Lynn set a great vision for MCCA: improve its operations business to provide customer receptivity and cash flow to build its information management technology products (in Chapter 1), and Greg similarly did well for FinServia (in Chapter 2). Rallying cries such as "we need to be Agile" or "let's be Lean to cut out the waste" aren't terribly motivating, and they emphasize the means, rather than the goal.

Development teams generally get excited about helping customers. It is ironic that many development team members never see or hear customers directly; their connection is indirect, conveyed through formal, dry requirements documents written by intermediaries. If at all possible, find a way to make these connections personal, as Wes did with his company's customer, San Diego National Insurance (SDNI).

Build a Supporting Coalition

Change draws opposition, so be prepared for it, by recruiting others early and often.

In Wes's case, he naturally reached out to his peers to gain shared ownership of the changes he believed he needed to make. He recruited Connie in Operations, Sasha in Finance, and Cynthia in Human Resources, and he did his best to recruit Jack Langley in Sales as well. Wes appealed to the goals the leaders all shared, and tried to find win–win cooperative opportunities. This coalition of support resulted in getting the right people into the right slots, cooperation and shared leadership of the improvement initiative, and when the crisis emerged with Jack and Alpha Health, Wes had a supportive team behind him.

In contrast, Mary was less of a natural bridge builder than Wes. She focused on "getting on with it," ensuring that she had the support of her boss but not worrying too much about how the rest of her peers were engaged. One consequence was that her relationship with her key partner, Mervin, became frayed, and she needed her boss to rescue her.

As you start a change initiative, think strategically about which leaders you would like firmly on your side, and reach out to them to ask for commitment and help.

Make a Plan, Specific to Your Reality

We've seen in Wes's and Mary's tales that although both leaders were headed toward a similar place, they began at very different starting points. Accordingly, the steps to move ahead were different: Wes's was initially a collaborative, people-oriented one; Mary's was a tools-and-process, directive one. Although a more sophisticated organizational study could identify patterns, for now, assume that every organization has its own starting place—a compendium of people, culture, process, history, tools, customer relationships, market realities, shareholder pressures, and organizational boundaries and requirements.

Additionally, the positions of the change agents vary. In these tales, Mary and Wes were highly placed organizational leaders with good support from their managers, whereas you may not occupy as lofty a role or have such stalwart support. The process of building organizational support for change was beyond the scope of this book (in fact, it was assumed away in favor of more focus on the actual mechanisms of driving change once the general direction was accepted), but will in most cases be critically important.

A change plan, tailored to the situation and your position in it, should be simple and easy to communicate, like Wes's and Mary's five-point plans in Chapter 3. Be Agile with it; pick off the most critical ones, get them implemented, and move on the next ones, updating the plan as you go.

Use Integrating Events

With Neville's urging, Wes and Mary selected events on which to focus their change efforts, in addition to relying on the events inherent in the Lean and Agile approaches. Wes set his sights on the DocWorld conference (described in Chapter 10); this provided an immovable target for his team, a public commitment to deliver, and a checkpoint for his constituencies. Mary relied more on the routine integrating events of Agile development, notably the sprint-end demonstration and retrospective.

Accelerate Delivery

The promise of Lean and Agile development is faster, cheaper, higher-value delivery. In any Lean and Agile transformation, the team must demonstrate this right out of the box. The Agile Manifesto puts emphasis on working code over documents, so demonstrate that—fast! Be sure to pick the smallest possible release of working code that adds business value on the strategic development path, and build, test, and release that. There should be, and can be, no time-out to learn and implement new techniques.

The ideal first implementation of Agile is to reorient a long, drawn-out traditional waterfall project. Can you find something of value ready to go in the piles of requirements and design, and get it built and into production?

Find Outside Wisdom

Luckily, your Lean/Agile transformation won't be the first. The intellectual foundation for Lean and Agile was laid down in manufacturing companies over the last several decades, and Agile software techniques have been in development for almost that long (although the label is newer). Rather than reinventing everything for yourself, draw on the experience of others, through reading, attending conferences, hiring, and using consultants.

Both Mary and Wes used consultants in their efforts. Wes relied on them more extensively, because he had less experience himself, had less opportunity for dramatic reorganization, and hired fewer people from outside the company. The assistance from GRI was important to MCCA's success, notably in training and mentoring (Chapter 8). Mary's use of GRI was somewhat different: she relied on GRI more for help in planning and executing her dramatic change (Chapter 7), and in facilitating sensitive events like the first sprint retrospective (Chapter 11).

Remember that Lean product development is mostly about *learning*. Use consultants to help accelerate learning, not to do for you what you could do for yourself.

Encourage Engagement and Debate, within Limits

Effective facilitative leaders ensure that their teams have their fingerprints on the critical decisions that they will be expected to implement. This requires that teams be allowed to engage with ideas, to express themselves, and to work through decisions together. For a leader who knows what he or she wants, this can be frustrating and appear to be a waste of time. It is not; if the leader simply dictates what she wants, she may get it, but only that; her teams' willingness and ability to think and act for themselves, and to express their opinions and belief to her, will be compromised.

This does not mean that the leader cannot, or should not, set limits and some absolute requirements, or intervene where the team members cannot get the job done themselves. For example, in Chapter 1, Lynn Hollander listened intently to Jack Langley's concerns with Connie's operations realignment, then she laid out in no uncertain terms the boundaries within which Jack's complaints could be considered. She also pushed Jack and Connie to get back together and work it out themselves, within the boundaries she had set. Similarly, in Chapter 11, Mary related how she listened to her team debate many items over the past several weeks, and how in some instances, she stepped in to make decisions. Mary used the retrospective to reinforce the extent to which she cares about the opinions of her team, being very careful not to "turn them off" by taking too much authority on herself.

There is an element akin to parenting in this dimension of leadership. The team needs to become self-sufficient, as does a child, but there always remains a role for the parent.

Understand Your Boundaries

In every business situation, there are boundaries that proscribe certain actions and require others. Sometimes, the boundaries are *people* (for instance, Jack is the head of Sales, so you need to deal with him). Sometimes, the boundaries are *deliverables* (for instance, "no matter what, don't blow the SDNI account deliverables for August!"). Sometimes the boundaries are *the process* ("inform Lynn of meaningful events in a weekly e-mail, involve peers"). Finally, sometimes these boundaries are explicit, but sometimes they're unstated. It's best to explicitly understand and accommodate or work to move the boundaries, rather than run into them and be surprised.

Both Wes and Mary tested their boundaries with their bosses early on (in Chapters 1 and 2), and Wes continued to try to understand both the formal and informal boundaries in MCCA by working with Connie, who had tested the boundaries prior to him.

It's (Almost) Always about the Money

Change is often about money, one way or the other—for example:

- speeding up delivery to save or make money
- becoming more efficient
- reducing the spend rate
- bringing in consultants and tools
- improving training and learning
- hiring experienced people

As you begin or work to sustain a change initiative, do the math on the money, and communicate it explicitly to those who need to understand and approve (i.e., Management, Finance, Accounting, your customers). You must be able to make the business case that Lean and Agile will make money for the organization, or don't start down the path.

Both Wes and Mary were cognizant of money issues: Mary justified bringing development in-house from GRI and transforming to a Lean/Agile approach largely through a promise to reduce spending and accelerate delivery. Similarly, Wes understood his budgetary parameters and lived within them.

PEOPLE

Give Existing Leaders a Chance

When considering the state of an organization (if it's not so good ...), it's tempting to assume the inadequacy of the people who comprise it. That's probably true to some extent: they may not possess towering technical competence, be facilitative leaders, be focused on driving out waste and delivering value, or know anything about Lean or Agile techniques.

This doesn't necessarily mean that they don't have potential to learn and contribute. Give them a chance! Make it clear that change is expected, expose them to opportunities to learn, give them support to implement new ideas. The business knowledge and relationships in the existing team are invaluable, if they can be harnessed to power your change.

Perhaps the best example in this book is Lynn Hollander with Jack Langley. It was clear from the beginning (Chapter 1) that Jack wasn't really on board with the changes that Lynn, Connie, and Wes were driving at MCCA. Lynn set boundaries for Jack, stating some absolutes that she would insist on. She listened to his objections and opinions, and she hoped, futily as it turned out, he would climb on board the train. More positively, Wes saw that Phillip had some outstanding qualities as a development manager, but that he had been put into a position ill suited for his disposition and skills. Wes gave Phillip the opportunity to modify his position to be a better fit and to learn new ideas and techniques. Phillip adopted the direction well, and became a valuable part of the new way of doing business. Max is another example at FinServia (Chapter 7, Week 4): he was comfortable in his siloed, document-driven, slow-moving data management processes, but when pushed, he was able to change.

Let Obstructionists Continue Their Careers Elsewhere

Giving existing team members a chance doesn't mean giving them infinite chances, however. As a manager, once you reach a confident conclusion that a team member won't sign up for the new culture, or doesn't have the skill set or the ability to adapt well, do both yourself and the team member the kindness of helping him or her to move on to another organization.

Mary immediately saw how poorly fit her FinServia team was for the new mission and methods she was imposing, and she did a wholesale reevaluation of the entire group, putting some "keepers" into new roles and giving the rest the freedom to continue their careers elsewhere (Chapter 7). At MCCA, Lynn gave Jack a much longer rope, but when he finally did hang himself, Lynn didn't hesitate to kick his feet off the stool.

Nothing builds confidence in a leader more than seeing them remove poor performers or bad fits from the team. Don't wait too long to help your team succeed if they need your help.

Stir Up the Pot by Adding Some New Blood

It is very difficult for a group of people to make fundamental change to themselves. Over time, groups develop comfort zones, topics that are too sensitive to readdress, long-simmering resentments and accommodations that can prevent forward movement. Additionally, if a group does not have the critical Lean and Agile values— towering technical competence, zealous waste elimination, single-minded and common focus on delivering value, and the rest—the process of development can be extended and uncertain.

This is not to say that change without adding new people to the mix is impossible; if some of the team members "catch the fever" and have the leadership skills to help the organization move forward, especially if they have management support and access to external help, progress can certainly be made.

At MCCA, President Lynn Hollander started at the top, adding Connie, who had experience in Lean manufacturing, Wes, and others. However, Wes didn't add many new people; instead, he focused more on giving his people exposure to new ideas and external expertise, and then helping them lead themselves. In contrast, at FinServia, Mary relied heavily on bringing in new people, judging that the existing group would not be able to get the company where it needed to be.

Get Them to Do It Themselves

People learn best by doing, not by being told how to do something. Similarly, they tend to implement ideas that they were involved in originating more effectively than those directed at them. Finally, the very nature of Lean and Agile development is about getting people to be expert at their disciplines, work effectively together, and continuously drive improvement. Add it up, and the imperative of getting the development team to own the plan and make change themselves is compelling.

The challenge, of course, is how to do this. Several options are presented in Wes's and Mary's stories. Wes relied on giving his team members the information they needed to guide the change, and he established the Lean Team management scrum. Mary was much more directive at first, but as her story unfolds she ensures that her team members do an in-depth retrospective and refresh their problem management skills. The risk is that the team makes the "wrong" decisions; it's a risk that must be taken, while of course management reserves the right to intervene if needed.

Build Chief Engineers, but Adapt to the Situation at Hand

The practice of Lean product development at Toyota depends on the Chief Engineer, or CE, but that structure is not necessarily a good fit, or even possible, in many organizations. The essence of the CE is the combination (in one person) of engineering, marketing, organizational, and leadership skills. The CE has worked in the organization for an extended period, is well regarded (the word *revered* has been used), has deep informal networks, and is highly expert in the business at hand and the professional disciplines. It's probably fair to say that most organizations embarking on a Lean and Agile journey have no one (or at best, very few candidates) who fits this bill.

At MCCA, Wes had no one close to able to fill the CE role. He chose an entirely different approach, building a team of the people who had the right skills. In contrast, Mary chose to appoint CEs even though they didn't have all the requisite qualifications, and even though the marketing role was formally outside their area of responsibility, in the hope that the appointees would grow into the (very large) shoes.

What's the right arrangement for your situation? It depends. But don't give up on the idea of creating people who have CE characteristics—multidisciplinary knowledge combined with organizational clout. And above all, be sure that leaders of software engineering groups are expert in software engineering!

Teach to Lead, and Lead by Teaching

Leadership is a combination of intrinsic personal characteristics and learned behavior. Leadership can be taught, and for a Lean/Agile environment, it must be. Lean and Agile leaders must be expert, they must teach, they must listen, they must help their people work together effectively, they must insist on rigorous decision making.

Consider Mary's boss, Greg, and how he dealt first, with Mary's reorganization proposal (in Chapter 7), and second, with the dispute between Mary and Mervin on commitments to project costs and schedules (in Chapter 9). Greg used both events as opportunities to teach, the first by modeling the behavior of injecting rigor and options into decision making, the second by setting up a dialogue in which his team would learn from each other under his guidance.

The idea of leaders as teachers is central to Lean, as practiced at Toyota and other companies. This means that they must have more or different knowledge than their team members, and that they must be expected and taught to teach. Find opportunities to reinforce these ideas.

Spreading Knowledge—Institutionalize Knowledge and Learning

It is widely cited that the difference between a good and a bad programmer is 10X in productivity.[1] My experience confirms this for some items, usually the hardest ones. The variation for other areas of software development is at least as much, I would say. For example, in architecture and design, a bad architecture or design might never work, whereas in requirements analysis, a poor understanding of needs can result in bad prioritization decisions, wasting development efforts entirely on a system or function that is never used. In a large software development project, dozens of people are making hundreds of decisions every day, and it is impractical, if not impossible, to provide enough controls and reviews to ensure that the decisions are adequate, much less optimal. The best way to ensure good decisions are made is to ensure that our team members have the expertise (along with the motivation and support) to make them.

A useful model for helping people learn is presented in Chapter 13, in the section on sustaining towering technical competence.

A final thought on this topic: match the knowledge level required of the team to the scale of the problem being faced. If you are dealing with a routine issue in well-known solution space, you probably don't need towering technical expertise—you just need adequacy. However, if you are in a demanding, top-class space, you need to have the skills to match. For Toyota, they wanted to be the best car manufacturer on the planet, so they had to have the best engineers, up and down the chain.

What does *your* organization want to be?

"You Go to War with the Army You Have"[2] or Build Your Capability before You Build Your Software

Donald Rumsfeld's famous quotation applies equally well to software projects. An organization's ability to deliver software projects depends on its *people, process,* and *tools,* as we have seen (Chapter 3). So, in some material ways, the success of any particular project is determined before it ever starts! Of course, *people, process,* and *tools* can be changed during the course of a project, and they usually will be, but material changes in these factors inevitably disrupt the smooth operation of a development team.

Mary certainly saw this, as expected (in Chapter 11): the results of her first sprint were more about the gelling of her *people, processes,* and *tools* than about productively delivering software.

If you want your organization to be effective at software development, don't focus solely on the projects in flight; that is too late. Instead, focus on the *people, processes,* and *tools* in the organization, and prepare to be successful at the next generation of projects. (Of course, don't ignore or give up on the current projects; but remember Mr. Rumsfeld's dictum: the projects in which you can succeed are determined by the team you have going in, or how quickly you improve that team.)

ORGANIZATION

Customer Focus

Lean thinking demands that customer value be understood and that value be delivered with no waste. This requires that the customer understanding be well linked to product development. Although this sounds like it might be straightforward, in practice, it is anything but. Product development planning requires deep understanding of technology and the organization's capabilities, and often the people who have this type of knowledge are far removed from customer contact. As organizations grow, and as people and departments specialize, the risk of disconnects between customer needs and product development activities grows.

Lean product development and Agile software techniques each provide their own "answer" to this conundrum. LPD relies on the Chief Engineer, combining in one person (with a small team) the engineering, organizational, customer focus, and leadership skills required. Agile posits the Product Owner, someone able to speak definitively on behalf of the customer and the organization with respect to priorities and product features. Either model can work, although both present serious issues and obstacles.

As Wes approached this problem, he was attracted to the idea of the Chief Engineer, but he had no one available who could fill the role. This is likely a common issue: Toyota addresses it by growing these people over decades. Wes solved his problem by adopting an alternative structure, using a Product Manager and a Customer Experience Manager within his development group along the model of the Microsoft Solutions Framework, and ensuring the entire team spent time with customers. In contrast, Mary was prevented from implementing a CE model by her lack of knowledge in a new business area and her boss's desire to split product management from the technology development function. Mary had to rely on product management residing outside the development group, and find a way to make her partnership with Mervin work.

Ultimately, a variety of structures can accomplish the linkage of the customer voice with product development priorities and capabilities. Getting it right for your company or organization is critical to your success. And however you choose to do it, don't give up on creating multifunctional leaders, grounded in engineering, on the model of the Toyota CE, or on getting all your team members as close to customers as you reasonably can.

Demolish the Barriers: We Are All "The Business"

Whatever organizational structure you have or choose, Lean/Agile requires that everyone (OK, maybe not *everyone)* be focused on value creation and end-to-end flow. How often do you hear the *technology department* trying to align with what *the business* wants? Or see a *business* project manager and a *technical* project manager? As you drive Lean/Agile change, stop using this type of language; everyone is serving the customer and the shareholder, we are all *the business*!

We don't want developers to be "code-bots" taking overly detailed specifications and trying to figure out what to do with them. We want them thinking like business owners about customer and shareholder value.

Small Intact Teams

Organize as closely to Mary's model as you can (Chapter 7): entrepreneurial leaders owning business or system areas with the resources they need to drive results, not just play a bit part as a cog in huge impersonal code assembly line. If you can't affect the organization directly, do it informally.

PROCESS

Process Can Drive Lean/Agile Change, but It's Not Enough by Itself

We saw Mary and Wes make different choices on how to make change, one focusing on people first, the other on process and tools. We also saw that process and tools alone cannot bring the results we seek; that takes all three sides of the Lean product development triangle: *people, process,* and *tools* (Figure 3.1 and Figure 3.2). Lean or Agile change programs that seek to move an entire organization to become Lean or Agile by changing the required methodology, forcing people to do scrums, or the like can result in improvements, but they are unlikely to be sustainable. Although Lean/Agile favors certain processes, it must be understood at a higher level—helping groups of smart people deal together with uncertainty by accelerating learning, eliminating waste, and driving rigorous decision making.

Start Slow and Simple

The preceding is not to argue that you shouldn't drive process change. Changing process is a great way to spark the learning process. For example, even in his most team-friendly moments, Wes imposed the scrum process on the overall change effort, helping the group learn how to plan in smaller increments and make frequent adjustments along a strategic path. In your own organization, there are likely to be opportunities to pick a process that adds value and begin there. Start with your own understanding of Lean and Agile principles (for example, by reading *A Tale of Two Systems*) and determine where the biggest benefit to your projects can be derived. Build a backlog, hold daily scrum meetings, build a knowledge sharing website and lunch and learns, begin doing test-driven development. You can't go from where you are today to where you want to be quickly, but you can start the journey.

PDCA Yourself!

Plan, do, check, act. It applies to your transformation effort as to any process improvement endeavor. Your situation, your goals, and your team are unique, so any advice or plan is probably only partially correct. The best illustration of this is Mary's experience of failure in her first sprint, and the powerful learning that resulted from the retrospective (in Chapter 11).

Methods—Don't Overprescribe

Methodology should be considered a tool for learning, not a requirement for compliance. Must all backlog items be complete units of work that add direct customer value? Or can the backlog include some tasks that need doing but aren't that directly customer related? Does every backlog item have to be defined such that it can be completed in one sprint or can they cross sprints? Does the scrum have to be fifteen minutes and be limited to the specified topics, or can the team make it a half hour and deal with more issues? Who is to say what is right for your team, other than your team (assuming for the moment the team is capable of making good decisions; if not, there is a different set of issues to address).

Our goal is to have a team of towering technical experts, rigorously making good decisions, informed by customer and shareholder value, adjusting continuously as they learn. Don't straitjacket them and short-circuit their ability to form and perform.

But Do Insist on Some Basic Practices

One of the foundational values of LPD is towering technical competence. Each of us steeped in product and software development no doubt has some very strong beliefs (call it technical competence) in certain processes that must be done to ensure success, and as leaders, we have an obligation to teach our teams to adopt these processes. It is an abdication to just let a team go off on its own and make its own decisions, just as it is poor management to dictate detailed process to a product development team. There must be a balance between empowerment and leadership.

I personally insist on high-quality product visions including costs and benefits, project statements of work, master test plans, as much test-driven development as possible, and visual status reporting. As a leader, I also always strive to make sure we have thoughtful team alignment on technical architecture/design, the requirements => design => code => test flow, and roles/responsibilities.

TOOLS

Tools Can Help, but Be Careful!

Because growing and sharing knowledge is so critical to Lean/Agile software, tools to assist team members in doing so can be important contributors to success. Some valuable tools include:

- A3 one-page issue/problem documents
- Visual management charts in a wide variety of formats

- Knowledge sharing platforms, such as websites, checklists, or common space
- Automated testing tools
- Agile project management tools, ranging from stand-alone tracking systems, small point-solutions, such as backlog managers and burn-down chart makers, all the way to integrated development management environments
- People selection and development tools, such as Mary's interviewing guides (see Chapter 7)

Be wary of overreliance on complex tools. For example, when just starting out on a scrum, it may be more effective to do everything by hand or use paper cards on a wall. This is similar to beginning Lean operations and visual management; some experts advise having the operations teams build their control charts by hand even if the data is available electronically, just to prevent the tools from getting in the way of true human engagement.

Mary discovered how a tool can get in the way during her first sprint (Chapter 11). She had hoped that the tool, an Agile project management system, would provide the structure and central communication required to accelerate the transformation to Agile, but in fact, it did just the opposite. The effort to implement the tool consumed the full attention of Mary's most valuable team member (Alex), and by forcing the other team members to focus on the constraints of the tool, diverted them from the substance of their work. Although Mary was dismayed by this result, she remained committed to the tool, and she expected that eventually, the investment would pay off.

Vendor Partnerships

Toyota is well known for its powerful leveraging of its vendors, who are often deeply involved in product development work as full partners. This requires sharing information at the vision and goals level, so the objectives of both firms, buyer and seller, can be aligned.

Migrating to Lean/Agile software development in many organizations will involve vendor relationships, as Mary's did with GRI (in Chapter 5). Sometimes, as Mary saw, moving in a Lean/Agile direction can require fundamental changes in existing relationships, whereas in other cases, only modest tweaks are needed. Work hard to find a win–win relationship;

dictating change on unwilling partners is unlikely to bring the results you seek.

A likely change in software vendor relationships will be deeper integration of requirements, design, and testing between firms. There is often great waste to take out of the system in a typical handoff oriented approach in which the customer develops system-agnostic requirements, hands them off to the vendor, and doesn't see anything until the code is ready for user acceptance testing. A more collaborative, Agile approach is difficult to reconcile with fixed-price, fixed-functions bids; I wish I had simple solutions to offer on this conundrum!

FINAL WORDS

The rewards of leadership in the software business can be compelling and exciting. These rewards may include the thrill of seeing new software in productive use; the intellectual challenge of working through complex design trade-offs; and the pride in development of talented team members. Fifty years into the software era, Lean and Agile development approaches have become a movement, borrowing techniques from manufacturing and product development, and adapting them to the unique circumstances of developing products with no physical instantiation. I encourage each reader to take stock of his/her own situation, and, as Mary and Wes did, make your own plan to become Lean and Agile.

ENDNOTES

1. A good summary of the research is found in Steve McConnell's online blog, as of this writing at http://forums.construx.com/blogs/stevemcc/archive/2008/03/27/productivity-variations-among-software-developers-and-teams-the-origin-of-quot-10x-quot.aspx.
2. Donald Rumsfeld, in a Town Hall meeting with soldiers in Kuwait, December 8, 2004. As of this writing, the official transcript can be found at http://www.defenselink.mil/news/newsarticle.aspx?id=24643.

Index

Page references followed by *f* refer to figures.